THE
ROUEN CAMPAIGN
1590–1592

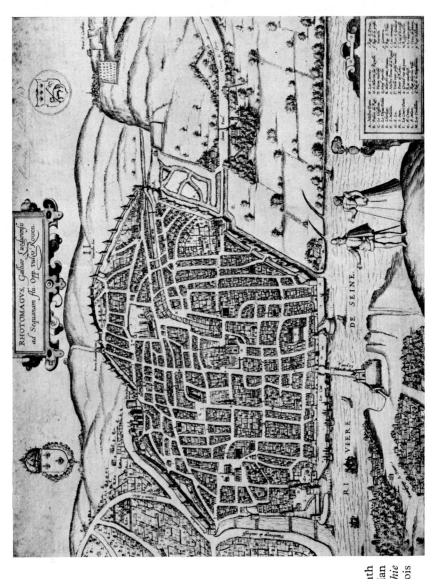

Rouen in the later sixteenth century. (After Sebastian Muenster, *La Cosmographie universelle*, ed. François Belleforest, Paris, 1575.)

THE
ROUEN CAMPAIGN

1590–1592

*Politics, Warfare and the
Early-Modern State*

BY

HOWELL A. LLOYD

CLARENDON PRESS
OXFORD
1973

Oxford University Press, Ely House, London W.1

GLASGOW NEW YORK TORONTO MELBOURNE WELLINGTON
CAPE TOWN IBADAN NAIROBI DAR ES SALAAM LUSAKA ADDIS ABABA
DELHI BOMBAY CALCUTTA MADRAS KARACHI LAHORE DACCA
KUALA LUMPA SINGAPORE HONG KONG TOKYO

ISBN 0 19 822411 7

© OXFORD UNIVERSITY PRESS 1973

PRINTED IN GREAT BRITAIN
BY RICHARD CLAY (THE CHAUCER PRESS) LTD
BUNGAY, SUFFOLK

for
SUSANNA

PREFACE

It was in the course of studying the career of Robert Devereux, second Earl of Essex, that I decided to write this study of the campaign in which he held his first major command. I felt that Essex's own conduct had been seriously misrepresented in historical writing. I also came to feel that the conduct and aims of the other principals had fared little better. Increasingly, it seemed to me that many of their modern interpreters had not taken adequately into account the circumstances in which political decisions were made and military affairs conducted: nor, indeed, the very nature and interrelationship of diplomacy, warfare, and the early-modern state. Thus, from a particular beginning I found myself forming a picture of the campaign in its general setting, and drawing from it still more general inferences. The book is the outcome of this process of broadening inquiry and reflection.

Owing to my initial point of departure I have dealt most fully with English aspects. Nevertheless I have endeavoured to deal with other states sufficiently to sustain the general themes of the book. Since one of its aims is to show how the participants had to contend with continually changing situations, in preference to an analytical I have adopted a narrative approach. To believe, as I do, in the merits of those modern approaches that seek to reconstruct *structures mentales* by means of sophisticated methodologies, is not to disbelieve in the complementary merits of old-fashioned political narrative as a means of illuminating the roles and attitudes of individuals in their changing *milieux*. There is currently, especially in France, no lack of exponents of the former approach in the field of early-modern history. All the more reason, therefore, to exercise the latter from time to time in relation to French matters.

The book is based largely upon primary sources. The principal source is those papers of Lord Burghley and his secretaries that were recovered from private possession in the early seventeenth century and now form the relevant volumes in the Foreign Series of State Papers at the Public Record Office. But I have also drawn upon an extensive range of other manuscript materials in English and continental national and provincial repositories. Bias, of course, affects all such materials: subjectively in the sense that those who composed them were interested parties in the affairs to which they relate, objectively in the sense that their availability to modern historians has been so

much a matter of chance and random survival. It is always worth re-
calling that Burghley looms so large in the political history of Elizabethan England partly, at least, because he hoarded a great many of his
papers when most of his contemporaries would seem to have been
neglecting a great many of theirs—or even, as is known in the case of
Essex, deliberately destroying them.

But however enthusiastic his search for manuscripts, every student
of episodes in the French civil wars has at some stage to consult published editions of the writings and documentary compilations of contemporary historians and memorialists. These too have their bias:
sometimes undisguised, sometimes covert. On the one hand, the vigorous Calvinist Simon Goulart, who between 1587 and 1599 compiled
that 'veritable library' the 'invaluable' *Mémoires de la Ligue*,[1] was
explicitly concerned to discredit the 'cursed and bloody League'. On
the other, the great historian Jacques-Auguste de Thou strove con-
sciously and unremittingly for objectivity. Between these extremes,
Enrico Davila sought out fresh sources, though not as many nor as
scrupulously as he pretended; while Palma Cayet sought out more
and reproduced them for the most part faithfully if uncritically. But to
a greater or a lesser degree it is as true of all of these as it is of Burghley
that their sentiments flowed with history's victorious tide, the tide of
the emerging state, of the *politiques*, and also in effect of the heroic
legends of Elizabeth and Henry *le Grand*.

Although this book proposes some modifications of those legends, I
find myself after all in the company rather of these monarchs' apolo-
gists than of their detractors. Nevertheless I would claim to have been
diligent in guarding against the bias of the sources. I have also endeavoured to guard against the editorial imperfections of the published
works which I have used. As Professor Kinser has recently shown,
there exists no satisfactory edition of de Thou's masterpiece; even the
best available edition, the London edition published by Samuel
Buckley in 1733, has significant defects.[2] Goulart's commentary is best
ignored, and his transcripts remain faulty despite the corrective efforts
of their eighteenth-century editor, the Abbé Goujet. The sins committed by Jules Berger de Xivrey in collecting Henry's *Lettres Missives*
were mainly ones of omission; but Sully has only very recently found,
and Villeroy still awaits, editors devoted and competent enough to

1. H. Hauser, *Les Sources de l'histoire de France: XVIᵉ siècle (1494–1610)*,
vol. iii (Paris, 1912), p. 106.
2. S. Kinser, *The Works of Jacques-Auguste de Thou* (The Hague, 1966).

present what pass for their respective memoirs in a form acceptable to modern scholars. At all events, in preparing this book I have tried to use the best available editions, and to verify matters both of fact and of judgement not only by means of critical and comparative evaluation but also by reference to manuscripts. I will record that in doing so I have been as often impressed by the soundness of the writers and editors concerned as I have been disturbed by their errors. Carelessness apart, even Goulart, no doubt confident that the words of the unrighteous were sufficient to condemn them, does not seem to have tampered excessively with his texts. In the case of Davila I have relied upon Ellis Farneworth's English translation from the Italian edition published in London in 1755 and commended by that considerable literary figure, Giuseppe Baretti, friend of Samuel Johnson and lexicographer in his own right. In the case of de Thou, I have compared the relevant passages in the French translation with which I began (the so-called London edition of 1734) with Buckley's Latin edition, and, whatever the former's defects in terms of textual scholarship, have for the most part found it adequate for my purposes. Even so, in every case where I have cited de Thou I have added in parentheses page references to Buckley's edition.

The plan of Rouen is published by permission of the Trustees of the British Museum. For permission to consult and to publish material from the Devereux Papers at Longleat House, I am obliged to the Marquess of Bath. Dr. R. B. Outhwaite and Dr. Neville Williams kindly made their unpublished theses available to me. Numerous librarians, archivists, and other scholars in this country and abroad have given me generous assistance in the course of my work. I thank them all, and especially the staff of The Brynmor Jones Library, University of Hull. Two of my colleagues at this University have placed me particularly in their debt. Dr. K. R. Andrews has helped me at every stage with expert advice and constructive criticism. Upon the judgement, time, and friendly encouragement of Dr. Gordon Connell-Smith I have been privileged to draw at will. If I have failed to profit from such scholarly support, the fault is certainly not theirs. My best thanks are reserved for my wife, Gaynor, my obligation to whom is exceeded only by my delight in recording it.

Dates are given throughout in New Style. Spelling and punctuation have been modernized in all quotations, but not in the titles of books.

University of Hull,   H.A.Ll.
Innocents' Day, 1972.

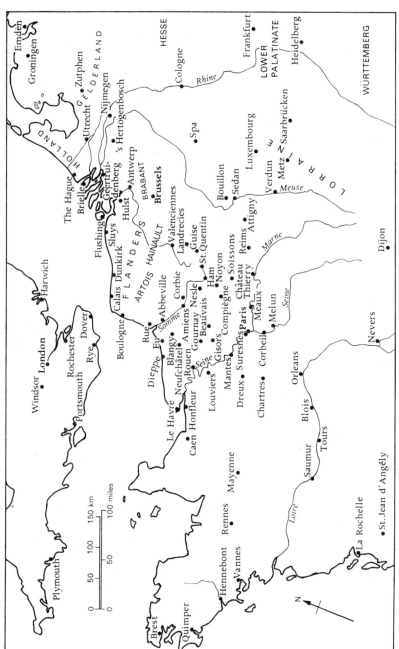

Northern France and its neighbours

CONTENTS

LIST OF MAPS

ABBREVIATIONS

Add	British Museum, Additional Manuscripts.
ADSM	Archives Départementales de la Seine-Maritime, Rouen.
AFF	Bibliothèque Nationale, manuscrits français, fonds français, ancien fonds.
AGR	Archives Générales du Royaume, Brussels.
AN	Archives Nationales, Paris.
Ancaster	Historical Manuscripts Commission, *Report on the manuscripts of the Earl of Ancaster*, London, 1907.
APC	*Acts of the Privy Council*, New Series, ed. J. R. Dasent, London, 1890–.
Bagot	Historical Manuscripts Commission, *Fourth Report* (Appendix, pp. 325–44), London, 1874.
BM	British Museum, London.
BN	Bibliothèque Nationale, Paris.
Carey	*Memoirs of Robert Carey, Earl of Monmouth*, ed. C. H. Powell, London, 1905.
CM	*Correspondance du Duc de Mayenne, publiée sur le manuscrit de la Bibliothèque de Reims*, eds. E. Henry and C. Loriquet, 2 vols., Reims, 1860–2.
Coningsby	T. Coningsby, *Journal of the Siege of Rouen, 1591*, ed. J. G. Nichols (*The Camden Miscellany*, vol. i), London, 1847.
Corbett	J. Corbett, *Drake and the Tudor Navy*, 2 vols., London, 1899.
CPR	*Calendar of the Patent Rolls, 1569–72*, London, 1966.
CS	'Copies de Simancas', being transcripts made by L. P. Gachard of documents in the Archivo General, Simancas, and now deposited in the Archives Générales du Royaume, Brussels.
CSPD	*Calendar of State Papers, Domestic Series*, London, 1856–.
CSPF	*Calendar of State Papers, Foreign Series*, London, 1863–.
d'Aubigné	T. A. d'Aubigné, *Histoire universelle*, vol. viii (1588–93), ed. A. de Ruble, Paris, 1895.
Davila	E. C. Davila, *The History of the Civil Wars in France*, trans. E. Farneworth, vol. 2, London, 1758.
de Croze	J. de Croze, *Les Guise, les Valois et Philippe II*, 2 vols., Paris, 1866.
d'Estaintot	Vte Robert d'Estaintot, *La Ligue en Normandie, 1588–1594*, Paris, 1862.

De L'Isle	Historical Manuscripts Commission, *Report on the manuscripts of Lord De L'Isle and Dudley*, 6 vols., London, 1925–66.
de Thou	J.-A. de Thou, *Histoire universelle depuis 1543 jusqu'en 1607*, vol. xi (1589–93), London, 1734; (*Historiarum sui temporis*, vols. iv and v, London, 1733).
Devereux	W. B. Devereux, *Lives and Letters of the Devereux Earls of Essex*, vol. i, London, 1853.
Discourse	Sir Roger Williams, *A Briefe discourse of Warre*, London, 1590.
E 351	Public Record Office: Exchequer, Declared Accounts (Pipe Office).
Egerton	F. H. Egerton, *A Compilation of Various Authentic Evidences*, London, 1816.
EHR	*The English Historical Review.*
Félix	J. Félix, *Comptes rendus des échevins de Rouen*, Rouen, 1890.
Finch	Historical Manuscripts Commission, *Report on the manuscripts of Allan George Finch, Esq.*, 4 vols., London, 1913–65.
Floquet	A. Floquet, *Histoire du Parlement de Normandie*, vol. iiiᶜ Rouen, 1841.
HMC	Historical Manuscripts Commission.
LD	Longleat House, Devereux Papers.
Lefèvre	J. Lefèvre (ed.), *Correspondance de Philippe II sur les affaires des Pays-Bas*, vols. iii and iv, Brussels, 1956–60.
LM	Jules Berger de Xivrey and J. Guadet, *Receuil des lettres missives de Henri IV*, 9 vols., Paris, 1843–76.
Lodge	E. Lodge, *Illustrations of British History*, 3 vols., London, 1838.
ML	*Mémoires de la Ligue*, ed. S. Goulart, 6 vols., Amsterdam, 1758.
MM	Philippe de Mornay, sieur du Plessis, *Mémoires et correspondances pour servir à l'histoire de la Réformation*, 12 vols., Paris, 1824–5, especially vol. v.
Palma Cayet	P. V. Palma Cayet, *Chronologie novenaire*, 2 vols. in 3, Paris, 1608.
Patry	R. Patry, *Philippe du Plessis-Mornay: un huguenot homme d'état (1549–1623)*, Paris, 1933.
Poole	R. Poole (ed.), 'A journal of the siege of Rouen in 1591', *The English Historical Review*, vol. xvii (1902), pp. 527–37.
PRO	Public Record Office, London.

PRS	Archives Départementales de la Seine-Maritime: Parlements, registres secrets.
RD	Rouen: Bibliothèque Municipale, Archives Communales, Série A (Délibérations).
RO	Record Office.
Rymer	T. Rymer, *Foedera*, vol. xvi, London, 1615.
Salis	Historical Manuscripts Commission, *Calendar of the manuscripts of the most honourable the Marquis of Salisbury*, 22 vols., London, 1883–1971, especially vols. iv and xiii.
Sommènil	L'Abbé Sommènil, *Campagne de Henri IV au Pays de Caux*, Rouen, 1863.
SP 12	Public Record Office: State Papers, Domestic Series, Elizabeth.
SP 78	Public Record Office: State Papers, France.
SP 81	Public Record Office: State Papers, German States.
SP 84	Public Record Office: State Papers, Holland.
SP 94	Public Record Office: State Papers, Spain.
Sully	*Les Oeconomies Royales de Sully*, eds. D. Buisseret and B. Barbiche, vol. i (1572–94), Paris, 1970.
Unton	J. Stevenson (ed.), *Correspondence of Sir Henry Unton*, London, 1847.
Valdory	G. Valdory, *Discours du siège de la Ville de Rouen*, Rouen, 1871.
van der Essen	L. van der Essen, *Alexandre Farnèse, Prince de Parme*, 5 vols., Brussels, 1933–7.
VCH	*The Victoria County History of England.*
VM	Nicolas de Neufville, seigneur de Villeroy, 'Mémoires d'Estat', *Nouvelle Collection des mémoires pour servir à l'histoire de France*, eds. J. F. Michaud and J. J. F. Poujoulat, Ser. i, vol. xi (Paris, 1838), pp. 89–263.
Zerotin	L. Leger, 'Le Siège de Rouen par Henri IV d'après des documents tchèques', *Revue historique*, année iii, vol. vii (May–June, 1878), pp. 66–77.

The Pays de Caux

PRELUDE

ROUEN

MODERN Rouen sprawls over both banks of the Seine, flanked by prosperous suburbs: a busy provincial capital, thriving, as in past centuries, on commerce and administration. At the core of the modern conurbation an older Rouen is still manifest, not only in narrow streets about the cathedral of Nôtre Dame and in carefully preserved monuments and public buildings, but with its very outline traced by five modern boulevards. These follow the line of the old walls and link the sites of the five gates, four of which each gave access to one of the *quartiers* of the town. The first boulevard runs from the north bank of the Seine past the site of the great Martainville gate which opened on the *quartier* of that name and looked eastwards, across marshy ground, towards the steep slopes of St. Catherine's Mount and, beyond it, upstream towards Paris. The gate to the second *quartier*, St. Hilaire, faced the valley on the north side of the Mount, towards the village of Darnétal; and from it the modern thoroughfare swings westwards, running below the northern hills towards the site of the third gate and *quartier*, Beauvoisin. So to the fourth gate, Bouvreuil, on whose western side stood the castle erected by Philip Augustus, guarding the northwestern approaches to the town, and now marked by little other than the *Tour Jeanne d'Arc*, where the Maid was held and tortured. The fifth gate, Cauchoise, looks downstream towards Caudebec and Le Havre; and from it the modern boulevard proceeds alongside the *quartier* Cauchoise, south to the river once more. There on the riverside stood the Old Palace. Behind its site a street of that name connects the old market-place, where Joan was burned, with another, relatively insignificant and undistinguished, square: the *Place Henri IV*.

Along the riverside from the Old Palace to the one bridge across the Seine in the sixteenth century lay the quay, partly paved, partly of trodden earth. Here were moored the little hundred-ton vessels upon whose success in navigating the difficult tidal waterway of the lower Seine depended the prosperity of the town. For Rouen lived principally by trade.[1] Her fine churches, her archiepiscopal status, might testify to

1. For an analysis of Rouen in terms of historical geography, see J. Levain-

her significance in the ecclesiastical life of France. Her judicial and administrative prominence might stand displayed in the gothic palace that housed the *parlement* of Normandy. Yet Rouen remained, as the name itself implies, a town of markets and of merchants. For Normandy, among the richest of French provinces, she was the distribution centre for grain, salt, fish, the products of an agrarian and maritime economy. But she did not rely only upon her own hinterland. For Paris she was a vital point along the line of access to the coast. Elsewhere in France trade was impeded and costs were inflated by the multiplicity of charges exacted by different authorities who controlled sections of the country's rivers. Together, the Rouennais and the Parisians had made significant strides towards overcoming such obstacles to the movement of cargoes along the Seine. They had established in commercial matters a greater degree of mutual collaboration than had been attained by any other town with which the capital had direct dealings.[2] But the movement of cargoes was also affected by other, physical obstacles. Silting, that notorious affliction of France's westward-flowing rivers, had virtually destroyed the usefulness of Harfleur on the Seine estuary. This was ominous for Rouen. At the beginning of the century her merchants had pressed for the construction of a new port at the river's mouth, where ships bound upstream might await a flowing tide, where commodities destined for Rouen might be laded and unladed—and from where, moreover, the defence of the coast might be organized. Hence Le Havre, the fortified port founded by Francis I, an outport even more necessary to the welfare of Rouen than was the Norman capital to the capital of France.

Yet Rouen was more than the leading provincial market, more than an *entrepôt* in national trade. As the sixteenth century unfolded, her involvement grew, in international commerce and in international finance. Both a symptom and a cause of this development were the increasing numbers of foreign dealers settling in the town: Italians and, especially, Spaniards, representative of the nations whose influence was

---

ville, *Rouen: étude d'une agglomération urbaine* (Paris, 1913). On commercial matters, see especially F. Braudel, *La Méditerranée et le monde méditerranéen à l'époque de Philippe II* (2nd edn., 2 vols., Paris, 1966); H. Lapeyre, *Une Famille de marchands: les Ruiz* (Paris, 1955); M. Mollat, *Le Commerce maritime normand à la fin du Moyen Âge* (Paris, 1952).

2. Though such collaboration is least apparent in relation to the marketing of grain, the medieval tendency to insist upon distinct trading areas remaining pronounced in the case of so basic a commodity (A. P. Usher, *The History of the grain trade in France, 1400–1710* (Cambridge, Mass., 1913), pp. 53–6).

formative upon the general expansion and quickening pace of European trade. Prompted by them, Rouen was drawn further and further into the swirls and eddies of business coursing along the great trade-routes of western Europe, whether northwards across the continent from the Mediterranean to Antwerp, or north-eastwards across the sea, from west Africa, from the Iberian ports, into the English Channel and beyond. Yet it was with Spain that her foreign trade was most voluminous, and Spanish practices that were chiefly emulated in the more sophisticated business methods adopted by her merchants as they engaged in increasingly ambitious and complex ventures. And not in private matters alone. In 1556, by royal edict, a consular tribunal on the Spanish model for regulating trade was set up at Rouen, in the teeth of opposition both by the *vicomte de l'eau*, who controlled river traffic and charges arising from it, and by established courts and lawyers, who pointed to the existence already in the town of an appeal court under the jurisdiction of the Admiralty. The guidance laid down by this tribunal in the important area of liability and compensation for cargoes lost at sea again followed Spanish precedents, and was widely influential. Furthermore, the same edict instructed the Rouennais to designate within the town a place for centralizing exchange and credit dealings. So Rouen acquired her *bourse*, situated again on the quayside; and thereby in time a status in international finance comparable with that of the leading centres of northern Europe.

The divergent attitudes of merchants and lawyers towards the consular tribunal typifies the conflicting interests and multiple authorities so characteristic of sixteenth-century France. At Rouen, organs and officials of municipal, provincial, royal, ecclesiastical, and commercial administration jostled one another and sought to discharge functions which in theory were distinct and in practice frequently overlapped, stimulating mutual suspicion and animosity on the part of those concerned. To all such aggravations the liveliest response was provoked when royal government tickled the sensitive nerve of local authority. Seeking to improve its financial administration in the province the Crown repeatedly attempted in the fifteenth and sixteenth centuries to set up at Rouen a permanent *chambre des comptes*. Until 1580 it was repeatedly frustrated by local opposition led by the Estates of Normandy,[3] who chose to regard as an invasion of their liberties an

3. 'Tables des registres mémoriaux de la Chambre des Comptes de Normandie', *Mémoires de la Société des Antiquaires de Normandie*, Ser. 2, vol. 8 (Paris, 1951), p. xii.

institution geared solely, as it seemed to them, to the convenience of
the agents of royal taxation. In 1584 information that the Crown
intended to establish an *intendant* in the town prompted the municipal
councillors to instruct one of their number to work by every possible
means for its prevention.[4] Measures at this time under royal commission to reform and codify customary law throughout the province
met significant opposition from the Duke of Guise, who, as Count of
Eu, insisted upon the immunity and independence of that particular
locality. Royal appointment of the commissioners' leader, Claude Groulart, as their *premier président* drew protests from the members of
the Normandy *parlement*.[5] In 1540 Francis I had dissolved that recal-
citrant *parlement* for four months.[6] At that time the King had commanded sufficient strength to discipline what he could not cow. By the
later 1580s this was no longer true. And as relations between Crown
and province deteriorated afresh, so did relations between authorities
and groups of several kinds within the town, the province, and the wider
world beyond.

In this complex of deterioration religious controversy had played
its part. For Catholic and Protestant alike it was both an issue of
burning disagreement in itself and the metaphor for other discontents
and aspirations. Through it, heat generated in many different quarters
became concentrated upon single issues whose subtleties fell away as the
fire of religious passion consumed the protagonists. At Rouen Protestant reformers operated from a comparatively early date. Prominent
Rouennais joined the movement, including leading members of the
parlement.[7] In the 1550s pastors from Calvin's Geneva were present
in the town and used it as a base from which to evangelize other parts
of Normandy. Dieppe's first Genevan pastor came there from Rouen,
and was succeeded by others who likewise transferred to Dieppe and

4. Félix, p. xxxi.
5. Floquet, pp. 180–210. Owing to the early centralization of the duchy of
Normandy, codification presented fewer technical problems in that province
than elsewhere; cf. Marc Bloch, *French Rural History: an essay in its basic
characteristics* (London, 1966), p. 207.
6. R. Doucet, *Les Institutions de la France au XVIe siècle*, vol. i (Paris,
1948), p. 222.
7. For examples, see F. Vindry, *Les Parlementaires français au XVIe siècle*
(2 vols., Paris, 1909–12): notably, Antoine de Saint-Anthost, *président* of
the Rouen *parlement* from 1550 and friend of Theodore Beza (see H. Aubert
(ed.), *Correspondance de Théodore de Bèze*, vol. i (1539–55) (Geneva, 1960),
p. 42).

worked there in association with other international evangelists.[8] By 1560 religious feeling was running high, as the Calvinists extended their activities, their opponents resorted to violence, and authority exerted repressive measures.[9] During the next two years the municipal authorities lost control of the situation. In April 1562 Anne de Montmorency, Constable of France, one of the Triumvirate endeavouring to govern the kingdom in the minority of Charles IX, sent forces under two captains to Rouen, ostensibly to assist them. The action was variously interpreted. It was an extension of arbitrary rule, a betrayal of the town by its *bailli*, a pre-emptive occupation by government troops fearful of the growing strength of French Protestantism, a recruitment drive by the Constable in support of his collaborator, the Duke of Guise, against the Protector of the French reformed churches, the Prince of Condé. Montmorency's captains were assassinated. Seizing the initiative, the Rouen Protestants rose in strength. They replaced the existing town councillors with a council of twelve elders, ejected the loyalist members of the *parlement*, who took refuge at Louviers, and, following attacks by government forces, appealed for assistance to Condé, Dieppe, Le Havre, and the Queen of England. To this last they declared themselves to be 'her natural subjects, as we were formerly'.[10]

Despite the arrival of assistance—or of intervention—from all these quarters, government troops recaptured the town within a month of their arrival there in force. Punitive measures followed; normal government was restored, blindly surveyed from a stake upon the bridge by the severed head of Augustin Marlorat, dynamic advocate of Calvinism in France and now executed for having preached sedition at Rouen.[11] Despite such grisly warnings, reformed churches continued to flourish in Normandy. But never again during the civil wars would the Huguenots control Rouen, where persecution of them broke out afresh in the

8. G. and J. Duval, *Histoire de la Réformation à Dieppe, 1557–1657*, ed. E. Lesens, vol. i (Rouen, 1878), pp. 8–10. For the activities of John Knox at Dieppe, see J. Ridley, *John Knox* (Oxford, 1968), pp. 308–9.

9. For example, the riotous rescue by his co-religionaries of a native of Bayeux, condemned to be burned at Rouen for heresy (A. Pottier (ed.), 'Journal d'un bourgeois de Rouen', *Revue rétrospective normande: documents inédits pour servir à l'histoire de Rouen et de la Normandie* (Rouen, 1842), item 8, pp. 7–10).

10. L. de Duranville, *Rouen, ville forte* (Rouen, 1867), p. 46.

11. R. M. Kingdon, *Geneva and the coming of the Wars of Religion in France, 1555–1563* (Geneva, 1956), p. 127.

later 1560s and again in 1572 on the notorious occasion of St. Bartholomew. Yet the damaging interruption caused to their trade by these
disturbances made a profound impression upon the Rouennais. Hence-
forth they sought to cultivate in commercial matters an intermediary
role between parties in Europe at large whom religious and political
principle and expediency impelled into opposition towards one another.
It was a problematical role, exemplified in the town's ambivalence
towards England.

On the one hand complaints multiplied concerning the activities of
English pirates and privateers in the Channel, preying upon vessels
freighted to and from Rouen and evoking retaliatory measures there.[12]
Through reports of movements of shipping and perhaps of troops on
and about the English coast, men were put nervously in mind of the
English intervention of 1562 and its possible recurrence. Indeed, so
nervous were the Rouennais that every ship arriving at the quayside
was searched for arms and munitions; while within the town attempts
were made to restrict possession of arms to the *bourgeois* militia, 400
strong.[13] And yet, on the other hand, the year of St. Bartholomew had
seen the Anglo-French treaty of Blois and the possibility that Rouen
might be designated the location of a staple for the vent of English
cloth: England's major export, until recently relying upon the Netherlands, and now driven by circumstances there to explore alternative
points of access to the continent. In the event this did not materialize,
though it was again under consideration in 1581.[14] But dealings with
England remained an important branch of Rouen's trade. Indeed, its
importance grew. English merchants were invading the Normandy markets in increasing numbers; in 1584 an official argument for measures to
protect French trade turned on the extraordinary quantities of English
cloth being brought into that province.[15] Yet apart from the unfinished

12. *CSPF* (1569–71), p. 23; (1575–7), pp. 401–2; (1581–2), p. 433; (1583),
pp. 276–8; (1584–5), p. 515; (1585–6), pp. 412, 555–6; (1586–8), pp. 50, 81, 96,
361, 632.
13. F. Blanchet, 'Actes concernant la Normandie dans le série KK des Archives Nationales', *Cahiers Léopold Delisle: revue trimestrielle de la société
parisienne d'histoire et d'archéologie normandes*, tome xiv, fasc. 1 (1965),
pp. 31–2, 41; F. de Fréville, *Mémoire sur le commerce maritime de Rouen*
(Rouen, 1857), p. 350; Floquet, pp. 33, 146.
14. *CSPF* (1581–2), p. 309.
15. J. Lair, *Histoire du parlement de Normandie* (Caen, 1860), pp. 25–6, cit-
ing the archives of the *chambres des comptes* and the MS. *Discours* of *maître
des requêtes* Séguier.

cloth of various kinds, lead and tin, which they sold there, English
merchants bought, at Rouen, linen, haberdashery and Corsican wool,
oil and cochineal from Spain; and above all, they looked to Normandy
in general, and to Rouen in particular, for that increasingly vital commodity, canvas.[16] So, strained though it might be by political misgivings
and religious distrust, the commercial bond between England and
Rouen held.

It held until the late 1580s, despite recurrent stress and near-fracture
in years of acute political and religious tension.[17] When in 1587 the complaints of English merchants regarding their treatment there reached
a new crescendo and culminated at last in their quitting the town, this
breach was a feature of the crisis towards which Rouen had steadily
been drifting, not only in her dealings abroad but also in her relations
with the royal government of France. At the Estates of Normandy in
1578, a canon of Rouen had painted a dreadful picture of provincial
miseries brought about by civil disturbance, misgovernment, and high
taxation, and had implied that the people might be driven to take
independent steps to remedy their condition even if these impaired
their loyalty to the Crown.[18] Fresh revenue demands by Henry III in
1582 drew protests and threats of rebellion from Rouen.[19] As the decade
wore on, concessions were demanded, and some wrung, from the King,
without improving the townsmen's temper. In 1587 difficulties and
disaffection intensified; money was scarce, the harvest bad, trade in
recession, and royal taxation resisted more strenuously than ever.[20]

16. See C. Read, 'English Foreign Trade under Elizabeth', *EHR*, vol. xxix
(1914), p. 518; B. Reynolds, 'Elizabethan Traders in Normandy', *Journal of
Modern History*, vol. ix (1937), pp. 289–303; P. Boissonade, 'Le Mouvement
commercial entre la France et les Îles Britanniques au XVIᵉ siècle', *Revue historique*, vols. 134–5 (1920), pp. 1–27, 193–228. No canvas was manufactured in
England until about 1590 (N. J. Williams, 'The Maritime Trade of the East
Anglian Ports, 1550–1590' (unpublished Oxford D.Phil. thesis, 1952), p. 132).
17. Notably in 1569 and 1572, when English merchants complained bitterly
of their treatment by the Rouen authorities (Blanchet, op. cit., pp. 49, 55). In
1577 and 1582 their protests were renewed against augmented impositions and
aggravations there (*CSPF* (1577–8), pp. 59–60; (1582), pp. 330–3). But as one
of them commented regretfully after the breach, 'all Spanish commodities were
had there in as good sort as in Spain and [we] sold to the Spaniards our
English cloth as well as though we did carry it into Spain' (PRO SP 78/20/118).
18. C. M. de Robillard de Beaurepaire, *Cahiers des États de Normandie sous
le règne de Henri III* (Rouen, 1887), pp. 323–7.
19. cf. below, p. 75, note 66.
20. Lapeyre, op. cit., pp. 455–6; RD, vol. 20 (1578–91), fos. 340 sqq.

Alarmed by the mood of the town in the summer of 1588, the King sent letters denying rumours regarding his intentions towards it. In June, a fugitive from Paris, he arrived there in person. But sympathies at Rouen were inclining decisively elsewhere, drawn by other attractions than those of Henry III. Spanish agents were at work; it was one of these who reported in August to the Spanish ambassador at Paris that the Invincible Armada had lived up to its name.[21] English Catholic *émigrés* were active in the town, the chief of them, Robert Parsons, finding it a 'most convenient city' from which to conduct 'this spiritual war' and to send to England devotional books, chalices, and all the apparatus of the Roman mass to raise the spirits of the English faithful.[22] Meanwhile, derisive of the King's presence at the Normandy capital, Le Havre and other key places on the lower Seine were joining Spain's client in France, the Holy League, in open rebellion against him.[23]

Rouen's own loyalty was longer-lived only by a matter of months. At the Estates-General of Blois in December 1588 the leader of the League, the Duke of Guise, and his brother, were assassinated on royal orders. At once Henry wrote to the provincial governors and municipal authorities of the realm, giving justifications for his action, assurances for the future. But delegates from those same localities were returning home to make their reports in person. Opinion polarized. At Rouen, by contrast to 1562, it was the turn of dissidents of Catholic beliefs to seize the initiative. Again the *bailli*, assisted by the governor of Dieppe, endeavoured to preserve order and loyalty to the Crown. Again he failed. And again the loyalist majority of the *parlement*, headed by *premier président* Groulart, quit the town, this time for Caen. On the first Sunday in February 1589 barricades appeared in the streets. So Rouen declared for the League: rebellious as before, with ample fervour as before, and with as little unanimity. And as before, in striving to shrug off the hand of the central government she involved herself directly in a game of kings.

21. G. Mattingly, *The Defeat of the Spanish Armada* (Harmondsworth, 1962), pp. 370–1.
22. L. Hicks (ed.), *Letters and Memorials of Father Robert Persons, S.J.*, *Catholic Record Society*, vol. 39 (1942), pp. lxvi–lxvii.
23. *CSPF* (1586–8), p. 642.

CHAPTER ONE
WESTERN EUROPE
NOVEMBER 1590

In November 1590 Alexander Farnese, Duke of Parma, governor-general in the Netherlands for the King of Spain, withdrew his army from Meaux, thirty miles to the north-east of Paris, and made for the Netherlands frontier. In military terms the withdrawal was executed with the technical efficiency characteristic of the greatest general of his age. Obedient to his strict orders against breaking ranks, the infantry marched in four divisions in battle formation, each flanked by protective walls of baggage-waggons; while outriders of light cavalry reconnoitred the immediate neighbourhood to guard against surprise attack.[1] But if militarily the withdrawal was successful, in political terms it was much less propitious. Rather than military niceties, it was the appearance of events that impressed observers in the interested states of western Europe. Parma was returning to the Netherlands with Henry IV's army snapping at his heels. He was returning in spite of instructions from his King that he should not leave France. In that kingdom satirical comments circulated, and resounded elsewhere, that Philip of Spain's general 'hath ill done his master's business in this voyage (having spent him a million of gold and lost him many thousands of men, returning blamed with the grief and reproaches of them to whose succour he came) [and] he hath yet done worse in those countries that are under his government'.[2]

In reply to such strictures which, he knew, reverberated in Spain, Parma did not lack strong arguments. He could argue that before his departure he had clearly advised the King of the desperate condition of the Netherlands and of the impossibility of effecting a decisive intervention in France with the means at his disposal. It was the urgent appeal of the King's French allies, the Holy League, for aid to relieve the besieged city of Paris that had finally persuaded him to intervene. He had relieved that city. He now repeated that to accomplish Philip's plans would necessitate a threefold or fourfold increase in the resources

1. van der Essen, vol. v, pp. 308–10.
2. BM Cotton Vespasian F V, fo. 352; cf. PRO SP 78/22/181.

made available to him. In principle his opinion remained that expressed at the end of the previous year by his councillor, Peter-Ernst van Mansfeld (who was later to succeed him as governor-general), and reaffirmed at a council of war at Brussels in August: that if the King were to devote his men, money, and munitions primarily to foreign war rather than to reconquering his rebellious provinces, he would consume his substance to no profit.[3]

Even so, Parma's adherence to this principle had wavered from time to time, as Philip was willing enough to remind him. But in any case the King had grown distrustful of his great servants with their narrow involvements and their partial views. Detached and distant within the Escurial, he had grown increasingly reliant upon his Castilian-based and Castilian-staffed bureaucracy. With that reliance his broad conviction had also grown, that the intransigence of resistance in the Netherlands to Spanish rule owed more to international machinations than to resilience on the part of the rebels themselves. That conviction had an empirical foundation, in the information that ceaselessly reached him concerning changing attitudes and events within Europe at large— information which he so painstakingly pondered and assessed. Yet it had a dogmatic foundation too: in the unchanging dictates of law, of conscience and of God. And upon these two foundations Philip had developed a greater conviction, firmer than Parma's opinion and irreconcilable with it. Owing to the very nature of the Netherlands problem and the issues to which it related, Spain's rights and the rule of law in north-western Europe could be safeguarded only through the exercise of force on an international scale: specifically, *vis-à-vis* England and, by 1590, France.

In the 1570s three successive governors-general, applying alternating policies of conciliation and repression, had succeeded only in inciting the Netherlands rebels to unlikely unity. During that decade, however, a major share of Philip's attention had been diverted elsewhere, by the need to combat the Turkish threat in the Mediterranean. By the end of the decade that threat had been disarmed: the Turkish face turned away towards the east, and Spain's towards Portugal and the Atlantic. For a time, while the process of annexing his neighbour kingdom had taken precedence in Philip's eyes, the view northwards from Castile had not been discomforting. Parma, recently appointed governor-general in the Netherlands, had already recovered the southern provinces within his charge and was crowding the remainder in promising style. Em-

3. Lefèvre, vol. iii, pp. 512, 514, 543–4, 454; van der Essen, vol. v, p. 311.

battled, the northern Union of Utrecht had formally offered sovereignty to the Duke of Alençon, heir to the French throne; and negotiations of marriage between Alençon and Elizabeth of England had taken on fresh momentum. Still, Philip had not been excessively disturbed, either by Alençon's inept incursions into the Netherlands or by Elizabeth's indecorous posturings. Then in the summer of 1584, with Alençon dead and their own leader, William the Silent, assassinated, the United Provinces offered their sovereignty to the king of France himself. Henry III had the good sense to decline, but Henry's good sense could not be relied upon. More important, the heir to his throne was now the Huguenot leader, Henry of Navarre. The prospect grew sharper of a multiple alignment, under Protestant colours, of states hostile to Spain and encircling her Netherlands territories.

At the close of 1584 Philip formalized his hitherto furtive support for the Guise faction and the Holy League in France, in a treaty which guaranteed him in return their support in the Netherlands. For him, the move redressed the adverse balance in north-western Europe. Yet its effect was to accelerate the drift towards open war. At first the move had seemed sufficient. By July 1585 Henry III had delivered himself into the hands of the League in the Peace of Nemours. France, the traditional and principal enemy of Habsburg Spain, seemed neutralized. But England had reacted too. In August 1585 Elizabeth took the Netherlands under her protection; by the end of the year the Earl of Leicester was on his way there. In February 1586 he alarmed his own Queen and outraged Spain's King by himself adopting the title of governor-general. In April Parma, who had met earlier explorations by Philip of the feasibility of a combined naval and military attack upon England with reminders that Netherlands reconquest ought to take precedence, wrote that success in the former would much facilitate the latter; indeed, that without it the situation of the rebellious Provinces and the obstinacy of those peoples would render their reconquest long, dangerous, and problematical.[4]

Perhaps Parma considered this a hypothetical proposition. Certainly the preconditions he judged essential for a successful invasion of England were not met; and in 1588 the Armada sailed to disaster. But during the following year, bewailing the drains upon his resources, acknowledging the risks of over-commitment on too many fronts, Philip none the less returned repeatedly to his English theme. Then events

4. Lefèvre, vol. iii, p. 105.

in France supervened. On 1 August 1589 Henry III was assassinated at Saint-Cloud. With the sudden termination of the line of the Valois, Philip's conviction of his European role was strengthened and enlarged. To Paris he promptly dispatched agents with more funds for the League; to Parma, views favouring open intervention in France and, for the time being in the Netherlands, reliance upon defensive measures. But his concern was not merely to ensure the exclusion of the dubious Protestant Henry of Navarre from the French throne and the succession of Henry's aged uncle, the sound Catholic Charles, Cardinal of Bourbon. Philip was also concerned to obtain 'whatever advantage possible along the English Channel'. And, coupling political aims with moral and legalistic righteousness, he was concerned as well for 'the rights of the Señora Infanta to those states acquired by their kings through force and by marriages'.[5] Moreover, with his genius for singling out those portions of his advisers' views that tallied with his own vision, he could again point to a 'decisive reason' tendered him by Parma: that Henry of Navarre was an avowed enemy, whose domination in France would be néfaste.[6]

So Philip reasoned. Yet no less ominous was the problem of finding the means to realize the vision. Owing partly to such cumulative losses as those sustained through Drake's raid on Cadiz in 1587 and the Armada itself, partly to factors other than English interference with her shipping and its movements, the years 1588 to 1592 saw a crisis in Spain's Atlantic trade. In this regard, 1590 was a year of extreme imbalance in numbers of vessels arriving at and departing from the key port of Seville.[7] The pattern of trade was undergoing disruption. In order to ensure a continuing, and increasing, inflow of American silver Philip was to be driven to disregard the needs of other vital branches of maritime commerce, and to concentrate Spain's naval resources blinkeredly upon this sector. This was important for the future. For the present, his growing commitment in France prompted an intensification of taxation in that part of his kingdom where his increasingly bureaucratic administration was strongest and upon which his war

5. De Lamar Jensen, *Diplomacy and Dogmatism: Bernardino de Mendoza and the French Catholic League* (Cambridge, Mass., 1964), pp. 194–6.

6. Lefèvre, vol. iii, p. 452.

7. P. Chaunu, *Séville et l'Atlantique, 1504–1650*, vol. viii$_2$ (Paris, 1959), pp. 767–840, especially 808–13. For the effect of privateering activity upon Spain's circumstances, see K. R. Andrews, *Elizabethan Privateering* (Cambridge, 1964), pp. 224–6.

effort principally depended: Castile, whose Cortes ratified in 1590 a new tax, the *millones*.[8] This again was ominous. Moreover, new measures were taken at this time not only to ensure but more effectively to control supplies of money for Parma.[9] Enviable though his wealth might seem to his rivals, Philip was no stranger to financial problems. His manner of responding to them would in the long term exacerbate the weaknesses of his country's economy without, in the short term, attaining his European ends.

But those ends grew steadily greater and less resistible; for events drew Philip on. The uncrowned Charles X was the prisoner of the principal enemy, Henry. In January 1590 Philip's ambassadors in Paris concluded with the leaders of the League an agreement by which the King of Spain was recognized as Protector of the Crown of France.[10] They were guaranteed material assistance; they were required to negotiate no further alliance other than with Philip, his ally the Duke of Savoy, or the Pope. In May Charles died. In June Philip wrote once more to Parma: 'I neither ask for nor desire words, but actions.'[11] So Parma marched to relieve Paris, but 'his master's business' now encompassed far more than that limited object. It involved no less than the claim of the Infanta, Isabella Clara Eugenia, daughter of Philip and his third wife Elizabeth of Valois, to her grandfather's throne of France. And whatever his justifications Parma's retreat now jeopardized the attainment of that end.

To attain so great an end—if it were attainable at all—continuous pressure must be applied upon France. The pressure was growing. In the south, in November 1590, Charles-Emmanuel of Savoy entered Aix-en-Provence, to be recognized by the *parlement* there as protector

8. For general comment upon the centralisation of government in Castile and the significance of the *millones*, see J. H. Elliott, *Imperial Spain, 1469–1176* (London, 1963), pp. 76–87, 279–81; cf. J. Lynch, *Spain under the Habsburgs*, vol. i (Oxford, 1964), pp. 196, 128–9. For analysis of the development there from 1586, owing to 'the obvious and avowed pressures of war', of 'a crucial step in the emergence of a recognisably modern, bureaucratic state system', see I. A. A. Thompson, 'The Spanish Council of War in the reign of Philip II', *EHR*, vol. lxxxii (1967), pp. 698–725.

9. H. Lapeyre, *Simon Ruiz et les 'asientos' de Philippe II* (Paris, 1953), pp. 59–80. cf. the suggestion that such measures were provoked by suspicions of corruption in Parma's administration (van der Essen, vol. v, pp. 260–1).

10. Rymer, vol. xvi, pp. 33–4. League-held coastal towns were to receive Spanish shipping and no enemy vessels, with reference to Spain's prosecuting the war against England or Scotland.

11. Lefèvre, vol. iii, p. 503.

and governor-general of the province.[12] In the west, Spanish detachments had arrived to assist the League in Brittany and, mastering the Blavet estuary and recapturing Hennebont, established control over most of the south-west Breton coast.[13] Meanwhile in Rome, with famine and riots disrupting the eternal city, Philip's agents were renewing at a stormy conclave the efforts which two months earlier had procured the election of a candidate acceptable to Spain as Pope Urban VII—and which, within a fortnight, had been rendered abortive by Urban's death.[14] Each of these endeavours bore upon the central issue. Yet each was marginal, and its outcome uncertain. The papal election was proving difficult. The dukes, of Savoy and of Mercœur in Brittany,[15] each had at heart interests of his own which might well obstruct the furtherance of Spain's. As Philip had advised his agents in Paris, their diplomatic moves and legal arguments must be backed by an impression of overwhelming force deployed by Spain herself: 'what would give warmth and life to the negotiations' concerning the Infanta's claim was 'the presence of his Majesty's army'.[16] It was that presence that was now being withdrawn, enabling Henry to boast how he had 'hunted the Prince of Parma and his army out of my kingdom'.[17]

It was a proud boast, typical of Henry's flamboyant style, so different from Philip's. By contrast to the withdrawn and suspicious manner of the Habsburg, Henry was affable, carelessly informal to the point, it seemed, of irresponsibility. Munching meat and drinking wine, he would discuss affairs of state amidst a babble of *primero*-playing soldiers, or greet early morning visitors 'all untrussed, and what he had been doing God knoweth'.[18] Where Philip had his monks, Henry had his mistresses; and actions explicable in the one by his desire to please God were readily attributable in the other to less exalted passions. While Philip sought privacy, scrupulously weighing his ser-

12. de Thou, vol. xi, p. 223 (vol. iv, p. 893).
13. Davila, p. 188; de Thou, vol. xi, p. 212 (vol. iv, p. 888).
14. L. Pastor, *The History of the Popes*, vol. xxii (London, 1952), pp. 320–3, 333–48.
15. On Mercœur, see especially G. de Carné, *Documents sur la Ligue en Bretagne: Correspondance du Duc de Mercœur et des ligueurs bretons avec l'Espagne*, Société des Bibliophiles Bretons, vols. 11–12 (Vannes et Rennes, 1899); and below, pp. 50–1.
16. van der Essen, vol. v, p. 302.
17. *LM*, vol. iii, p. 309.
18. Coningsby, p. 45.

vants' written words and distrustful of their opinions, Henry consulted freely and would follow where his advisers led—or so he would have them and others believe. By his own account, 'the manner of proceeding in his Council was always to conclude by the more part of voices which at that time carried the resolution that way, and was of the most grave and experienced Councillors, though contrary to his own opinion. And yet as well as that in all other consultations his custom is to prefer the opinions of his greatest and best counsellors before his own, and all other resolutions so taken he putteth in execution as his own.'[19] In the circumstances of 1590 Henry needed all his friends. Whatever its effect upon his kingly image, this appearance of human responsiveness and of malleability had advantages for a king who lacked the power to enforce, or even openly to declare, his own will and his own intentions.

For despite his bravado, Henry's tenure of his kingdom in November 1590 remained precarious. Only in part was this because of objections to him on legal grounds, though these were strenuously argued. Hostile lawyers stressed that his relationship in blood to the deceased Henry III was no better than that of twenty-second cousin. The crown of France should pass by hereditary succession to males in the direct line by primogeniture and, in default of such, to collaterals in accordance with degree of kinship. Since Henry's relationship to the late king was more remote than the tenth collateral degree, his claim was invalid in law. Further, it was irrelevant that upon his deathbed the last of the Valois had acknowledged Henry to be his successor. However proprietorial the attitudes of kings and their servants towards lands and offices within the realm, the crown at least was no king's property and could not be willed by one to another. More important still, profession of the Roman faith was essential to the title of the kings of France. In 1577 the deputies at the Estates-General of Blois had declared this a principal and fundamental law of the kingdom.[20] Henry of Navarre was a Protestant—worse, a relapsed heretic who, having in 1572 sought and been granted papal absolution from his earlier errors, had afterwards reverted to Calvinist doctrines. The

19. PRO SP 78/27/285.
20. R. Villers, 'Aspects politiques et aspects juridiques de la loi de catholicité, 1589–93', *Revue historique de droit français et étranger*, Ser. 4, année 37 (1959), p. 197. For discussion of rival claims, see R. Mousnier, *L'Assassinat de Henri IV* (Paris, 1964), pp. 91 sqq.; A. G. Williams, 'The Abjuration of Henry of Navarre', *Journal of Modern History*, vol. v (1933), pp. 143–71.

sincerity of his convictions was certainly questionable. It was shortly afterwards reported that he was a man of no beliefs, who laughed at his Huguenot ministers even when they were in the pulpit and had been known to bombard them with cherry-stones even as they preached.[21] But lightheartedness in these matters was hardly a recommendation.

Henry, of course, had lawyers of his own, and they had serious arguments at their command. According to them, his opponents' objections in law to his title derived from confusion on their part of the laws governing inheritance to private property with the fundamental law governing succession to the throne; and indeed, the distinction was implicit in any discounting of Henry III's deathbed recognition. But such precise debates, vastly stimulating though they might be to lawyers, were impotent in themselves to resolve France's differences. Moreover, the religious case against Henry was a compelling one for political reasons. As Protector of the reformed churches he headed a minority group, singularly weak in northern France, controlling few important towns, and tainted with a reputation for resistance to established authority. Reconciliation with the Catholic church offered not only conformity with the religious beliefs of most Frenchmen, but also the prospect of coronation in accordance with traditional rites, consecration with holy oil—ceremonies in which, as Henry himself would later write, the people reposed great confidence. And although his Catholic opponents were divided among themselves, collectively they enjoyed weighty endorsement. Ultramontane opinion would be guided by the papacy. In 1585 Pope Sixtus V had pronounced Henry excommunicate and incapable of succeeding to the throne—a ruling which, together with the Pope's authority, was upheld by the Sorbonne in 1590. Gallican opinion, favouring conciliar above papal authority, resentful of the pretensions of popes, of their interference in French affairs, and of their subservience to Spain, would prefer the guidance of the institutions of the realm. In 1588 the Estates-General and the *parlement* of Paris had both reaffirmed Henry's exclusion.

Even so, the fact that his opponents were divided and that there were many shades of opinion upon these questions itself served to deny Henry a straightforward solution to his dilemma. He could not risk a spontaneous switch of religious allegiance. Such a switch would cost him the basis of his existing support. There was no certainty that

21. M. N. Tommaseo (ed.), *Relations des ambassadeurs vénetiens sur les affaires de France*, vol. ii (Paris, 1838), p. 637.

it would win him a greater. Indeed, it might win him little beyond fresh strictures that, with cynical disregard for all religious values, he acted purely from motives of self-interest. On this issue he could only temporize, seeking to gain credibility and to beguile the confidence of every opinion while irrevocably alienating none. It was an intensely difficult task. In August 1589, making his first public pronouncement following his predecessor's death, Henry had declared that for no kingdom would he exchange the 'religion which I have, so to speak, drunk with my mother's milk ... except for that which will be proposed to me by an ecclesiastical Council'.[22] Even this had provoked the Protestants in synod at St. Jean d'Angely the following month to express profound misgivings and to threaten to elect themselves a new Protector.[23] Henry had written letters of reassurance; he had also commented on the impatience of those who would have him 'bend the bow of my affairs to the string of their passions'.[24] But rhetoric was not enough. In November 1590 Philippe du Plessis-Mornay, the sober and distinguished founder of the Protestant academy at Saumur and *surintendant* of Henry's hereditary lands, submitted to the King's council a formulary calling again for guarantees for Protestants and for an ecumenical assembly to iron out religious differences.[25] Meanwhile, direct approaches had been made to the papacy. In December 1589 Sixtus V, made uneasy by Spanish manoeuvrings, had received in audience the Duke of Luxembourg. Ostensibly the Duke represented the Catholic princes in France; in fact, as everyone knew, he was acting on behalf of Henry himself. In response to Luxembourg's plea that Henry 'protests that he is no heretic, and that if his error is proved to him he will retract', Sixtus had exclaimed, 'It is true, it is true!'[26] But hopes so raised were sustained neither by Sixtus's subsequent vacillations, nor by the manifest pro-League sympathies of his legate in Paris. In any case, in November 1590 Sixtus was three months dead; and the success of Spanish pressure in his immediate successor's election did not augur well for future developments at the Holy See.

But it was chiefly in the direction of Gallican opinion that Henry had aimed that declaration of August 1589. It was Gallican opinion

22. de Thou, vol. xi, p. 13 (cf. vol. iv, pp. 795–6).
23. Patry, pp. 183–5.
24. *LM*, vol. iii, pp. 70–3.
25. Patry, pp. 194–5.
26. M. de Bouart, 'Sixte-Quint, Henri IV et la Ligue', *Revue des questions historiques*, vol. cxvi (1932), p. 83.

that he hoped to encourage, both by appointing Catholics to positions about him and by emphasizing a view he had long since aired: 'We are all Frenchmen, fellow-citizens of the same nation.'[27] The League leaned upon Spain. More, the League was inherently divisive, a centrifugal force within the realm. While its leaders claimed to stand for Catholicism and the state, its members—lawyers and artisans, clerics and great feudatories—stood in reality for provincial and municipal liberties even to the extreme of autonomy, and against centralized, hierarchical government, even to the extreme of republicanism. The League aimed to reduce to fragmentation and to foreign subservience the state to whose mastery Henry aspired. By comparison with what was involved in the tendencies of the League, Henry's deficiencies were scarcely more than technical, given that his religious position was negotiable. Certainly such a viewpoint was gaining adherents. In 1590 the distinguished jurist Guy Coquille, the lawyer Pierre Ayrault, Henry's cousin the powerful Duke of Nevers, each published an assessment of the situation from the standpoint of the interests of the state. They insisted that the state's security depended upon acceptance of Henry as king, if he would declare himself a Catholic. And Nevers had since declared for Henry even without that prior concession. Moreover, peace negotiations were being covertly explored on behalf of prominent Leaguers by the influential administrator Villeroy, formerly the late king's secretary of state. In October 1590 a conference took place between him and some of Henry's closest advisers.[28] In November Henry wrote to Nevers that Villeroy had again 'sent to ask for a passport in order that he may come to see me'.[29] Thanks to his own moderation, moderate opinion, anxious for the preservation of the state, was gravitating towards Henry.

But not sufficiently so. To consolidate such political opinion about him, Henry must carry political conviction: which, especially in a situation of war, meant military conviction too—the ingredient that had escaped the later Valois. Without it, his legal position remained acutely problematical. Among the sovereign courts of the realm he was supported only by that section of the Paris *parlement* that had earlier removed to Tours, and by its counterpart in Normandy that had

27. *LM*, vol. i, p. 116.

28. J. Nouaillac, *Villeroy, secrétaire d'état et ministre de Charles IX, Henri III et Henri IV* (Paris, 1908), pp. 177, 195. The trade of Paris had been a consideration at these talks.

29. *LM*, vol. iii. p. 297.

transferred from Rouen to Caen. None of those that still resided in the established seats of government recognized his claim. Only the *parlement* of Bordeaux, under the influence of the astute Marshal Jacques de Matignon, retained for the present an equivocal position. It was to Matignon that towards the end of 1590 Henry outlined his view, that if he should relax military pressure upon his enemies 'they will usurp all the rest of this state, or at least leave me only a small part of it; and if I should intensify the war, I can ruin and destroy them'.[30] But this was precisely what he lacked the necessary resources to achieve. In November 1590, declaring that 'nothing is so necessary to us as to raise money towards maintaining the armed forces we must assemble', he issued his warrant to Mornay to sell his hereditary lands to the value of 100,000 *écus*.[31] It was a desperate remedy. The King's right to alienate lands in this way was questionable. Prospective purchasers lacked confidence to buy: the Crown's credit had fallen to abysmal depths and there was no certainty that they would be able to enjoy what they were offered.[32] Lacking means of his own to put adequate forces in the field, Henry must seek support where he could find it.

With misgivings he had looked to those European states which themselves felt menaced by Habsburg power. The choice was limited. In Italy, Spain was paramount in Sicily and in Naples. Her influence was liable to challenge further north. The papacy had already proved restive. In Milan, Borromeo aspirations had long caused vexation in Madrid. Most encouraging of all, Venice had promptly recognized Henry as king of France. But the Republic's lead had not been followed by her neighbours. The leaders of Genoa and Florence would not exchange the real dividends of association with Spain for risky dealings in the affairs of France.[33] For the rulers of Tuscany and Savoy,[34]

30. ibid., p. 316. cf. the letter by the essayist and former magistrate Michel de Montaigne, associate of Matignon, to Henry in January 1590: 'We could not possibly draw from the justice of your cause such strong arguments to confirm or subdue your subjects as we do from the news of the prospering of your campaigns' (D. M. Frame, *Montaigne: a biography* (London, 1965), p. 285).

31. AN K 104, no. 27.

32. *MM*, vol. v, pp. 59–62.

33. HMC *Salis.*, vol. xiii, pp. 418–19, for a reminder in December 1589 to the Florentine authorities that once secure upon the throne Henry might prove aggressive towards Italy.

34. The wife of Ferdinand I, Grand Duke of Tuscany, was Christine of Lorraine, daughter of Charles of Lorraine and Claude of France, and niece of Henry III. For a discerning note on Savoy, see A. Dufour, 'Charles-

disorders in that kingdom roused ambitions of their own, which success for Henry must disappoint. More might be hoped of divided Germany than of divided Italy. The princes of Hesse and Württemberg, Brunswick and Saxony, Brandenburg, Mecklenburg and the Palatinate—all these in the course of the century had opposed themselves to the Habsburg Emperor and had sought assistance in France. Henry's father had cultivated the friendship of the Rhineland princes who, during the last twenty years, had frequently intervened in France and had aided Henry himself. Their inclination in this regard persisted. Protesting at Brussels and at The Hague in the summer of 1590 against extension into their territories of Parma's struggle with the northern Provinces, delegates from the Rhineland principalities had been reminded by the latter, and were disposed to believe, that all was attributable to Habsburg Spain's tyranny and ambition.[35] More still might be hoped by Henry of those same United Provinces. There had long been collaboration between them and his party in France. Close associates of his had fought and had suffered imprisonment in their cause. The widow of their late leader, William the Silent, was the daughter of Coligny, late leader of the Huguenots and confidant of Henry's own mother. And Louise de Coligny's stepson, Maurice of Nassau, rapidly strengthening his own position of leadership in the Provinces, was widely credited with enough sympathy for Henry to wish to co-ordinate his own activities with his.

But the German princes were unreliable. Moreover, without remuneration they could not, or would not, serve. As for the Provinces, although Maurice had exploited Parma's absence in the summer of 1590 to good military effect, their position was by no means so secure as to make them more able to give assistance to others than needful of it themselves. One state remained: England, sensitive to developments among her continental neighbours, believed to have great resources at her disposal, a declared opponent of Spain's. But there were political disadvantages in open reliance upon England, traditionally the enemy of France. England's queen, who called herself Queen of France, was freely abused on the continent. She was Jezebel, persecutress of English Catholics, murderess of a rival queen, territorially ambitious.[36]

Emmanuel Ier, duc de Savoie, et la Ligue', *Bulletin de la société d'histoire et d'archéologie de Genève* (1954), p. 301.

35. de Thou, vol. xi, pp. 250–1 (vol. v, pp. 8–9).

36. G. Ascoli, *La Grande Bretagne devant l'opinion française* (Paris, 1927), pp. 206–8.

In consequence of her assistance the Provinces had experienced meddling by her representatives in their affairs, occupation by her troops
of important towns: towns from which, as some still believed despite
her reassurances, she intended to move towards imposing upon the
Provinces her own brand of tyranny.[37] Henry's political credit was far
from sound enough to allow him casually to add England to his
liabilities—if this could be avoided.

It could not be avoided altogether. Like his predecessor, Henry had
already received English funds; he had also been assisted by English
troops. But use by sixteenth-century monarchs of foreign money and
foreign mercenaries was common enough. Formal commitments to
potentially hostile states in return for aid, of the kind already concluded by the League with Spain, were a different matter. Such commitments betrayed the state. The League threatened its dismember-
ment. Henry drew political strength, and hoped for more, from such
capacity as he possessed to project himself by contrast as its defender.
Political concessions to England in exchange for assistance must as
far as possible be avoided. Hitherto he had managed to avoid them.
Indeed, earlier in 1590 it had seemed for a time that his need for
assistance would shortly end. Control of Paris and of northern France
had seemed within his grasp. But Parma had intervened. Although he
was now withdrawing, undoubtedly he would shortly return; and
Henry's army was disbanding. If the League's political discredit was
greater than ever, so too was Henry's need to demonstrate con-
vincingly not merely his title to the throne but his power to hold it,
and to hold the kingdom. His conviction remained, that such a demonstration in the military sphere must precede resolution of the religious
difficulty. So he must turn to England, in quest of maximum financial
and military aid at minimum political cost. While his advisers
clamoured, for an ecclesiastical council, for conversion, for negotiations,
for war here or there, Henry laid his plans. In November 1590
his envoy, the Viscount Turenne, arrived at Dover.

Whatever Elizabeth's reputation among her continental contemporaries, she herself insisted that, 'carrying ever a single eye to justice
and truth', she 'never gave just cause of war to any prince ... nor
had any greater ambition than to maintain my own State in security

37. HMC *Salis.*, vol. iv, pp. 32–3, 56; cf. R. B. Wernham, 'The mission of
Thomas Wilkes to the United Provinces in 1590', *Studies Presented to Sir
Hilary Jenkinson*, ed. J. C. Davies (London, 1957), pp. 423–55.

and peace'.[38] Her self-appraisal has been widely endorsed by subsequent historians, with the partial reservation that what she ascribed to scruple and concern for law ought perhaps to be credited to political craft. Judgements upon her political skill have varied, but few would deny her general reluctance to resort to the exercise of force or her general preference for other means of maintaining her state's security against external threats. Earlier in her reign the likeliest aggressor had seemed to be the traditional enemy, France: where Guise influence dominated the sickly successors of Henry II and reached behind England into Scotland, in the shape of James V's widow, Mary of Lorraine, and her daughter, the unpredictable Queen of Scots. Later, with French energies dissipated in internal strife, it was the power of Spain, amassing perilously near in the Netherlands, that appeared the more menacing. One means of insulating England against these two potential threats lay in manipulating their mutual hostility. But more was required than a simple version of that dangerous game, difficult as it was to control. Elizabeth had two further potential safeguards.

The first involved exploiting factions hostile to the established governments within those uncomfortable neighbour states, with a view not to overthrowing those governments but to neutralizing their ability to direct a challenge against England. In Scotland the available instrument was the protestant Lords of the Congregation; in the Netherlands, the rebellious Provinces; in France, the Huguenots. Elizabeth exploited these principally by means of diplomatic activity, sometimes surreptitious, but also formal, as in her dogged representations to Spain that the Provinces' case had merit in law. Apart from intervening in Scotland at the very outset of her reign, only once, before 1585, did she resort to force. That occasion relates to her second safeguard. It needed no extraordinary perspicacity to discern that unimpeded control by either of her potential enemies of the coastline across the English Channel would constitute, in strategic terms, a major threat to England's security. When Calais fell to French arms under Guise command in 1558 England lost her last direct impediment to such control. In 1562 Elizabeth attempted to repair that loss. At the invitation of the Huguenots, English troops arrived at Le Havre, Dieppe, and Rouen, with the object of holding these until Calais should be returned. The outcome was an ignominious withdrawal. But despite this costly failure the strategic consideration remained. Its importance increased with the

38. From her closing speech to her last parliament in 1601, printed in J. E. Neale, *Elizabeth I and Her Parliaments*, vol. ii (London, 1965 edn.), pp. 428–9.

international developments of 1584–5, which went far to undermine Elizabeth's diplomatic safeguard and drove her to intervene openly in the Netherlands. As security for her support she obtained from the Provinces, by the Treaty of Nonsuch, control of the towns of Brielle and Flushing: the latter a deep-water port such as the Armada would have found so welcome after beating through the Straits of Dover in 1588.

The assassination of Henry III in 1589, and subsequent events, exacerbated Elizabeth's problem without altering its essential nature as she saw it. The danger that had forced her to act in 1585 was intensified: the danger that Spain would be dominant over France, that the Netherlands would be contained even if the Provinces did not submit, and that the two continental giants would together assail England. In 1585 she had agreed to subsidize Henry of Navarre. Now in 1589 she paid him a further £20,000 and sent 4,000 troops, under a commander experienced in Netherlands affairs,[39] to Dieppe to assist him. There was also the possibility that a firm understanding, undesirable and unpropitious for England, would develop between the Provinces and the new *régime* in France. In the summer of 1590 a special English envoy reported that for the time being this could be discounted. The Netherlands were self-absorbed. France was absorbing the attention of Philip of Spain. Following his lead, Elizabeth could concentrate her own attention upon the situation there.

By this analysis, Elizabeth's policy—as distinct from incidental exploits—was solely to maintain disunity and a balance of forces, in general among the continental powers and in particular along the littoral from Quimper in Brittany to the estuary of the Ems. That policy, if unambitious, was realistic.[40] Unlike her father, unlike many of her subjects, Elizabeth dreamed no expansive dreams: or, if she dreamed them, she permitted them little intrusion upon reality. What she accomplished was what she had set out to achieve: the safety of her government and the security of her state. If her achievement was indeed so exactly the measure of her considered intentions, she must surely have stood first among her contemporaries in clarity of judgement and in maturity of statesmanship. And yet contemporaries, even

39. But disinclined to resume his own service there (HMC *Ancaster*, p. 282).
40. Present-day English historians have broadly concurred in this view of Elizabeth's aims. It has recently been criticized, in terms which challenge her claim to be credited with a 'policy' at all, by C. Wilson, *Queen Elizabeth and the Revolt of the Netherlands* (London, 1970).

in her own kingdom, had considerable reservations regarding Elizabeth. They detected in her regrettable traits of hesitancy and indecision, a failure to recognize the possibilities of the international situation from the standpoint of England's interests, a dithering parsimoniousness which meant that everything was done by halves. To them, her policy —if such it was—damaged her reputation abroad and gained her nothing in return beyond continuing cause for nervous apprehensiveness as to what, at any moment, might befall.

In many cases such views as these were matched by notions of what the Queen ought to do. She should seize the initiative in the maritime sphere, in one of several ways. She should cut off at source the flow of American silver upon which Philip's war effort was believed to depend, by sending her ships in force to range the Caribbean. She should interrupt that flow, by operating from the Azores to intercept the treasure *flotas* on their inward voyages. She should, by blockading the Iberian coast and even occupying locations upon it, interfere with Spanish commercial shipping, promote disorder within Philip's own realm, carry the war to him. She should concentrate her naval resources in home waters, again disrupting Spain's sea-borne trade, breaking Philip's communications with the Netherlands, and ensuring freedom of movement behind this defensive screen for her own merchants and for her continental allies.[41] Alternatively, she should certainly attempt more by way of land operations. The opportunity existed for her to head a protestant coalition on the continent. Conversely, by the implications of history and her own reasoning, all 'neighbouring nations would be in happier case when France should be subject not to one sceptre but to twenty petty kings';[42] and so Elizabeth should join with Spain and the League in partitioning that kingdom. None of this was beyond England's means. Private adventurers would collaborate, as they already did, in plundering Spain's

41. For strategic alternatives in general, see R. B. Wernham, 'Elizabethan War Aims and Strategy', *Elizabethan Government and Society: Essays presented to Sir John Neale*, ed. S. T. Bindoff *et al.* (London, 1961), pp. 340–68. For the advantages of concentrating ships in home waters, BM Cotton Caligula E VII, fos. 338–9.

42. W. Camden, *The History of the most renowned and victorious princesse Elizabeth, late Queene of England* (London, 1688), p. 444. cf. Robert Naunton's comment to the Earl of Essex in January 1597, that 'England had never a fitter time to think of recovering its ancient rights in France which will be much easier to do than to support this broken estate' (BM Harleian 288, fo. 245).

seagoing traffic; and 'it is possible to find the ability of six or twelve of
her subjects at the most to be well able to discharge the charge of a
great war, and yet a sufficient estate received to themselves to maintain
the port of their fathers' children.'[43] And in addition to the seamen and
soldiers, peers and administrators, determined Protestants and other
visionaries, who aired their opinions on the basis of practical experience
or, indeed, on the basis of none at all, there were some very practical
men, whose concern over these matters was essentially neither political,
religious, nor strategic. England's merchants who engaged in overseas
commerce were deeply concerned over the condition into which their
trade had fallen.

The cloth trade with Antwerp had formerly been their mainstay.
Circumstances since the 1560s had driven Antwerp and this trade into
decline. Seeking alternative outlets in north Germany they had run
into difficulties with the Hanseatic League.[44] Covetous of Mediterranean and Iberian riches they were frustrated by the enmity of
Spain. The years 1586–7 had been years of crisis in the export trade.
Problems persisted: the structure of the trade itself was changing, and
this brought difficulties to many merchants.[45] France had remained
viable, and increasingly attractive to them—especially her southern
Atlantic ports which gave access to Spain, but also those of Normandy.[46] But by 1590 trade with France was problematical too. Dealings with League-held towns were prohibited by the government.
Elsewhere, as at Bordeaux, trade was far from trouble-free. Some
bold, far-sighted merchants could think in terms of seeking to wrest
a share of the Atlantic trade from Spain, of engaging in fresh southward drives into the Mediterranean, of profit from expanding commerce and from plunder. Such prospects were beyond both the vision

43. BM Lansdowne 63, fo. 112^v; cf. Essex's expenditure 'in the Queen's service', below, p. 190.
44. These difficulties are summarized in PRO SP 12/231/77.
45. The crisis is discussed by J. D. Gould, 'The crisis in the export trade,
1586–1587', EHR, vol. lxxi (1956), pp. 212–22. PRO SP 12/238/122, 129,
illustrate the continuing difficulties of the Merchant Adventurers and of the
Muscovy Company in April 1591, the latter bemoaning scarcity and price
inflation of unfinished cloth in England owing to 'murrain of sheep' and the
fact that 'much wool is turned into . . . other kinds of foreign wares of late years
made here by divers workmen strangers that are come over and do inhabit
here'.
46. See above, pp. 6–7. For illustration of difficulties at Bayonne in 1590, PRO
SP 78/22/95, 99.

and the means of many more. As Burghley wrote to Walsingham in December 1588, 'when their trade to all other parts for the most part is stopped' the loss of their trade to Rouen was a crippling blow to some of these.[47] For them, to abide by governmental prohibition might mean ruin; to defy it meant running the risk of having their ships and cargoes impounded in the Normandy ports.[48] They required a remedy.

All these opinions and considerations reached the Queen, or at least her closest adviser, Burghley. For Elizabeth's style of rule was very different from Philip's and from Henry's. If by comparison with the latter she cultivated majesty and formality, by comparison with the former she was approachable if temperamental. She roved about England from manor-house to manor-house, seen by her people, moving among them though always with appropriate ceremony. Not for her the seclusion of the study, the agonizing over paper, pen in hand, where Philip spent his days. The politics of personal confrontation were Elizabeth's *forte*—though only a very few participated with her in those innermost counsels that led to the decisions which she herself would take. Throughout her reign Burghley had always been one of them; after more than thirty years he was still 'old Saturnus ... a melancholy and wayward planet but yet predominant here'.[49] And among his personal memoranda all these conflicting views were recorded.

They scarcely helped the Queen to make up her mind with resolution and to abide by her decisions with conviction. In foreign affairs, policy and decisions were no doubt her prerogative. As she laboured towards them, there was always plenty of advice to hand, and with it plenty of seductive rumour. But like all contemporary rulers, what Elizabeth lacked most keenly, and knew she lacked, was trustworthy information and reliable means of obtaining it. While she could and did take steps to obtain first-hand experience of England, of her own subjects and of domestic matters, she remained throughout her reign

47. PRO SP 12/219/46.

48. For example, as happened to merchants of Great Yarmouth in 1590. The special circumstances of their case won them some compensation from their town; but anyone who subsequently might sustain such a loss in France 'shall bear the same loss himself without any manner of recompense to be given him by the town' (Norfolk and Norwich R.O., Great Yarmouth Assembly Book (1579–98), fos. 199–200; Audit Book (1582–1619), fo. 130ᵛ).

49. HMC *De L'Isle*, vol. ii, p. 123.

entirely without first-hand experience of Europe, and was palpably ignorant of circumstances abroad.[50] Ignorance made her distrustful, which was often salutary; over the years her advisers had grown wise in the arts of persuasion, knowing that to implant their ideas in the Queen's mind they must first make 'the soil seasonable to receive seed.'[51] But ignorance also made her vulnerable to misleading information. In part, this could not be helped. News, like the conduct of war itself, was perennially affected by factors beyond human control: bad communications, adverse weather conditions, accidents, disease. But it was also affected by the intrusion of uninvited persons, often associates of prominent personages and groups: persons avid to exercise upon great affairs an influence beyond merely stating their points of view, and sufficiently energetic and ingenious to exploit circumstances to their own advantage. However marked her ignorance of other matters, Elizabeth was well enough aware of this. Surely she was guarded enough to take it into account in pondering her decisions.

So, the fact that her Court buzzed with them is no reason for believing activist recommendations stemming from interested parties to have influenced her policy very far. Neither she nor Burghley tired of reminding such advisers at home and abroad of how limited her resources in reality were, notwithstanding all rumours to the contrary. Military expeditions were dauntingly expensive and showed no cash return. Naval expeditions might yield windfalls, but equally might be ruinous to all who adventured in them. Two years' aid to the Provinces alone between 1585 and 1587 had cost her a sum approximately equivalent to her entire ordinary revenue in a single year. If Elizabeth's policy was indeed to undertake as few positive commitments as possible, and those as near home as possible, this was as much as she could afford. If occasionally she did permit herself more ambitious measures, this was to act boldly in her circumstances. If her policy was conceived in terms of defensive operations on the home front with use further afield from time to time of surplus naval and military capacity, rarely did she have any such surplus at her disposal. And if she had committed herself in any degree to a programme of foreign

50. Thus, for example, in the summer of 1591 the English government had no maps adequate to enable it to follow the reported movements of its own armies either in Brittany or in Normandy, and did not even know whether the army in Brittany itself possessed one (PRO SP 78/25/101, 127; Unton, pp. 87–8). For the significance of this factor, see below, p. 65.

51. BM Harleian 6994, fos. 187–8: Walsingham to Burghley, July 1589.

conquest by sea or by land, this would surely have been outrageous folly.

Or so it might appear. But in fact, in the two years following the Armada Elizabeth did sponsor a series of measures which together approximate more closely than at any other phase of her reign to a general counter-offensive, well beyond what she would seem to have been able to afford—certainly in terms of her previous financial ability. Such measures were premeditated, as is evident from her preceding them with an energetic programme of fund-raising. Money flowed in through parliamentary subsidy, through a special commission for the sale of Crown lands, through loans on the City of London, through loans from the country on privy seals. Management of the customs was altered.[52] Even the possibility of borrowing from abroad was explored—a measure abandoned since 1574.[53] Neither the need to repay existing debts nor a desire to restore a healthy balance in the ordinary revenue account is sufficient to explain so extraordinary a degree of fiscal activity on the part of the notoriously parsimonious Queen. In the aftermath of the Armada the Elizabethan state, whether encouraged by success or alarmed by narrow escape, was going seriously to war. Asking parliament for a subsidy in February 1589 Elizabeth's Lord Chancellor, briefed by Burghley, said as much, in a rousing call to arms: 'England hath been accounted hitherto the most renowned kingdom for valour and manhood in all Christendom; and shall we now lose our old reputation? If we should, it had been better for England we had never been born.'[54] His mistress seemed eager to suit the action to the word.

In April 1589 a fleet of 150 ships sailed for Portugal under the command of Drake and Sir John Norris, with instructions to destroy surviving Armada vessels in the Biscay ports, to attempt to seize Lisbon if local support for the Portuguese pretender were strong enough to warrant this, and to capture islands in the Azores.[55] That

52. H. A. Lloyd, 'Camden, Carmarden and the Customs', *EHR*, vol. lxxxv (1970), pp. 776–87.

53. On royal finance in general, R. B. Outhwaite, 'Studies in Elizabethan Government Finance: Royal Borrowing and the sales of Crown lands, 1572–1603' (unpublished Nottingham Ph.D. thesis, 1964); pp. 59–60, 70, 116–17, discuss the 1589 inquiries abroad (I do not altogether agree with the author's view of the implications of Milwarde's tour).

54. Neale, op. cit., p. 201.

55. R. B. Wernham, 'Queen Elizabeth and the Portugal Expedition of 1589', *EHR*, vol. xlvi (1951), pp. 1–26, 194–218.

expedition's failure did not deter the Privy Council from seeking, within a fortnight of its return, the commanders' opinion as to 'what present service may be done either for the Islands or for Santander'.[56] At the end of August Sir Martin Frobisher was sent with a cruising squadron on 'certain special service in the south and west seas' off Cape St. Vincent.[57] Meanwhile, orders to Sir Francis Vere in the Netherlands inaugurated there a phase of more active English participation in offensive measures in the field.[58] Although the force of four thousand sent into Normandy in September achieved nothing of note,[59] Elizabeth enthused to its commander, Willoughby, 'that it is to our no small comfort to perceive the forward endeavours and valour both of yourself and of those under you'.[60] In the summer of 1590 a fleet of thirteen ships and 2,500 men, commanded by Sir John Hawkins and Frobisher, was licensed to implement the policy advocated by the former and Walsingham since 1587, of patrolling between Spain and the Azores to harass Spain's commercial shipping and to intercept her treasure fleets.[61] And Elizabeth was seriously considering fresh exploits by land.[62]

Thanks to England's increasing involvement, France's *impasse* and Spain's aspirations, by November 1590 the western European war was escalating on all fronts. But the fact that Elizabeth was adopting more positive measures did not guarantee Turenne success in his mission. Nor is that adoption sufficient in itself to disprove doubts regarding purposefulness and ability on Elizabeth's part as a war-leader and a strategist. Sound strategy hardly consists in random exploits: still less, in euphoric switches from defensive to offensive war. Yet in the developments that stemmed from November 1590, Elizabeth was indeed to show herself at least the equal of her fellow-monarchs in ability to convert varying and questionable advice and information

56. M. Oppenheim (ed.), *The Naval Tracts of Sir William Monson*, vol i (Navy Records Society, vol. xxii (1902)), p. 216.

57. ibid., pp. 237–8.

58. *APC*, vol. xviii (1589–90), pp. 6–7.

59. The campaign is summarized in C. G. Cruickshank, *Elizabeth's Army* (2nd edn., Oxford, 1966), pp. 236–51.

60. HMC *Ancaster*, p. 297; also Egerton, pp. 28–9, where Elizabeth writes appreciatively to Henry for his care of her troops and assures him of their future availability to him.

61. H. A. Lloyd, 'Sir John Hawkins's Instructions, 1590', *Bulletin of the Institute of Historical Research*, vol. xliv (1971), pp. 125–8.

62. See below, chapter 3.

into policy decisions conceived in coherent strategic terms. Whether her own and her contemporaries' decisions were to be vindicated by events was another matter, as was their ability respectively to anti-cipate contingencies or to satisfy the needs and demands of their servants and their allies. Those same developments resulted in military activity about the capital of Normandy that followed a course and assumed a significance unforeseen by any of the principals involved. There, as many observers grew increasingly to believe, the destiny of France and even of western Christendom would be determined.[63] That destiny took the form of a system of states to whose evolution these monarchs contributed but by whose current limitations they were bound as, by reference to law and by means of force, they discharged their conflicting roles.

63. See, for example, below, pp. 69, 183.

CHAPTER TWO

TURENNE'S MISSION

THROUGHOUT Elizabeth's reign the kings of France maintained a resident ambassador at her Court. The current ambassador, Beauvoir-La Nocle, accredited there since August 1589, was the eighth of their number. A reputable and experienced diplomat, his limitations were basically those of his office. Resident ambassadors easily became objects of suspicion. Sometimes justifiably, their hosts were quick to suspect them of sinister activity, while their own governments suspected them of double-dealing. Inadequately and irregularly paid, constantly apprehensive of injuries done them by rivals at home, they consoled themselves by playing at politics, and thereby heightened such suspicions. Their governments' intentions altered too frequently, advice and instructions passed to and fro too unreliably, to allow them to function satisfactorily over long periods or to handle important matters without assistance. And so, throughout the reign, a stream of extraordinary envoys traversed the English Channel, authorized to conduct particular negotiations which could not be left to the discretion of the residents. During the decades before Beauvoir's appointment Elizabeth had received well over a score of such missions; already, since his arrival, there had been two more.[1] The arrival of Turenne as extraordinary envoy was hardly an unusual occurrence.

But Turenne himself was a personage of unusual importance and distinction. His mother was the daughter of the Constable Anne de Montmorency, one of the French Triumvirate of thirty years before. Her first cousin was the Admiral Gaspard de Coligny, late leader of the Huguenots, whose attempted assassination had precipitated the events of St. Bartholomew's Day. Shortly before that massacre Turenne had accompanied his uncle Francis, Duke of Montmorency, to England, and had witnessed his installation at Windsor as a knight of the Garter, at the ceremony in which Burghley himself and Walter Devereux, first Earl of Essex, had been similarly honoured.[2] His other maternal

1. A. Baschet, 'List of French Ambassadors, etc., resident in England', *37th Report of the Deputy Keeper of the Public Records* (London, 1876), pp. 185–7.
2. *CSPD* (1547–80), p. 446.

uncle, Henry de Montmorency-Damville, had, after some vacillation, emerged as defender of Protestantism in Languedoc.[3] Turenne had served under him in Guienne and elsewhere in southern France, where his own personal influence was considerable.[4] He had tended to associate himself with the more extreme wing of Protestant Bourbons, led by Condé, King Henry's former rival. Captured when fighting in the Netherlands he had, by his own account, valued his duty to the reformed church above the freedom on *parole* that was then offered him. Walsingham had once described him as 'one so earnestly devoted to her Majesty as no nobleman in France more'.[5] In terms of his birth, his religion, and his reputation in the countries with which Henry now intended to deal, Turenne was excellently qualified to act as his representative. In terms of the Viscount's own aspirations,[6] his record of personal loyalty, and even his physical health, those qualifications may have been rather less convincing. Nevertheless it was he whom Henry chose to send, considering him attractive to those countries' leaders,[7] appropriate to the image he himself wished to project abroad, and necessary to the attainment of ends which the flimsy machinery of ordinary diplomacy would not suffice.

After some difficulty in obtaining shipping at Dieppe,[8] Turenne arrived in England to a reception so elaborate 'that some suspected (by reason that all the gentlemen of Kent were commanded to attend the sheriff to receive him, and Sir Richard Baker sent from London, where he intended to have lain this winter, to lodge him the one night, and Mr. Lennard the other; the Queen's coaches and barges both sent; the Lord Cobham to meet him at Rochester and the Earl of Essex at Gravesend) that the French King was secretly in his company'.[9] The Queen herself entertained him at Windsor, the Lord Chancellor in London; 'but from the first to the last the Earl of Essex doth lodge him,

---

3. H. Dubled, 'Un Soutien de la Réforme en Languedoc: Henri de Montmorency-Damville (1563–1594)', *Bulletin historique et littéraire de la société de l'histoire du protestantisme français* (April–June, 1947), pp. 51–8. Montmorency-Damville had married, in 1558, Antoinette de La Marck, daughter of Robert, Duke of Bouillon, Prince of Sedan; cf. below, pp. 112–13, 121–2.

4. 'Mémoires de Henri, Duc de Bouillon', *Nouvelle Collection des mémoires pour servir à l'histoire de France*, ed. J. F. Michaud and J. J. F. Poujoulat, vol. xi (Paris, 1838), p. x.

5. N. H. Nicolas, *Memoirs of the life and times of Sir Christopher Hatton* (London, 1847), pp. 186–7.

6. cf. below, pp. 112–13.   7. Egerton, pp. 30–1.

8. PRO SP 78/22/88.   9. Lodge, vol. ii, pp. 425–6.

and the best about him, and defrayeth his diet', and that of his atten-
dants, at York House.[10] Hospitality there was so lavish as to cost
Robert Devereux, second Earl of Essex, £2,200.[11] The Earl was investing heavily in his own political recovery. Recent events had clouded
his prospects of succeeding his late stepfather, the magnificent Earl
of Leicester, in position at Court and in inward influence upon the
Queen. Participation, against her wishes, in the Portugal expedition
the previous year had damaged his already tottering finances with a
blow of £7,000, and had earned him a reputation for foolhardy love of
adventuring that would be difficult to shake. Earlier in 1590, without
Elizabeth's knowledge, he had married Frances Walsingham, widow of
the admired Sir Philip Sidney. Only within the last month had the
Queen's indignation subsided sufficiently to enable Lady Essex to return from her mother's house to the environs of the Court.[12] Yet by
these actions Essex had asserted even more clearly than before his
claim to the leadership of activist opinion about the Queen. By entertaining Turenne he was consolidating that position.

For Turenne, association with Essex was an obvious course. If only
by way of marriage-relationships, the mantles of three of England's
major political figures, each now dead, appeared to have fallen upon
the young Earl: Leicester, Sidney, and Walsingham who, for all their
respective individuality and their differences, had cultivated contacts
upon the continent to a greater degree than most—contacts involving
many prominent figures from the overlapping realms of politics, religion, and culture. More than this: Essex's own childhood companion
was the son of the Huguenot captain, Montgomery, and protégé of the
Earl's father.[13] He had himself seized early opportunities of serving in
the Netherlands; he had corresponded with associates of Turenne's—
the Duke of Bouillon, François de La Noue[14]—and, following the Portugal affair, had declared to the latter that he was 'idle here' and eager
for 'some opportunity by which we could together win honour and

10. ibid., pp. 419, 422; HMC *Ancaster*, p. 307.
11. LD, vol. ii, fo. 84.
12. loc. cit.; Lodge, vol. ii, pp. 415–18.
13. LD, vol. i, fo. 28; vol. v, fo. 29ᵛ. In his will, dated 14 June 1576, Walter
Devereux, first earl of Essex, bequeathed 'to Gabriel Montgomery, one of the
Count Montgomery's sons, whensoever he shall depart from my son Robert
... towards the realm of France, four hundred French crowns' (ibid., box iv,
no. 59). In 1577 Montgomery was with the second Earl at Cambridge University (BM Lansdowne 23, fo. 131).
14. LD, vol. v, fo. 64ᵛ; HMC *Salis.*, vol. iii, p. 445.

serve the common weal'. Essex was listed first among those English magnates whom Turenne was instructed to approach and to whom he carried personal letters from his King.[15] If the Viscount's mission presented the Earl with a fresh political opportunity, Essex's attitude and influence were believed in France to be important for its furtherance.

For both of them it was essential to win the Queen. To all outward appearances the auguries were favourable. By the middle of the month Beauvoir could write that she, like her principal Councillors, had received Turenne 'with all the affection that could be wished for'.[16] On 27 November, the anniversary of her accession, when marks of her favour were especially to be prized, Turenne sat beside the Queen 'at the foot of the stairs under her Gallery window in the Tiltyard at Westminster', saw twenty-six noblemen, knights, and gentlemen run courses in her honour, and saw presented to her gifts by three virgins from 'a Pavilion made of white Taffeta, containing eight score ells, being in proportion like unto the sacred Temple of the Virgins Vestal'.[17] Nor was Essex overshadowed. Among the presents received by the Queen that day was his, of five diamond pendants.[18] Among those who jousted before her he stood out, apparelled all in black: perhaps in memory of Walsingham, perhaps, as at least one poet thought, in memory of Sidney,[19] perhaps in mourning for his own late disgrace, perhaps even—who could tell?—in memory of the Black Prince who, over two centuries before, had led English arms victoriously to western France and to triumph at Poitiers at a time when England's ally had been an earlier king of Navarre and count of Evreux. It seemed within a fortnight that such a symbol was indeed relevant. Turenne was by then about to leave; according to Beauvoir he 'goes away much pleased, not only with the Queen and the great men of the kingdom, but with England altogether; and her Majesty has promised him to spare no efforts to assist the King, my master'.[20]

But all this masked the real difficulties of Turenne's task and the complexities of the political game in which he played, the current phase of which had begun a good many months before.

In the summer of 1589 another extraordinary envoy had arrived in England, seeking a loan of 100,000 *écus* to raise an army in Germany

15. Egerton, pp. 29–30.   16. HMC *Ancaster*, p. 307.
17. D. H. Horne (ed.), *The life and minor works of George Peele* (New Haven, Conn., 1952), p. 167.
18. LD, vol. iii, fo. 47.   19. Horne, op. cit., pp. 235–6.
20. HMC *Ancaster*, p. 311.

for the allied French kings, Henry III and Henry of Navarre. Elizabeth
had received him without enthusiasm. German mercenaries were expensive. Their performances on their numerous incursions into France
in the course of the civil wars had been unimpressive, testifying mostly
to lack of discipline on the part of the troops and to preoccupation with
their own self-interest on the part of the German princes concerned.
Outstanding in its futility had been the expedition of 1587, which had
achieved nothing beyond pillage and which had cost the Queen 100,000
écus.[21] Nevertheless, she did consider sending again on an exploratory
mission into Germany Horatio Palavicino, the financier of Genoese
extraction whom since 1580 she had frequently employed in foreign
negotiations.[22] Then in August Henry III was assassinated, and circumstances in France were transformed. Within a month the French
envoys in England had been advanced £20,000.[23] At the end of the following month another extraordinary envoy obtained a further loan of
£15,000.[24] Meanwhile, as Elizabeth knew, Henry IV's representatives
in the Provinces had negotiated a loan of 30,000 écus. His emissary
there, the *intendant des finances* Incarvile, had hoped for more and
in fact obtained rather less.[25] No sooner had he conveyed this sum to
France than Henry dispatched him to England,[26] acknowledging that
Elizabeth, after her recent advances, could scarcely be asked again for
money, but requesting permission to negotiate a loan from the City of
London, to be repaid through the customs and imposts of Bordeaux
and La Rochelle.[27] Permission was granted, but Incarvile was coolly
received in the City, where the merchants trading to Bordeaux complained of maltreatment in France.[28] By June 1590 he had managed to
raise only a matter of £2,000;[29] and so he left for Holland once again.[30]

But in the meantime, Palavicino had gone to Germany after all, to
assess prospects for levying a fresh army for Henry at the expense of
the princes and possibly of the Queen. He reported favourably; yet

21. cf. below, p. 112.
22. L. Stone, *An Elizabethan: Sir Horatio Palavicino* (Oxford, 1956), pp. 4–5.
23. PRO SP 78/22/48.
24. PRO SP 78/20/150.
25. PRO SP 84/35/27. Charles de Saldaigne, sieur d' Incarvile, was *intendant* in Normandy, and later held key central office in the French financial
administration; see below, p. 190.
26. PRO SP 78/20/190.
27. PRO SP 78/21/120; BM Lansdowne 104, fo. 126.
28. HMC *Salis.*, vol. xiii, p. 432.
29. PRO SP 78/22/48.
30. PRO SP 78/21/216, 233.

Elizabeth had serious reservations. In less than a year Henry had cost England, by way of money, munitions, and Willoughby's expedition of 1589, a sum of at least £60,000. He had also received assistance from elsewhere, and was known to be negotiating for more. Moreover, in the summer of 1590 his political and military position seemed greatly improved. Although in July Palavicino was allowed to set off once again for Germany, via France, to work for the raising of troops, he was not to commit the Queen to 'any farther expenses thereabouts'.[31] Then Parma's intervention, together, as Elizabeth saw it, with Henry's mismanagement of his campaign, reduced the French king yet again to desperate straits. Again both she and the Provinces had rallied round: they responding to Incarville's pleas with powder, wheat, and warships,[32] she immediately following suit with a fresh loan of £10,000.[33] And Palavicino had been sufficiently moved by circumstances in France to return to England in quest of more explicit financial assurances from the Queen before picking up the threads of his negotiations in Germany. It was in his company, with this end in view, and hot from the conference with Villeroy,[34] that Turenne had come.

Turenne's instructions[35] seemed perfectly clear and straightforward —indeed, almost naïvely so. The occasion of his mission was 'what Sir Horatio Palavicino had communicated to the King on behalf of the Queen of England and also of the Duke of Saxony'. The burden of that advice was that the Queen wanted Henry to be assisted from Germany; that Saxony felt likewise; and that what remained to be settled was not the principle of an army's coming from that quarter but the means by which it should be paid. So confident was Henry of this that he invited Elizabeth to amend Turenne's instructions as she saw fit before he went on to Germany to complete arrangements. But the instructions stressed that on this mission he should be accompanied by Palavicino, who should be furnished with 'sufficient means and credit from her to aid the levying and paying of the forces with which she desires that his Majesty be assisted'. In short, Henry represented himself as believing that the initiative had come from the Queen and her envoy, with

31. PRO SP 78/21/292. It is noteworthy that Palavicino's favourable May report had nevertheless recorded strictures by the princes on French mismanagement of earlier German levies (PRO SP 81/6/7).
32. PRO SP 78/22/20.
33. PRO SP 78/22/35, 41.
34. See above, p. 18.
35. BN Béthune MSS., no. 8682, printed in Egerton, pp. 29–30; copies in BM Add. 5455 and 30622.

whose attitude he was delighted and with whom he was eager to co-operate. Indeed, he had already written to Christian of Saxony in terms which implied that his assistance and the Queen's were virtually assured.[36]

Yet Henry knew perfectly well that the matter was not so simple. All past experience showed that when Elizabeth could be persuaded to lay out money, she did so circumspectly, upon conditions and in expectation of some tangible return. No less well known was the importance of the Channel littoral in her strategic thinking. Accordingly, Henry had taken care to prepare the ground, partly by means which he had tested before. In August 1589, very soon after his accession to the throne, he had come into Normandy and, in conjunction with de Chatte, governor of Dieppe, had made a demonstration before Rouen.[37] In the following autumn, when the September loan and Willoughby's troops had been gained but before the October loan had been concluded, he had sent for the English merchant Otwell Smyth, recently expelled from Rouen[38] and now resident at Dieppe. By Smyth's account, Henry had avowed himself ready to besiege Rouen if he had the money to pay his army for that purpose. The merchant had replied that many English merchants would be glad to stake him in this, for the benefit of their trade. Repayment could be assured through customs dues payable at Rouen. Henry had spoken of this plan to the English ambassador, Sir Edward Stafford.[39] In fact, in the ensuing campaign the King had concentrated his efforts and Willoughby's elsewhere. Yet his agents in England had been granted the October loan, and had promised in return to recommend Henry to busy himself with regaining the sea-coasts of Picardy and Normandy, 'and not to withdraw his forces from thence other wise than to the recovery of the towns of Rouen and Paris or either of them'.[40] Now at the end of September 1590 Stafford reported from Mantes that he

36. *LM*, vol. iii, pp. 259–61.

37. PRO SP 78/19/265. According to Mornay, this was a feint by means of which Henry simultaneously deferred to a suggestion emanating from Dieppe and succeeded in attracting League forces away from Paris and the towns he had taken in that region (*MM*, vol. v, pp. 8–9).

38. Where, after having been briefly imprisoned in 1586 'because he would not kneel down to their elevation at mass time', he had nevertheless held his ground throughout the maltreatment of English merchants in 1587 (*CSPF* (1585–6), p. 300; (1586–8), pp. 206, 329–31, 416).

39. PRO SP 78/20/118.

40. PRO SP 78/20/154; BM Lansdowne 60, fo. 152, and 149, fo. 26.

had 'had a great deal of conference' with Henry, who had 'made a motion to me to desire at this time to have 5,000 foot and pioneers for two months only that he would besiege Rouen'. In Stafford's judgement, 'we should reap some good by it, by opening a place of traffic'; and afterwards 'put Le Havre to a siege so that all Normandy and that coast might be assured from the enemy'.[41] And Stafford was also returning to England,[42] avid to put this case. His intention was to convince his government that he could persuade Henry to decline with thanks an offer of money for German troops, in preference for the means of taking Rouen.[43]

Despite his considerable ambassadorial experience, Stafford was not the most reliable of diplomats. In the past he had been suspected of selling information to Spain; he had also expressed deep distrust of Henry, as well as hostility towards Walsingham and Leicester.[44] The French king had little reason to trust him above the others engaged in the current negotiations. But Stafford was principally Burghley's man, and would lose no opportunity of transmitting to that quarter information likely to enhance his own importance.[45] But in addition to him, and to Palavicino and Turenne, yet another party was hastening towards England with views as to what needed to be done in France: views based upon first-hand experience there and also upon confidential discussion with the King. Sir Roger Williams, forthright, irascible, veteran of the continental wars, opinionated observer of the military scene, and close associate of Essex's, was *en route* from Mantes to Dieppe in the last week of September.[46] Following his share in the

41. PRO SP 78/22/60. In all references to the town I have substituted 'Le Havre' for 'Newhaven', the name by which contemporary Englishmen commonly referred to it.
42. PRO SP 78/22/101.
43. PRO SP 78/22/70.
44. C. Read, *Lord Burghley and Queen Elizabeth* (London, 1965 edn.), pp. 386–90. For debate regarding Stafford and the implications of his conduct, see C. Read, 'The Fame of Sir Edward Stafford', *American Historical Review*, vol. 20 (1915), pp. 292–315; and articles under the same title by J. E. Neale, *EHR*, vol. xliv (1929), pp. 203–19; C. Read, *American Historical Review*, vol. 35 (1929–30), pp. 560–6.
45. For Burghley's special concern for the Normandy coastline, see below, p. 70.
46. PRO SP 78/22/39. For Williams's temperament, see Camden's comment, BM Harleian 6845, fo. 100; in the war of words after Portugal he snapped at one of his critics, 'Where Sir Walter Ralegh speaks of my hulk, I cannot stop his mouth to belie him—for he belied the Ark of Noah, which was the best ship that ever was.'

Portugal affair he had suffered Elizabeth's censure. In May he had
gone to France. He had served at the siege of Paris, where the King's
supporters 'all hearken to him what he sayeth and is accompted a great
soldier, and the King will talk with him in his ear and confer with
him'.[47] And at the end of November, back in England, making no secret
of his close ties with Essex,[48] and with Turenne's negotiations actually
in train, Williams submitted to Burghley another assessment of what
needed to be done. 'The German army,' he wrote, 'all men must
confess will stand the action of France to good purpose ... But to
speak to the purpose: what is the state of England the better for that
army?' In his judgement, its effect in France would be to bring about a
build-up of forces on either side and a military deadlock which neither
would be able to break. In such circumstances the advantage must lie
with Spain and her allies, for 'their great means will eat our small'.
But far more urgent was the danger that Spain would 'possess the
seaports. It were better for us that he had five other provinces than
Brittany. For all the best ports of France is in that province, and without [Spain's] possessing either those ports or them of the Low Countries our dangers cannot be very great. In all reason there is no means
to save it but presently to send eight thousand soldiers either into
Brittany or into the Low Countries.'[49]

All these opinions reached Burghley and, in all likelihood, the Queen
herself. All were tuned to measures which she was known to have
danced before. She had contributed to German levies; she had intervened in the Netherlands; she had cast covetous eyes upon Rouen; she
was acutely concerned over the Channel littoral. All were conveyed by
parties who had each an interest in the particular case he favoured. Not
for nothing did Palavicino tour the continent to arrange transfers of
large sums by exchange. Stafford was a compulsive intriguer, anxious
to carry a view of suitable French dealings different from Palavicino's,
and so to restore his own diplomatic reputation. In competition with
other professional soldiers, Williams sought an independent military
command. And each of them had recently conferred with Henry and

47. BM Harleian 6995, fo. 3; PRO SP 78/21/276.
48. To whom in 1590 he dedicated his *Discourse*.
49. PRO SP 78/22/134. cf. below, pp. 53, 56–8, 67–73, for other attitudes of Williams's and their importance; and chapter 6 for his influence upon
Essex in military matters. He also advocated naval war in the Caribbean, in
terms similar to those favoured by Sidney, La Noue, and others (F. Greville,
Life of Sir Philip Sidney (Oxford, 1907), pp. 110 sqq.; H. Hauser, *François
de la Noue* (Paris, 1892), pp. 315–19.

appeared to have drawn a different conclusion as to what England ought to undertake. Perhaps the French king had simply got his diplomatic lines crossed, through carelessly playing with ideas in the company of foreigners. But those lines had one common strand. Whatever they may have suggested to Elizabeth and to these others, the current French negotiations in England were intended to secure for Henry the benefits of money and of men. The circumspect Queen must be persuaded. And numerous arguments would now be put to the English government which, if it accepted any or all of them, would have precisely that effect. It was the charge of Turenne, Henry's heaviest diplomatic gun, to win him a German army: for Elizabeth, the least immediately attractive of these various alternatives. But whether or not the Viscount was successful, Henry had diversified his approaches in, it could be argued, no random fashion.

Turenne began promisingly. He delivered his several letters, with some encouraging results. On 22 November Lord Treasurer Burghley was composing one of his detailed memoranda, in which he noted that 'if the King may not have an army out of Germany he shall not be able to pass over this next summer' and resist the various enemies threatening his kingdom.[50] Lord Chancellor Hatton was a shade more guarded, recommending that 'the negotiation of Viscount Turenne be well digested, that he may receive a sound answer'.[51] But by 27 November Burghley had progressed to the point of listing the German princes to whom must be sent 'letters from the Queen's Majesty recommending the viscount's legation', letters of credence and instructions for the English envoy to accompany Turenne, and a 'warrant for money to be delivered, to be ready by exchange, at Frankfurt'.[52] Meanwhile, the Queen's own reply to Henry was drafted, assuring him of her admiration for his qualities and her eagerness to prove it 'with all possible care and diligence'.[53] The instructions which were actually prepared for the English envoy on 30 November must therefore have been all the more disappointing to the Viscount. They contained powerful arguments to persuade the German princes so to act that an army of '6,000 horsemen and 8,000 footmen might be ready to enter into France in

50. PRO SP 12/234/11. The negotiation is described in Stone, op. cit., pp. 165 sqq.; my own interpretation differs from his in important respects.
51. PRO SP 12/234/15.
52. PRO SP 12/234/16.
53. PRO SP 78/22/164.

the month of April *if possible it may be*'.[54] But in so far as a contribution towards its cost was expected from Elizabeth, 'we may not be chargeable with any such extraordinary charge towards that levy in Germany'.[55] The cost of the expedition must be met by contributions from within Germany itself.

Mere exhortations, however vigorous, were unlikely to stimulate the princes to act, as Henry had already implied. Yet despite the unequivocal tone of these instructions, Elizabeth was at this time already disposed to act, in a different way. The same draft declared 'that we must of necessity *give further* help *to* the French king either by sea or by land *or by both* to our unknown charge'.[56] On the following day she instructed her Lord Treasurer to raise in England by loans on privy seal an amount totalling (on paper at least) £170,000: 'in consideration as well of the great charges daily sustained by us both by sea and land for the necessary defence of our realm against foreign invasion, as also of the continuance or rather increase of like charges to be borne by us this year coming'.[57] Five days after the draft instructions were prepared she floated to Turenne the idea that the German army, towards which she avowedly did not wish to contribute, should cross the Rhine and march, via Cologne, into Brabant, Hainault, Artois: in short, westwards towards the southern Netherlands coast, rather than by the more southerly route, via Lorraine, directly into France, which Turenne was known to favour. If the Germans should come via the Netherlands they could be joined by the Provinces' forces—and also by the Queen's. This suggestion was amplified, in a form identifiable with a point made by Williams in his advice submitted five days before. Williams had said that it would not be possible for Henry's enemies in France to prevent a junction between the Germans and the King's troops; for 'it is too dangerous for a great army to lodge betwixt two reasonable armies'.[58] Now Elizabeth argued that if the Germans should follow the route she preferred, which would take them towards France's northern frontier, 'the Spanish army will find itself as if in a strait between the German army and that which the King will raise and march to meet the said German army'.[59] That this was no passing

54. PRO SP 81/6/86ᵛ. The italicized phrase was added to the draft, in this instance and in the quotations that follow, by Burghley.
55. PRO SP 81/6/88ᵛ.
56. PRO SP 81/6/89.
57. PRO SP 12/236/1ᵛ.
58. PRO SP 78/22/134.
59. PRO SP 78/22/141.

fancy for military theory is evident from her reiterating the point at a later conference; and she was 'glad to perceive that the Viscount inclined greatly to this our opinion'.[60]

Elizabeth, then, had ideas regarding the uses of the troops Turenne was seeking. From the point of view of the French envoy and of those who favoured his cause, any ideas that might lead to his obtaining those troops were worth cultivating. But it was English money that he wanted now. Palavicino had estimated the cost of raising the army in question and paying it for one month at £57,000, of which the Queen must contribute £15,000.[61] On that essential point Elizabeth had seemed adamant on 30 November. Since then, however, she had herself promised money to the Viscount, but had 'not named particularly the whole sum'.[62] On 9 December Palavicino wrote to Burghley that at his last conference with the Lord Treasurer the unexpected arrival of Lord Admiral Howard had prevented Turenne from disclosing all that he had in mind; the Viscount would like another meeting, at which everything would be revealed.[63] On that same day Burghley submitted in writing to the Queen a series of points concerning the financial arrangements, and asked bluntly whether the English emissary's instructions were to include authority to advance up to £15,000 towards the levy.[64] The next day Elizabeth gave an affirmatory reply, but emphasized that Turenne must not know of it and that only in extreme circumstances should so large a sum be contributed.[65] That day revised instructions to this effect were at last drawn up for Palavicino.[66] If without money from the Queen the mission should prove abortive, he was secretly authorized to contribute up to £10,000, £8,000 of which had already been delivered to him, the remaining £2,000 to be issued by Burghley. A revealing sidelight

60. PRO SP 78/22/162. For further discussion of this plan and its implications, see below, chapter 3.

61. PRO SP 81/6/44 (Burghley's conversion into pounds sterling of Palavicino's estimates, expressed in florins).

62. PRO SP 81/6/99. Especially on this aspect of the negotiation, cf. the interpretation by Stone, op. cit., p. 167.

63. PRO SP 78/22/155.

64. PRO SP 81/6/97. There was news that Philip of Spain was dying of apoplexy. 'I wish', wrote Burghley with the dry humour that sometimes invaded his writings, 'that both he and I were in heaven, where I am sure he would not wish me.'

65. PRO SP 81/6/99.   66. PRO SP 81/6/110.

upon this arrangement was that £1,000 of the amount in question was to come from Essex, in repayment of a debt of his to the Queen.[67] The instructions continued, that if the total funds thus made available should still not suffice Palavicino might, with the utmost secrecy, raise an additional £5,000 in Germany on 'your own credit', meanwhile requesting further authority from England to pay this amount over as well.

The mission was completed. Accompanied by Palavicino, Turenne departed. By accident, or by design, their journey took them to The Hague. With them was a third envoy, charged with following up Turenne's English mission through negotiating with the Provinces on Henry's behalf. Paul Choart de Buzenval was as appropriate an emissary for that purpose as was Turenne himself. In 1587 he had represented Henry in England. Phillipe du Plessis-Mornay had recommended him warmly to Leicester,[68] and he had moved in the circle of courtly admirers of Essex's sister, Penelope Rich, Sidney's celebrated 'Stella'.[69] But of greater present relevance than these English connections were Buzenval's contacts in the Provinces. For he had studied at Heidelberg, with Mornay and also with Oldenbarnevelt,[70] the Advocate of Holland who had by now emerged as the Provinces' dominant political figure. Partly by virtue of that association, Buzenval was embarking upon a long phase of effective diplomatic representation in the course of which many of the political and cultural leaders of the Provinces would acknowledge him as friend.[71] More relevant still, Oldenbarnevelt's present policy was in line with Buzenval's present purpose. The former, though no lover of Leicester and his works, had taken care to maintain good relations with England; but he also saw the importance, for military success in the Netherlands,

67. PRO SP 81/7/1. Four bonds by Essex to Palavicino are extant, totalling £1,350, two of them dated January 1589, and all payable at Palavicino's house 'without Bishopsgate' (LD, box v, no. 71). A bond by the Earl in £1,000 is elsewhere recorded as having been 'assigned by Sir Horatio Palavicino unto her Majesty and is due May 1590' (LD, vol. ii, fo. 29). Essex subsequently declared himself unable to meet this obligation; cf. below, p. 46, note 83, and p. 123, note 93.
68. H. Brugmans (ed.), *Correspondentie van Robert Dudley, Graaf von Leycester*, vol. iii (Utrecht, 1931), pp. 41–2.
69. J. A. van Dorsten, *Poets, Patrons and Professors* (London, 1962), p. 86.
70. J. den Tex, *Oldenbarnevelt*, vol. ii (Haarlem, 1962), pp. 76–7. I am obliged to my colleague Dr J. L. Price for assistance with this Dutch work.
71. G. G. Vreede (ed.), *Lettres et négociations de Paul Choart* (Leyden, 1846).

of measures to promote Henry's victory in France.[72] The latter had come to persuade the Provinces to contribute 30,000 *écus* towards the German army.[73]

Like Turenne in England, Buzenval was instructed to approach specified dignitaries, and particularly to disclose his entire purpose to Louise de Coligny, the widowed Princess of Orange.[74] Of course, such contacts could not guarantee diplomatic success. Men might be linked by ties of family or friendship, culture or interest, regardless of the frontiers of states. Such ties were scarcely more resistant to the pressures of contending personalities and conflicting circumstances than were the formal relations of kings and governments. Yet they could give entry into circles where useful information was to be found, where helpful advice might be forthcoming, and possibly assistance as well. Buzenval and his two principal companions needed all the assistance they could find. In mid-December the French envoys made their appeal to the States-General.[75] They were courteously received, with expressions of goodwill and even, verbally, of support. But money was no more easily obtainable here than it had been in England. Like Elizabeth, the Provinces had grievances—grievances against England rather than against Henry, who none the less had instructed Buzenval to stress that Elizabeth backed his requests. They drew attention to the effect of the war upon their commerce and thereby upon their financial capacity. The English might complain of, and endeavour to prohibit, their trading with the common enemy; they themselves complained of the losses they suffered through the activities of English privateers.[76] Palavicino was deluged by their complaints. He and Turenne left for Germany with no firm promises gained. But Buzenval and the Advocate laboured on. After many vicissitudes during the fol-

---

72. den Tex, op. cit., p. 78, where the Advocate is represented as even more strong a supporter of aid for Henry.

73. BN AFF 3956, fos. 85ᵛ–91 (Buzenval's instructions).

74. The Princess had been another of Sidney's intimate friends, and wrote to Leicester upon learning of his death at Zutphen, 'which I regret, and shall regret all my life, as if he had been my brother' (J. Buxton, *Sir Philip Sidney and the English Renaissance* (London, 1964), p. 170). Turenne's relationship with her was later reinforced through his second marriage, to her second daughter. On the occasion in question she greeted him effusively, with the fallacious comment that an hour's diplomatic effort by him would accomplish more than a year's by Buzenval (L. Anquez, *Henry IV et l'Allemagne* (Paris, 1887), p. 34).

75. den Tex, op. cit., p. 78.

76. PRO SP 84/40/6, 7 and 9; and below, pp. 54-5.

lowing months, in May 1591 Elizabeth's ambassador at The Hague could report that 'There is now accorded by the States a contribution of £10,000 sterling towards the levy in Germany'.[77] Henry seemed after all to have judged aright, that those who counted in the Provinces would not surrender him to sole dependence upon the English queen.

By then Turenne and Palavicino had been negotiating in Germany for three months. Again they had entered upon prepared ground. They were following up Palavicino's earlier mission, renewing earlier dealings between the princes and the French, and also plucking at the international threads that linked politically conscious intellectuals. Mornay had helped draft Henry's letter to Christian of Saxony, recommending Turenne's mission.[78] Saxony's substantial support would be vital; and Mornay was a friend of the much-travelled scholar, the late Hubert Languet, patron of Philip Sidney and diplomatic envoy for Christian's father, Augustus. Again Turenne was instructed by his King to emphasize the support accorded to his mission by Elizabeth who, twelve years before, watched by the young Earl of Essex, had received at her Court with outstanding marks of honour and esteem the second in importance of these princes, John Casimir of the Palatinate.[79] But once more, favourable precedents and friendships were not enough. Casimir's more recent attitudes and activities had cost him much of the Queen's regard. Languet was dead; though some of his associates and influence lived on, he had in any case been no Oldenbarnevelt. Most important, the German princes' ardour had cooled since Palavicino's last visit. They insisted that assurances on money matters must precede military arrangements, adding that costs had risen. Despite Eliza-

77. PRO SP 84/42/48; BM Cotton Galba D VIII, fo. 57ᵛ. One illustration of the abiding difficulties encountered by negotiators with the Provinces is the separate agreement concluded by Buzenval with the States of Utrecht, which both ensured their formal support for the contribution and also conceded that they themselves would contribute a fictitious sum; as usual, the lion's share was Holland's (den Tex, op. cit., p. 80); cf. also, below, p. 126, note 108.

78. Patry, p. 192. On earlier Franco-German relations, see A. Waddington, 'La France et les protestants allemands sous Charles IX et Henri III: Hubert Languet et Gaspard de Schonberg', Revue historique, vol. xlii (1890), pp. 241–77.

79. Bagot, pp. 334, 337. Again there is a link with Sidney, who had met Casimir at Heidelberg in 1577 (Buxton, op. cit., p. 88). Among Languet's most significant directly political acts was his contribution, shortly before his own death in 1581, to the authorship of William the Silent's Apology.

beth's exhortations to Casimir, quoting Scipio on the superiority of deeds to words,[80] her fervour was not altogether convincing. Was she not herself reluctant over money matters? Did she not deserve the consequences of *ad hoc* arrangements, in view of her failure to pursue such proposals for a more durable Protestant alliance as had been postulated from time to time? Was it not the princes, rather than she, who must nevertheless endure the effects of rumours spread from France by the League's present leader, the Duke of Mayenne, among Imperial Catholics that his enemies were planning to create in Germany a successor to the Schmalkaldic League which had caused such difficulties for the Emperor Charles V?[81] Harassed, the two envoys separated, each touring the principalities in search of firm commitments to their cause. But late in February 1591 Palavicino informed Burghley that he had had to agree to advance the £10,000 and asked permission for the full £15,000.[82]

Permission was denied[83]—with expressions of politeness to Turenne, of annoyance to Palavicino. But letters travelled too slowly between London and Frankfurt for Elizabeth to be able to harmonize developments at the latter with fresh developments at home. In mid-April, before the Queen's refusal arrived, the question of money had been in some measure resolved, and agreement had been reached in Germany for provision of 6,000 cavalry and 9,000 infantry.[84] In June Turenne reported this success to Burghley, and at the same time expressed

80. HMC *Salis.*, vol. iv, p. 105.

81. *CM*, vol. ii, pp. 56–61. Proposals were recurrent for an alliance of protestant princes. Through her own envoys—and, especially, through the King of Denmark, a prince of the Empire—Elizabeth had herself explored its possibilities: notably, in 1577, to counteract 'a solemn assembly intended to be holden at Magdeburg ... with intention to condemn such as are not of the Augustan Confession'; and in the special circumstances of the spring of 1585, before she committed herself to the Treaty of Nonsuch (see *CSPF* (1577–8), pp. 89–90, 179–84; (1584–5), pp. 416, 433–4, 636–9). Whether she genuinely meant to include England in such an alliance, as distinct from exploiting the idea—much favoured by influential intellectuals such as Languet—as a means of promoting unity among continental princes, is very much open to doubt.

82. PRO SP 81/6/156. The contract between Palavicino and Turenne was not in fact concluded until 11 April (PRO SP 78/24/1).

83. PRO SP 78/24/193; 81/7/1. The most Burghley could concede was that Essex's contribution in the shape of his outstanding debt would be paid, though not by the Earl himself.

84. BN AFF 3980, fos. 238–40; PRO SP 81/6/188; Anquez, op. cit., p. 36. In France it was reported that Turenne had obtained 7,000 cavalry and 13,000 infantry (PRO SP 78/24/164).

consternation that Elizabeth wished 'to cut her loan by a third of what she promised me, instead, as I hoped by her goodwill, of adding to that sum'. He could explain such a change of heart only by a belief on her part that the mission had failed; whereas the princes' determination could in fact be cooled only by coolness on the part of the Queen.[85] These expostulations were certainly disingenuous. There had been no change of heart, for Elizabeth had simply reaffirmed her unwillingness to contribute so large a sum. During Turenne's stay in England she had been at pains to avoid so firm a promise; and the Viscount had long been aware of her attitude.[86] She may also have felt aggrieved that the army had been raised on the basis of contributions of which her share was paid while many others remained mere paper promises. But quite apart from pique, she now had other, heavy commitments; and Turenne was in effect contriving to force her hand with a *fait accompli* in a matter which, for her, had depended throughout upon contingencies. Even so, he was certainly embarrassed. In mid-June he was urgently requesting Count John of Nassau, William the Silent's brother, to bring his influence to bear upon the German reformed churches 'in order to increase our funds'.[87] Yet his embarrassment was as certainly no greater than Palavicino's. The financier, whose interests depended upon his ability to preserve international goodwill towards himself, had offended the Queen by exceeding his instructions and the princes by excessive parsimoniousness. From Duke Casimir the opinion flowed, to Beauvoir in London and thence to Henry, that Palavicino had not served the King's cause in Germany as he ought.[88] It sounded the knell to a busy diplomatic career.

So, with misgivings and recriminations on every hand, Turenne got his army. At last he mustered them, on 1 August on a plain near Frankfurt, and marched them across the Rhine under their commander, Christian of Anhalt, Casimir's nephew. At once he had to call a halt and distribute pay, the majority of the troops having received none. Already the pattern was set that was to hamper the effectiveness of the entire expedition. But for the time being the army marched slowly on, obedient to orders received from Henry, for Saarbrücken, for Metz, to Vandy near Verdun.[89] The campaigning season was near-

85. PRO SP 81/7/19.

86. For example, PRO SP 78/23/60; cf. above, p. 42.

87. G. Groen van Prinsterer, *Archives ou correspondance inédite de la maison d'Orange-Nassau*, Ser. ii, vol. i (1584–99) (Utrecht, 1857), pp. 167–9.

88. BN AFF 3645, fo. 15. 89. BN AFF 3618, fo. 103.

ing its end. Rumours circulated that the League had raised in Germany a comparable force of its own,[90] which would nullify any advantage brought from there towards Henry. Then at Vandy the King himself met his troops. The entire body swung northwards along the Meuse, towards Sedan. Momentarily it may have seemed that account was to be taken after all of the plan to take the Germans into the Netherlands, by a variation of the route favoured by Elizabeth. But that plan had been displaced several months before.

90. PRO SP 78/26/9.

CHAPTER THREE

THE FLANDERS PLAN

WHEN Elizabeth had suggested to Turenne that his German army should march via Cologne westwards through the southern Netherlands towards the Flanders coast, this was a serious proposal. No doubt it sprang partly from her regal habit of calling every tune when she paid the piper. Yet the proposal was firmly rooted in her broad strategic thinking and tallied with specific measures which she had been considering for some time. Parma's occupation of Flanders was, for her, a matter of keenest concern. It was from that coast, and notably from Dunkirk, that two years previously he was to have embarked his army to rendezvous with the Armada and thence to invade England. Of course that project had foundered, upon abiding natural obstacles. Yet Parma had earlier put forward a plan of his own, for direct invasion by his troops, in barges, at night, uncomplicated by any rendezvous at sea. As long as that section of the littoral remained in enemy hands, enemy commanders would entertain such schemes; some day they might be implemented, and might succeed. Several weeks before Turenne's arrival Elizabeth had suggested to the Provinces that if she were to land 4,000 men in Flanders to strike at Dunkirk and other selected targets in conjunction with their forces, this would quickly relieve France of Parma's presence.[1] In fact, Maurice of Nassau had made a premature attempt upon Dunkirk, and had failed. While this had removed the element of surprise formerly favoured in the enterprise, it had not destroyed the attraction of the plan itself.

It was an ambitious plan. It would require a high degree of collaboration between all those interested in bringing about Parma's discomfiture. Rewards might be correspondingly high. Combined operations in Flanders by the Provinces' forces led by Maurice, by the Germans

---

1. BM Cotton Galba D VII, fos. 272, 286; HMC *Salis.*, vol. iv, pp. 57–60; *APC*, vol. xix (1590), p. 432; PRO SP 84/39/88, 107, 131. Vere had approved this plan, with the reservation that the Provinces would not initiate the action but would join it when the Queen had made her move (PRO SP 84/39/133). In her concern for Dunkirk, subsequently a source of intense annoyance to English shipping owing to its use as a base by enemy privateers, Elizabeth anticipated Cromwell as well as later English strategists.

led by Turenne, and by the English led by Vere, could hardly fail to absorb the Spanish governor's attention. They might well succeed both in securing the Flemish coast and in removing Parma from France altogether. Moreover, if King Henry were simultaneously to operate northwards from Picardy, Parma might be caught in severe straits—certainly embarrassed, perhaps even destroyed. According to Turenne,[2] Elizabeth was sufficiently enthusiastic for this plan to have given him written assurances that 4,000 English soldiers would be sent to the Netherlands to release her veterans there for service in the field with his Germans—if he should march them by the proposed route. But before the Viscount was in a position to put these promises to the test, changes in the situation had nullified them. Chief among these were developments stemming from Brittany.

Barely a century had elapsed since the incorporation of the duchy of Brittany into the kingdom of France. Its privileges and liberties had been guaranteed in a series of contracts concluded between the Crown and the Breton Estates. Those Estates were dominated to an unusual degree by noblemen, of the peculiar Breton type—racially proud, fractious, and impoverished. Those contracts had endowed the province with a peculiar status within the imperfectly centralized government of the realm. Upon all such governmental arrangements the civil wars placed a dangerous strain. Weakness on the part of the Crown stimulated intensification of separatist tendencies on the part of provinces whose distinctiveness was already formally recognized. When such tendencies were linked with the ambitions of great potentates, royal authority, and prospects for its recovery, weakened still further. By 1590 situations of that kind were all too numerous in France. Moreover, as the Crown's power diminished so, in certain provinces and municipalities, did the powers expand of those noblemen who held lieutenancies and governorships: offices whose scope, strictly defined, was military, but whose holders took it increasingly upon themselves in the violent circumstances of civil war to intervene in every area of governmental activity, in effect on their own rather than on the Crown's account, and certainly rather to their own advantage. In Brittany such a potentate had emerged in a particularly menacing form. Philippe-Emmanuel, Duke of Mercœur, was through his father a member of the great Leaguer house of Lorraine; through his mother,

---

2. As reported to Burghley by Sir John Norris, at a time when this information ran counter to Norris's own purpose (PRO SP 84/41/52).

a blood relative of the houses of Bourbon and Montpensier; and through his wife wielded a claim to the duchy of Brittany. In July 1589 Henry III had revoked his office of lieutenant-general in that province, and had bestowed it upon Henry de Bourbon, Prince of Dombes, cousin of Henry of Navarre and son of the king's governor in Normandy, the Duke of Montpensier.[3] Dombes and Mercoeur now contended, with all the bitterness of rival kinsmen, for control in a Brittany ravaged by war, famine and popular unrest. Their struggle excited keen interest much further afield.

On the one hand, Mercœur had turned for assistance to Spain. He presented Philip with the prospect of a strong Spanish presence at the entrance to the English Channel. Moreover, Philip's own daughter, the Infanta, had a claim of her own to the duchy of Brittany. Whether the Duke would be content with the role of Spain's agent there was an open question. For the moment, his need for military reinforcements was great enough to make him willing to appear so. Some Spanish forces had already arrived. On 6 December 1590 Mercœur sent for more, reminding Philip of how convenient a base Brittany would be for 'the enterprise of England', and assuring him of every assistance for furthering that enterprise.[4] On the other hand, the French king could not remain indifferent to the needs of his cousin, Dombes. If Brittany was itself important in strategic terms, no less important to Henry in political terms was the continuing alliance of his powerful kinsmen. There had been hesitation on Montpensier's part before he had aligned himself with the Bourbon leader in 1589; and it was not to be forgotten that Montpensier's stepmother was a daughter of Francis, Duke of Guise, and had been a fervent opponent of Henry III's. So Dombes must be reassured and sustained. But beyond his royal commission—whatever practical advantage or otherwise he might derive from that—he could hope for little by way of practical assistance from Henry at the present time. Plainly, the solution lay in counter-balancing Spain's assistance to Mercœur with English assistance for Dombes, if this could be procured. Elizabeth might cavil at spending money on German soldiers. But with Spaniards multiplying upon the threshold of her realm, she would surely be more open to persuasion

3. BN AFF 3344, fo. 49. In relation to the French state, the constitutional position of the principality of Dombes itself—situated below Burgundy, to the east of the Saône—was obscure.
4. de Carné, *Mercœur correspondance*, vol. i, pp. 19–20.

that Dombes could not survive without her aid.

This was the situation when Turenne left France for England. But the instructions carried by the Viscount to the Queen contained no mention of Brittany. True, he had written to assure Dombes that in England he would endeavour to persuade her to send him aid.[5] But Turenne's formal representations to Elizabeth had included no such specific request. Meanwhile, however, Henry had dispatched a separate envoy, first to Brittany to consult with Dombes and thence to England, apparently in pursuit of Turenne.[6] At Rennes, in the last week of November 1590, Dombes prepared letters for Beauvoir and for Burghley, and instructions for the envoy. Des Mesnils was to ask, ostensibly through Turenne, for 2,000 footmen, and for powder, for shot, for pikes.[7] Moreover, Dombes stressed that the Spaniards in Brittany were concentrating their efforts upon Hennebont and the south-western coast—key maritime positions, which he himself had only recently recovered; their loss would be a serious matter for all concerned.

But by the time of des Mesnils's arrival, Turenne had departed with his own business done. It was left to des Mesnils and to Beauvoir to press these arguments and these requests. The Viscount's own task of persuasion had proved difficult enough. Theirs began much less propitiously. Des Mesnils had little of the personal distinction and personal connections that Turenne had been able to call into play. By 20 December he had seen the Queen and had met refusal; because of her extraordinary expenses at the present time she could not afford what he required. Following Turenne's example, he now appealed through Beauvoir to Burghley, craving a half-hour's interview.[8] This too, it seemed, was of no avail. Within a week, letters to Dombes had been drafted, assuring him of the Queen's high regard but explaining that the winter season, the danger of Spanish interception and her own heavy expenditure upon continental causes all precluded present assistance. Such assistance ought in any case to be sought from Henry himself, now that he was relieved of Parma's presence.[9] Beauvoir begged that she reconsider: if the Spaniards should hold Brittany they would have, in effect, a foot in England; and Turenne had promised Dombes that English aid would be forthcoming.[10] Whatever the merits of these arguments, it seemed that des Mesnils would have to be con-

5. PRO SP 78/22/129.
6. PRO SP 78/24/210 shows that des Mesnils came initially from Henry.
7. PRO SP 78/22/219.   8. PRO SP 78/22/189.
9. PRO SP 78/22/191, 193, 203.   10. PRO SP 78/22/214.

tent with a loan of powder, and even this upon security tendered by
Breton merchants.[11]

The matter was not allowed to rest there. Nothing if not persistent,
the French had available other avenues than those of formal ambassadorial representation. While further arguments were marshalled by
Beauvoir, further letters arrived from Brittany. Among them was a mis-
sive from Claude de Nau, former secretary to Mary Stuart. Following
the Scots' Queen's trial in which Nau's testimony had been so helpful
to her prosecutors,[12] his return to France had been arranged by her
greatest antagonist, Walsingham. Having served the family of Guise
with less than perfect loyalty, Nau was now serving the house of
Bourbon; some believed that he exercised too great an influence upon
Dombes.[13] On 14 December he wrote from Rennes to Sir Francis
Drake, referring to 'our old acquaintance and your gentle and courteous dealing with me at our first meeting in my Lord of Leicester's
house', conveying Dombes's thanks for the letter Drake had sent him,
and urging 'all possible means to prevent and stay the establishing of
the Spaniards in this country'.[14] Drake himself at this time signed a
memorandum recommending forces for Dombes to be coupled with a
naval assault upon the Blavet estuary, where the Spaniards were building fortifications.[15] Moreover, Sir Roger Williams was submitting to
Burghley a fresh memorandum. He advised that 2,000 English soldiers
—the very number des Mesnils had requested—would suffice to meet
the present emergency; and added, reminiscently of Drake's view,
'Whatsoever the troops be we must send such shipping as will be sufficient to stop the course from succouring their forces by sea : else our
men by land will be to small purpose.'[16]

However, the Queen and Burghley were neither so innocent of the
needs of the case nor so negative towards Brittany as they would seem.
They had already brought their own political perspective to bear upon

11. PRO SP 78/22/218.
12. Specifically, regarding the authenticity of incriminating passages in
Mary's letters to Anthony Babington; it was Nau who had been responsible for
their dispatch.
13. There were fears that Nau 'might be drawn to be a pensioner to Spain,
and to favour that party' ((HMC *Salis.*, vol. iv, p. 98). Others alleged that he
was fraudulently converting money entrusted to him by the Breton Estates
(PRO SP 78/24/5).
14. PRO SP 78/22/194.
15. PRO SP 78/22/107 (internal evidence invalidates the endorsed date).
16. PRO SP 78/22/233.

the situation there, and were taking steps accordingly. Five days before the submission of Williams's memorandum, draft instructions had been prepared for Bodley, the English ambassador at The Hague. He was to take confidential soundings as to how the Provinces' leaders would react if English veterans in garrison there were withdrawn for service in Brittany.[17] Within a week more instructions were drafted, this time for Sir John Norris. Extensively experienced in military affairs in the Netherlands, Norris was to arrange the withdrawal from there of 3,000 men, and to take command of them for Breton service.[18] As Sir John himself pointed out on leaving Margate for Flushing, such a redeployment of English troops would scarcely gratify Turenne.[19] Indeed, well before Norris's departure the Viscount himself had written from The Hague that existing English forces in the Netherlands were too depleted in numbers to permit the release of men for service in the field. If he brought his Germans by the projected route, Elizabeth must send fresh recruits to replace the veterans who would join them.[20] It was precisely the contrary that the Queen now appeared to intend, in a manner prejudicial to the Flanders plan and also to the Viscount's hopes of raising money from the Provinces. Had she simply changed her mind over that plan, and over the Brittany situation too? Was she merely trying to minimize expense by shuttling her troops to and fro, drifting thereby into doing everything by halves, going 'on in strange paradox, decided only to be undecided, resolved to be irresolute'?[21]

There is another explanation. The Flanders plan, for all its attractiveness on paper, depended upon serious co-operation by the Provinces and by the French. Their willingness so to co-operate could scarcely be taken for granted and everything left in amber until the instruments of war were prepared. Moreover, at this time Elizabeth had excellent reasons for bringing pressure to bear on the Provinces. In her judgement, they had recently displayed a disturbing lack of concern over the welfare of her garrisons and the security of the cautionary towns. Contrary to her wishes and to her advice, they had also persisted in trading with the enemy and even in supplying munitions to Spain. Even as des Mesnils was pressing his case, a delegation was arriving from the Provinces to argue the whole question of trade and to present objec-

17. PRO SP 84/40/91.   18. PRO SP 84/41/3.
19. PRO SP 84/41/52.   20. PRO SP 78/22/232.
21. Churchill's charge in 1936 against the Baldwin government, levelled against Elizabeth by C. Wilson, *Queen Elizabeth and the Revolt of the Netherlands*, p. 130.

tions to interference with Provinces' shipping by English privateers. There were to be sharp exchanges between these delegates and the Queen.[22] Further, the earlier version of the Flanders plan had been disrupted by Maurice of Nassau's premature move. All this suggested that the Provinces' willingness to co-operate to the full in the current version of that plan could not be assumed and should be tested. So should the staunchness of the French. Before he left for Flushing, Norris dined with Beauvoir and, on the Queen's direction, asked him for letters of recommendation to Buzenval.[23] Her general's mission, and the response it provoked, would assist the Queen towards the decision she must take as to where she should apply her military effort in the coming season. It was also another move in her continuing endeavour to remedy through diplomatic pressure what she regarded as irresponsible conduct by her allies.

For Elizabeth was not quite as parsimonious, nor as changeable, as she might seem. Before Norris left, stand-by instructions were issued to thirteen English shires for raising, as circumstances might require, from 1,500 to 3,000 fresh soldiers 'if this service shall take place'.[24] These could be sent directly to Brittany; alternatively, they could replace whatever veterans Norris might withdraw from the Netherlands. Evidently, at this stage the English government was thinking in terms of the latter alternative.[25] But this was not evident to the Provinces. At The Hague Norris met flat refusal to his proposal to withdraw 3,000 veterans. With a fine disregard for rancour, he nevertheless set about arranging withdrawals in accordance with the enabling clauses of his commission. Vigorous protests ensued. By their interpretation, the Council of State admonished the Queen, her agent was acting in breach of the Treaty of Nonsuch. More interesting to her was their reminder of their own strategic role, of diverting and distracting Parma when he should seek to re-enter France.[26] Interesting, too, was Buzenval's response. Amid complaints over Norris's high-handed dealing, he wrote of a project which the Provinces had in mind that would much impede

22. The delegates' letters of credence were signed on 13 December (PRO SP 84/40/6-9). They arrived in London on 30 December, and stayed for two months. On the issue of trade, see especially BM Cotton Galba D VII, fos. 47, 144; D VIII, fo. 52.

23. PRO SP 78/23/24.   24. APC, vol. xx (1590-1), p. 206.

25. ibid., pp. 210-11. The number of veterans that Norris would be able to bring away was uncertain, and the possibility envisaged that he might bring none.

26. PRO SP 84/41/128, 145.

Parma in his departure for France.[27] The Queen was sufficiently re-assured to issue Norris with fresh instructions. Now she openly declared that her intention was to withdraw veterans only up to a maximum number of 1,500, and that these would immediately be replaced by fresh recruits from England. What had persuaded her to this concession was the Provinces' declared intention to augment their forces in the field with a view to combining with English troops in pre-venting Parma's march for France.[28]

And yet the reassurance had been insufficient to consolidate her belief in the Flanders plan. Injurious to that belief were the attitudes of her own military commanders. Williams had already supported the claims of Brittany. Norris, consulted by Burghley, had given his opinion that 'the army preparing in Germany will not be able to pass through the Low Countries without the assistance of 6,000 or 8,000 footmen from her Majesty besides as many horsemen as her Majesty and the States do entertain there'.[29] This was a far greater requirement than the Queen had envisaged. Vere added his view, that nothing would be gained by bringing the Germans along that route unless they were to concentrate their efforts entirely on the Netherlands and abandon all pretence of proceeding into France.[30] From Elizabeth's point of view there was a good deal to be said for this. But it was still highly uncertain that her allies would co-operate to a degree sufficient to make that plan of campaign worth while. The effect of her revision of Norris's instructions was merely to confirm her doubts. No sooner had the Provinces approved withdrawal of veterans on the revised terms than Vere was writing to Burghley as to where he and Maurice intended to campaign in the coming season. He himself, he claimed, saw considerable merit in the Flanders plan and had tried to persuade Maurice to it. However, the latter was clearly determined to operate in and around Gelderland, arguing that such an operation would be generally more acceptable and perhaps more serviceable to the Provin-ces. Vere felt bound to agree, believing that it might even prove enough to keep Parma out of France.[31] But it was also well removed from Flanders,[32] and scarcely relevant to the implementation of that plan.

27. PRO SP 78/23/100.   28. PRO SP 84/41/168.
29. PRO SP 84/40/108.   30. PRO SP 84/41/36.
31. PRO SP 84/41/228.
32. In the event Maurice was to surprise everyone by the speed with which he moved his forces over great distances in related offensives; see below, p. 126.

None of the Queen's commanders was altogether disinterested. However strenuously they might protest the contrary, Elizabeth knew of the continuing rivalry between them. Williams made no secret of his own antipathy towards Norris[33]—an antipathy stemming from their days in the Netherlands with Leicester.[34] Burghley had suggested that Vere might accept a commission under Norris in Brittany.[35] On the likelihood of this, Williams had commented, 'I cannot believe it.'[36] And indeed, while Vere declared his willingness to serve anywhere the Queen might command him and conducted himself with scrupulous courtesy towards Norris during the latter's negotiations at The Hague, he found himself insufficiently recovered from wounds to be able to accept such a commission.[37] Characterized by strength of personality and independence of mind—the very qualities that made them effective as leaders of men—each of these commanders coveted a command of his own. This in itself did not augur well for co-ordinated action of the kind essential to the success of the Flanders plan. And as the weeks passed the practicability of that plan receded even further. The Provinces were dragging their feet over contributing towards Turenne's Germans. They saw little purpose in those troops coming through the Netherlands at all.[38] Into the month of April 1591 Turenne in Germany, unsure of developments at The Hague and at London alike, kept open the possibility of executing his march as had been planned.[39] Into the month of May Elizabeth retained her lingering affection for the notion of attempting Dunkirk.[40] By then, Maurice of Nassau was launching his famous Spring offensive: a feint southwards towards Geertruidenburg and 's Hertogenbosch, but a full-scale offensive in Gelderland. The Provinces' commander was going it alone.

Well before that offensive took place, the Flanders plan was little more than a dead letter. But Elizabeth's shift away from it—a shift

33. See especially his tirade against Norris, PRO SP 78/24/132.

34. *CSPF* (1586–7), pp. 47, 138, 173.

35. PRO SP 84/40/102; such an acceptance might improve other captains' attitudes towards Norris.

36. PRO SP 78/22/233.

37. PRO SP 84/41/36, 80, 126. Norris enjoyed the support of Lord Admiral Howard; cf. above, p. 42, and below, chapter 4, note 80.

38. PRO SP 84/41/281.

39. PRO SP 81/6/168. cf. Mansfield to Parma, 29 July: 'The rumour persists that the troops raised in Germany for Henry of Navarre will come to attack the Netherlands' (Lefèvre, vol. iii, p. 590).

40. PRO SP 84/42/33.

that directly affected her attitude towards Palavicino and Turenne[41]—
had not been impelled solely by attitudes among her own commanders
and at The Hague. Scarcely less relevant than the movements of
Prince Maurice to its implementation were the intentions of Henry of
France. If Parma was to be detained and squeezed in Flanders, Henry
must play his part from Picardy. If he failed to do so, and if the
Provinces also followed their own devices, Elizabeth might be left
contemplating Flanders while Parma marched briskly southwards. And
if he did march southwards unimpeded, there was the possibility of his
erupting into Brittany with harbours, shipping, and a large army freely
at his disposal—the very conjuncture that had been so narrowly
averted in the Armada year. Before Elizabeth could decide upon
her disposition of her forces, Henry's intentions must be ascertained.
Regarding them, all too little was known. It was from Dombes, not
from Henry, that des Mesnils had received his instructions—a fact
to which Elizabeth took exception, and not merely on grounds of
etiquette.[42] Nor was she merely concerned about expense. Certainly
she had insisted to Beauvoir that if English troops were sent to Brittany
Henry must give formal guarantees for reimbursement, supply, a
place of retreat in the form of a suitable harbour. Fresh arguments
from Williams, fresh news from Brittany of a rapid build-up there of
Spanish naval strength, were no substitute for these.[43] But above all
there was no substitute for hard information regarding what Henry
himself meant to do. To obtain that information, a reliable envoy
must be sent to consult with the King himself. On 9 February, while
Norris was still negotiating at The Hague, Edmund Yorke departed
from Richmond on this mission. Before he left Rye, two deputies
of the Breton Estates arrived direct from Henry, full authorized
to bind their principals to repay whatever aid Elizabeth might accord.
Yorke himself knew of their authority.[44] This did not prevent his own
departure.

Yorke's instructions[45] contained sharp comments on Henry's recent
silence and apparent inactivity.[46] They also recorded that upon receipt
of adequate guarantees Elizabeth 'could be content, if the King should
think it needful and require it, to prepare some two or three thousand

---

41. See above, pp. 46–7.
42. Though she never took kindly to attempts by subjects of a fellow-monarch
to conduct their own foreign policy in the manner of a sovereign state.
43. PRO SP 78/23/11, 15, 28, 43, 44.   44. PRO SP 78/23/83, 98.
45. PRO SP 78/23/48–58.   46. cf. below, p. 110.

or more men to be sent into Brittany'.[47] What she 'found it most necessary to inform him' was 'that when the power by sea shall be come out
of Spain, the Duke of Parma is ordered to come away into France,
and without staying about the winning of any towns, or to offer any
fight, to march as speedily as he can by the help of the Leaguers to
give him passage, directly into Brittany and there to join with the
Spanish forces, and thereby as they make accompt to be to recover all
Brittany'. She left it to Henry to consider 'how the same may be effected by the Duke of Parma'. But to test the King's position in the matter
of the Netherlands, her veterans and Turenne, she carefully observed:
'we would the king should understand it how our disposition is more
inclined to bring [the veterans] out of the Low Countries for Brittany
than to employ them to accompany the German army, which may be
doubted whether it shall be thought meet in Germany to come through
the Low Countries'. Yet she added, in a personal letter also carried
by Yorke, a rousing call to Henry to anticipate the danger from
Parma. 'Prevent his coming, do not wait for him to come', she expostulated. Henry must cover and command every route by which the
redoubtable Spanish governor might enter his kingdom.[48]

In Edmund Yorke an envoy had been chosen who, as he himself
shortly afterwards acknowledged, depended entirely upon Burghley,[49]
and who had every incentive to prove himself competent and reliable.
A younger son of a former Sheriff of London and Master of the Mint,[50]
Yorke had had his own way to make in the world. His brother Rowland
had helped neither his family's reputation nor his country's cause when
he sold the Sconce of Zutphen to the Spaniards in 1587. Still, Edmund
had persevered with military service to the Crown. In the Armada year
he had prepared plans for the defence of Yarmouth, and had been
quartermaster of the army assembled at Tilbury. He had since been
'clerk of the victuals' in Willoughby's army in France, and was now
employed on the fortifications in Munster.[51] The mission to King

47. Preparations to this effect were, of course, already in hand.
48. PRO SP 78/23/62.
49. 'I acknowledge my bondage to your Lordship so great as never any poor
man was ever so much bound to so great, so honourable and worthy a personage as I to your Lordship' (PRO SP 78/23/189).
50. J. Foster (ed.), *The Visitation of Yorkshire made in the years 1584/5 by
Robert Glover* (London, 1875), p. 382.
51. L. Boynton, *The Elizabethan Militia* (London, 1967), p. 129; HMC *Fifteenth Report, Appendix V (Foljambe MSS.)* (London, 1897), p. 52; PRO SP
12/226/31; *CSPD* (1581–90), p. 642.

Henry was his greatest opportunity hitherto to climb from the ranks of the Queen's minor servants through demonstrating ability in major affairs.

Yorke travelled by a circuitous route, through parts of Normandy where he had been some eighteen months before.[52] Eventually he reached Henry, at Chartres. The inexperienced envoy had some reason to believe that his work there was done well enough. To the specific points put to him, Henry made amiable replies. He wanted from the Queen 3,000 infantry for Brittany. He would himself send 3,000 more. They would be supplied locally with munitions and with victuals, at rates agreed by the French and English commanders on the spot.[53] He was delighted with the Queen's intention to send shipping to defend the coast. Of course, he was in no position to supplement her naval power with any of his own. But all his harbours in Brittany were at her disposal. As requested, he was willing to designate the harbour and town of Brest as a place of retreat for the English forces.[54] Perhaps they ought not to have the castle, lest the sensibilities of his Catholic nobility be offended. Even better for English purposes, he understood, would be the castle, admittedly half-finished, at the mouth of the Blavet —'if it can be taken, which ought to be the army's first enterprise'.[55]

All this might seem evasive—especially since Elizabeth had sought not verbal promises but formal guarantees, ratified by the French *parlement*, as Burghley had put it, 'in such a form that the French crown would be bound by its obligations'.[56] But as Henry fairly pointed out, his own ambassador and the Breton deputies were already fully em-

52. See also below, p. 64.
53. As always, drink was a problem; Henry admitted that it would have to come from England. Within a month of his arrival in Brittany, Norris complained of an acute shortage of beer for his men (PRO SP 78/24/109). According to him, all other provision was hopelessly inadequate too.
54. Yorke had announced in advance that in dealing with Henry he would 'stand somewhat for Brest' (PRO SP 78/23/119).
55. cf. BM Cotton Caligula E VII, fo. 382^v; PRO SP 78/23/232; Rymer, vol. xvi, p. 94, misreading 'Blavet' as 'Relaner'. Currently in Spanish hands (see above, p. 14), the mouth of the Blavet was thought by some informed contemporaries to constitute the best harbour in France, after Brest (Oppenheim, *Monson's Tracts*, vol. v, p. 29). At the end of June Norris was in fact encamped at Landernau ('Chateau Landry'), further up the estuary (PRO SP 78/24/273).
56. The English government's knowledge of foreign constitutions—not least, in the case of the *pays d'état* of Brittany—was throughout this period as unsure as was continental knowledge of the extent of England's resources.

powered in that respect. What he gave Yorke was not guarantees but a schedule of fresh demands. There was no hint in these of the Flanders plan. All the emphasis fell on measures which Henry would take, not to *prevent*—as the Queen had stressed in her letter—but to encounter Parma on his expected return to France. When this occurred, Henry would need an additional force of 4,000 English infantry, including the Netherlands veterans, to be sent to Dieppe. He would join them there with his own army, and, further reinforced by the Germans, he would confront the enemy.[57] He would deploy these troops on a line from St. Quentin through Corbie along the Somme. That defensive line, barring Parma's southward route, might win the Queen's approval. But Henry also wanted cavalry, sappers, artillery, and munitions.[58] In short, far from concurring in the Flanders plan he was proposing his own firm alternative without in the slightest degree reducing his demands upon the Queen.

Small wonder, then, that within a week Burghley should have informed Beauvoir that while Turenne might expect assistance from English veterans already there if he did after all bring his Germans via the Netherlands, there was no intention of sending extra forces to that area. If the Provinces wished to put the Germans to work, the Provinces must pay for them.[59] Small wonder, too, that on his return to England Yorke's was a cold reception, that left him miserable at Stratford-at-Bow, bewailing his 'great indiscretion'.[60] In a sense his efforts had helped the Queen towards a decision. But that decision was a frustrating one. Far from taking an initiative against Parma in coordination with her allies, she would have to wait and see what he would do. In fact, Parma had returned to the Netherlands with an army so reduced, with finances so depleted, and to a situation so disordered, that for him a prompt return to France was out of the question.[61] There is good reason to believe that circumstances were unusually favourable for such a plan as the Queen had entertained. But her in-

57. As Yorke was preparing to leave England, Henry had sent a fresh envoy to follow up Turenne and to obtain from the Queen fresh letters to the German princes. At that time he had advised Beauvoir that if she and they should insist upon bringing the Germans via the Netherlands, he would be agreeable to that route. But evidently his major concern was to gather as many forces as possible under his own command (PRO SP 78/23/81, 102).

58. PRO SP 78/23/146.   59. PRO SP 78/23/161.

60. PRO SP 78/23/189. Thanks to Burghley, however, his disgrace was by no means final; see below, pp. 148–9.

61. See van der Essen, vol. v, pp. 313–14.

formation regarding those circumstances was all too contradictory and unreliable.[62] Meanwhile, Parma's reputation remained, always a vital ingredient in the situation; and with it remained Henry's determination that the entire situation must be resolved in France.

Throughout Yorke's absence, the chorus of appeals from Brittany had been mounting to a crescendo. The Breton deputies, led by their Treasurer, had stressed that for the moment the Spaniards had not succeeded in penetrating north of the Blavet estuary. That favourable circumstance was unlikely to last very long. Dombes and Henry had reiterated their pleas.[63] More telling still, news was arriving from the Biscay ports of 'a new armada that [Philip] doth now make ready to go into Brittany'.[64] From Chartres came confirmation, that Spaniards were landing at the Loire estuary, that Brittany must soon be lost.[65] At last, on 27 March, the Privy Council confirmed the stand-by instructions sent two months earlier to the lords lieutenant in the English shires. Three thousand fresh soldiers were to be levied. Some were destined for Flushing, to replace the veterans released in accordance with the agreement with the Provinces. The rest, with the veterans, would go to Brittany.[66] Norris had his army, Dombes his aid. But whatever gratification they may have felt, however imperative the needs of Brittany may have been made to appear, the English government remained noticeably unenthusiastic. In those same orders of 27 March, Normandy was mentioned again.

62. Throughout the winter and spring months of 1590–1 a stream of hopelessly conflicting reports reached the English government regarding the condition and likely movements of Parma and his men—the key to the whole situation, which the unpredictability of Maurice of Nassau's movements did nothing to clarify. cf. below, pp. 171–2.

63. PRO SP 78/23/67, 139.

64. PRO SP 78/23/148.

65. PRO SP 78/23/179. On the same day Vere sent confirmation that Maurice of Nassau was intent upon campaigning in Gelderland (PRO SP 84/41/228).

66. APC, vol. xx (1590–1), pp. 361–3.

CHAPTER FOUR

NORMANDY

SINCE Stafford's report of it in October 1590, very little had been heard of the French king's proposal to attempt the recovery of Rouen. There were references to the town, during the months that followed, in letters sent to Burghley from Dieppe by the merchant Otwell Smyth, to whom Henry had earlier mentioned that proposal.[1] But despite his own special interest in Rouen, Smyth did not press that matter in those letters. He commented on depredations committed on English shipping by French and Spanish vessels operating from their base at Le Havre, and regretted that English merchants should continue to trade to the latter town. While Turenne was in England Smyth volunteered his view, that 'there is small account made of the Spaniards in Brittany, they be such poor fellows and there is such sickness amongst them.'[2] Shortly afterwards he thought, on the grounds of Parma's withdrawal and the arrival in Normandy of Marshal Biron, that 'the King doth mind to keep Paris blocked and Marshal Biron to keep Rouen blocked, so I do trust in God they will render shortly both of their towns'.[3] This was little more than general comment. Beyond requesting that English merchants should not participate in the temporary reopening of trade between Dieppe, Caen, and rebel towns, which Henry had authorized in order to raise money, Biron himself did not seek English assistance for his own campaign in Normandy.[4]

---

1. See above, p. 37.
2. PRO SP 78/22/131.
3. PRO SP 78/22/167. Armand de Gontaut, seigneur de Biron, of an ancient but impoverished Périgord family, was now aged about 65; godfather to Cardinal Richelieu, he was vastly experienced in French politics and warfare and at various times had had the ear of Henry III, with whose successor his earlier relations had frequently been discordant.
4. PRO SP 78/22/201. Notwithstanding the war situation and Elizabeth's censure of the Provinces, English merchants could still obtain licences in 1591 to trade to Le Havre and to Rouen (for example, *APC*, vol. xxi (1591), pp. 80–1, 103, 127). On the present occasion the English merchants trading to Dieppe and Caen, consulted by Burghley, thought that Henry's concession to those towns would benefit their own trade there (HMC *Salis.*, vol. iv, pp. 87–8).

A few weeks later, reportedly to Biron's vexation, Henry ordered him to quit Normandy and join him at the siege of Chartres.[5] Concern mounted in Dieppe. Stimulated by conversations with Yorke on his roundabout journey towards Henry, the governors of Dieppe and Caen reminded the Queen of their difficulties. There was a possibility that when Parma returned he might attempt Dieppe. There was a need for shipping to protect the sea-link with England. Yet these were still comparatively general remarks. Far more immediate and more specific were requests from the Duke of Épernon for munitions to enable him to secure Boulogne. Elizabeth was discouraging enough over this; as she pointed out to Épernon, having neither the eastern nor the western Indies she could scarcely cater for every emergency.[6] As for Henry, his requirements were for the time being limited to the case of Brittany, with a continuing eye to what he would want when Parma should return.

Then, at the end of March, the tone of letters from Dieppe was transformed. On the day following the issue of confirmatory orders by the English Privy Council for the levies for Brittany, the *intendant* Incarvile, Henry's former envoy to England and to the Provinces, wrote from that town to Beauvoir in urgent terms. According to him, Dieppe was now in jeopardy owing to the capture of the castle of Blainville-Crevon in a combined operation by the governors of Le Havre and Rouen.[7] On the following day Otwell Smyth wrote to Burghley, still more urgently. The fall of Blainville, he asserted, had placed Dieppe in serious danger and had reduced its governor to despair. Three thousand English troops were needed, paid for four months, to defend the town.[8] Five days later Smyth was intensifying his pleas. Spaniards, he claimed, were pouring into Le Havre (presumably fitter and fresher ones than the 'poor fellows' in Brittany). If 3,000 Englishmen were not available, 600 would do good service in Dieppe.[9] In view of the expense to which Elizabeth was already committed on behalf of the French, it was with some diffidence that Beauvoir passed these applications on to Burghley.[10] But the Queen's response was startlingly prompt

5. PRO SP 78/23/32.

6. PRO SP 78/23/113, 119–41. In mid-March Parma was relating Épernon's presence at Boulogne to Norris's recent activities in the Provinces, and envisaging that they would join forces for operations along the littoral (Lefèvre, vol. iii, p. 564).

7. PRO SP 78/23/188.   8. PRO SP 78/23/177.
9. PRO SP 78/23/181.   10. PRO SP 78/23/211.

and favourable. On the following day Beauvoir could notify the Lord Treasurer of his delight at learning of her decision to send some men to Dieppe, though the details were not yet settled.[11] They were settled very quickly. The next day instructions were issued for a detachment of 600 from Norris's force to be sent to Dieppe. Their commander was to be Sir Roger Williams.[12]

The Queen had acted without hesitation. Yet she had done so, it would seem, on the basis of questionable information. She could hardly have been oblivious to the fact that neither Incarvile nor Smyth was a disinterested observer of events in Normandy. True, she may not have been able to appreciate quite how disingenuous was their current clamour. Blainville-Crevon, captured several days before Incarvile's report of its fall, lay no more than nine miles east-north-east of Rouen. It was certainly relevant to the defence of that town. Indeed, the Rouennais were taking steps not to fortify the castle as a potential base for offensive operations but to destroy it as an actual threat to their own security.[13] Only to the most timorous mind could it have seemed an immediate threat to Dieppe, over thirty miles away. Whether or not Elizabeth was so timorous, or whether she was merely misguided through geographical ignorance, she had also been advised that Governor de Chatte of Dieppe, under pressure from Tavannes of Rouen and Villars of Le Havre, might arrive at some understanding with them. The possibility of de Chatte's weakening in his loyalist allegiance and perhaps changing sides, was certainly to be deplored and to be avoided. Again, the possibility was doubtful,[14] though it drew an urgent letter to him from the Queen.[15] But possibilities other than danger had been aired by Smyth. He had added to his appeals the significant rider, that the arrival of English troops in Normandy 'would be a means to bring the King to besiege the town of Rouen'.[16]

If the other arguments put to Elizabeth from Dieppe were speculative, this last was no less so. For Henry, still at Chartres, knew nothing of these developments. Far from considering an incursion into Normandy, he was at this very time summoning Montpensier and his forces out of that province to join him.[17] He did not even know that

11. PRO SP 78/23/217.
12. PRO SP 78/23/228. 13. RD, vol. 20, fo. 486; cf. below, p. 134.
14. See below, pp. 67, 135–6. 15. PRO SP 78/23/226.
16. PRO SP 78/23/181.
17. So Edward Grimeston, Stafford's deputy, wrote on 4 April from Chartres (PRO SP 78/23/213): the letter cannot have reached England in time to have

troops for Brittany had been granted. One week before the orders for
their levying had been issued in England, he had been pondering
whether to send there a fresh envoy for that very purpose. Puzzled
by conflicting reports of the Provinces' response to the proposal to
withdraw the English veterans, he had been undecided whether to
press upon Elizabeth his own demands for troops. To do so successfully might cost the Provinces the veterans, and himself the Provinces'
sympathy. It might also enable Parma to bring a larger army into
France.[18] Information that the difficulties with the Provinces were
resolved did not reach the King until Elizabeth had taken her decision
with regard to Brittany. It was on the strength of that information, and
in ignorance of that decision, that he finally sent off his envoy. Antoine
de Moret, sieur de Reau, was to negotiate for the Breton forces. He was
also to negotiate for additional forces to support Henry's in dealing
with Parma. Beauvoir was advised by the King of the urgency of both
requests. He was also informed that a further 3,000 Spaniards had
arrived in Brittany.[19] Yet Edward Grimeston, whom former ambassador Stafford had left to hover about the King, simultaneously picked
up and passed on news which had reached Henry of mutiny in Parma's
garrison forces, serious enough to prevent the Spanish governor from
sending any troops into France for the time being.[20] Evidently, Henry's
present concern was still principally to make sure of the Brittany contingent. Even with Chartres taken, a fortnight after Incarvile's first
appeal from Dieppe, Henry was still reported to be thinking not of a
Normandy campaign but of engaging Mayenne in battle.[21] A further
week passed before Grimeston gleaned at the King's camp 'some
meaning to go and besiege [Rouen]'.[22] On that same day Williams was

---

affected Elizabeth's decision. Three weeks earlier Henry had ordered Montpensier to recover Honfleur, as a matter of urgency (AN K 105, no. 2c).

18. PRO SP 78/23/174, 222; *LM*, vol. iii, pp. 827–9.

19. loc. cit.

20. PRO SP 78/23/215; the reported mutiny was at 's Hertogenbosch (cf.
above, p. 57). Earlier Grimeston had sent to England warnings of the growing
danger in Brittany, and explanations of Henry's inability at this time to 'have
retired himself into a corner of his realm, and abandon the heart of France
unto his enemies'. Using an identical phrase, Elizabeth had herself previously
interpreted Henry's retirement into Normandy in August 1589 as a sign of
weakness (PRO SP 78/23/174, 187; 21/293).

21. PRO SP 78/24/5, 6.

22. PRO SP 78/24/45. The town was denoted in cipher. Subsequently
Grimeston continued to note the desirability of such a siege, and represented
Biron as a particular advocate of it (for example, ibid., 118).

arriving at Dieppe with his company. The pleas that had brought him there had owed nothing to the French king, and had been made independently of him.

Thus, if Elizabeth's prompt response to those pleas had sprung from a belief on her part either in imminent danger to Dieppe from Blainville or in Henry's declared intentions towards Rouen, she was deceived. If she had acted from fear of what might follow from pressure upon or overtures to Governor de Chatte, she was scarcely better-advised. The collusion between de Chatte's antagonists, Tavannes and Villars, over the taking of Blainville, had been short-lived. Always the uneasiest of allies, they had promptly quarrelled. Tavannes had gone away on a futile adventure to relieve Chartres, leaving Villars to make advances of his own to de Chattes. Now Smyth and Incarvile wrote in unison to England once again. Dieppe was still in a dangerous predicament. But, they advised, until the outcome of these discussions between the governors were known it would be best to hold back Williams and his men. If the purpose of those troops was to stiffen de Chatte in his allegiance to King Henry, this was strange advice. It seemed that this was not their purpose after all. Their number, the Queen was told, was 'not enough for a big effort in the country, as is most necessary'.[23] Here was the heart of the matter. For the English merchant and the French official, troops from England meant not merely some additional defenders for Dieppe but the nucleus of an army for an offensive campaign in Normandy. Having as yet no indication of Elizabeth's views on this, they were disconcerted by the speed with which she had moved. Its immediate effect, with Williams's arrival, was the breakdown of the governors' discussions.[24] Yet the basic argument remained: as Smyth put it, Dieppe 'will still trouble her Majesty for help if the King do not come to take Rouen, and there is nobody can persuade the King to come to Rouen but her Majesty. That being taken, all the rest will soon yield.'[25]

That argument was now acquiring a fresh advocate. In her instructions to Williams Elizabeth stressed that he must limit his activities to assisting de Chatte in the defence of Dieppe, unless available

23. PRO SP 78/24/20.
24. De Chatte and Villars later reached a gentlemen's agreement to conduct their struggle with minimum disturbance and molestation of the peasantry (PRO SP 78/24/103); such agreements were by no means unusual in these wars.
25. PRO SP 78/24/10.

French forces were sufficiently augmented to justify an extension of combined operations into the surrounding countryside.[26] For a while Williams's conduct was consistent with these instructions. Less consistent were his opinions with views he had expressed earlier. While Dieppe's breezes did not instantly bear from his mind all thoughts of Brittany, that province's prominence was quickly reduced in Williams's assessment of the needs of France. On the day following his arrival he repeated his warning, that if a 'great navy' should 'enter the ports of Brittany, their meaning must be for England'. But, he remarked, 'I hear also that they of [Le Havre] looks for four galleasses and 24 galleys from Spain with Spanish soldiers, in great numbers.' He restated the possibility that when Parma returned he might 'march with a great army into Brittany'. But Parma might do other things. He might 'march to levy the first siege of importance that the King will attempt'. Certainly Henry ought to be encouraged to 'win some of his great towns, with the which means he should be able to make wars of himself'. Clearly the King's mind was on Paris. For that, a three months' siege would be needed, 'else his only way were to come to Rouen'.[27]

Within a week these ideas had hardened. Now Williams claimed to have learned that 3,000 Spaniards on their way to Brittany had been lost at sea. The strategic importance of the sea-coast was presented in a fresh light: 'There is no means comparable for the King and to us as the siege of Rouen; being won, the King will clear all the sea coast and be able to repay such treasure as her Majesty lent him hitherto, or at the least be able to maintain his own wars.'[28] The prospect of repayment was painted more glowingly by Smyth, writing the same day: 'If the King would grant her Majesty the receipt of the custom house of Rouen for two years after it should be taken, it would reimburse her Majesty of all the money she hath lent with the interest, the traffic would be so great to that town.'[29] The point was repeated by Williams a week later: 'let [the King] give your merchants the customs, it will repay her Majesty in a short time all that her Majesty hath lent him'. And in the same letter he neatly tied the threads of his old arguments to his new objective: 'You must,' he urged the Privy Council, draw [the King] and his forces to clear his sea coast, the which is

26. PRO SP 78/24/27; BM Cotton Caligula E VIII, fo. 93; *APC*, vol. xxi (1591), pp. 26–8.

27. PRO SP 78/24/49.   28. PRO SP 78/24/53.

29. PRO SP 78/24/55.

dearer unto England than the mainland. True it is, doth he lose his ports how shall you succour him? Wherefore your lordships must draw him to Rouen.'[30]

There is an obvious affinity between Williams's altered opinions and the ideas of Otwell Smyth, and clear evidence of collusion between them. In Incarvile they had another partner. All three had the advantage of being able to present their views in the guise of first-hand information. Even this was not all. Apart from his correspondence with Burghley, Williams was in touch with Essex in England.[31] On the same day that Sir Roger was marshalling his men and his preliminary arguments at Dieppe, the Earl was entertaining the latest French envoy at Wanstead in the county of Essex. Never a scrimping host, he was treating this guest very lavishly. De Reau was feasted on oysters and prawns, turbot and carp, pike and plaice, pullets and geese, mutton and lamb, fruits, preserves, and confectionery, consumed off polished silver and pewter dishes, in quarters bedecked with fresh flowers, lit by dozens of 'white lights'—and, significantly, equipped with a map.[32] Within ten days de Reau was given fresh cause for celebration. On 2 May Hatton and Burghley wrote to Williams that 'the Queen's Majesty liketh well of your opinion that the French King, now having won Chartres, should attempt the recovery of Rouen, for which purpose her Majesty hath lately written most earnestly to the King to induce him thereto, with offer of an aid of 3,000 or 4,000 more Englishmen to be waged by him, and with some aid of shipping also for that purpose'.[33]

De Reau's mission seemed accomplished. English troops both for Brittany and for Henry were obtained. He promptly returned to his master. At Dieppe there was rejoicing. As Smyth put it, 'the taking of that town [Rouen] is the greatest safeguard that the King can have and the greatest commodity for England'.[34] But the occasion for rejoicing was short-lived. On 12 May Elizabeth instructed Williams that he must after all join Norris in Brittany.[35] The next day Beauvoir expressed to Burghley his chagrin that the Queen had changed her mind. This, he claimed, with the consequences that must ensue, would be 'the ruin of France and thereby of all Christendom'.[36]

Perhaps the Queen had indeed changed her mind. Perhaps she had

30. PRO SP 78/24/78.   31. For example, PRO SP 78/24/122.
32. LD, vol. ii, grocers' bills preceding fo. 65; cf. above, p. 27, note 50.
33. PRO SP 78/24/70.   34. PRO SP 78/24/103.
35. PRO SP 78/24/96.   36. PRO SP 78/24/97.

once more reviewed strategic priorities in the light of fresh information from France. Certainly she chose to tell Williams that she had learned of the arrival at the Blavet a fortnight earlier of another large contingent of Spaniards.[37] Moreover, on 30 April a report had been sent from St. Jean de Luz indicating no relaxation in the Spanish naval and military build-up in Brittany;[38] and English territory might still be the enemy's main objective, as Williams himself had suggested earlier.[39] If Elizabeth was temperamentally changeable and indecisive, her mind may indeed have been subject to alteration with every courier's arrival. But again, there is another explanation. The English government's concern for Normandy was of long standing.[40] During the past month Burghley had been carrying out a review of military expenditure, scheduling the numbers and cost of troops stationed on the frontiers of the realm. There were garrisons at this time in Ireland, at Berwick on the Scottish frontier, in the Provinces and now in Brittany.[41] In this protective circle, Normandy was a yawning gap. In February, when Burghley had advised Grimeston to urge once again upon the King the importance of recovering his 'port-towns', he had itemized Le Havre before the ports of Brittany as key places.[42] In March he and the Queen had suggested to Beauvoir that some proportion of the force for Brittany might instead be employed in Normandy, 'as shall be thought profitable for the French King's service'.[43] What was uncertain in the present situation, from the English point of view, was not so much the importance of Normandy as the intentions of King Henry.

For whatever may have been imagined in Dieppe, Henry was by no means committed to any project so specific as a siege of Rouen. While de Reau was in England the King had written of 'some good enterprise' which, he believed, would be agreeable to the Queen and which he would undertake if Parma gave him leisure.[44] This was distinctly

37. PRO SP 78/24/96.   38. PRO SP 78/24/61.

39. See above, p. 68. In March a fleet of 75 sail was reported to be making ready at Ferrol, next door to Corunna from where the 1588 Armada had finally set sail. By mid-May this estimate would rise to 140 (PRO SP 94/4/7, 21).

40. For example, above, p. 37.   41. PRO 12/238/77–8, 88, 109.

42. T. Birch, *Memoirs of the Reign of Queen Elizabeth*, vol. i (London, 1754), p. 64.

43. PRO SP 78/23/161.

44. *LM*, vol. iii, pp. 381–2. On 26 April Grimeston sent Burghley information that Villeroy was again coming to the King to negotiate for peace which, in view of the weak state of the rival forces, was a distinct possibility (PRO SP 78/24/85).

vague. No more reassuring were indications that the King had it in mind to proceed from Chartres not north-westwards towards Dieppe but north-eastwards towards Château-Thierry, and thence further into Champagne.[45] In that event, Elizabeth might find herself acting unilaterally in Normandy, in a manner tantamount to invasion and all too likely to be represented as such by the King's enemies and by her own. That would be a serious military and political risk. It was a risk of the very kind that she had previously endeavoured to avoid, as in the Flanders plan. On that occasion, hopes in her allies' willingness to co-ordinate their efforts with her own had had a bearing upon her committing herself to subsidizing a German army—a commitment which she had soon regretted, and from which she was trying to win some reprieve. With money a continual matter of concern, she had not received from Henry the precise guarantees she had sought for the Brittany force. Now, in the case of Rouen, Beauvoir was told that while the Queen had agreed to send troops she did not mean to pay for them herself.[46] But this was only one consideration, and not merely a financial one. Her forces in France must be seen to be there as auxiliaries to the royalists. Beauvoir was also told that while 3,000 or 4,000 English would be held in readiness for Normandy they would be dispatched only when Henry had come there himself, and had also sent into Brittany all the troops he could spare.[47] These were Elizabeth's conditions. Her redirection of Williams's little force was a feint, calculated to secure them.

Feint or not, Beauvoir was in despair. All three of the ends he had been serving now seemed jeopardized. To Burghley he complained that Norris's force in Brittany was incapable of supporting Dombes adequately; that Henry, misdirected by de Reau, would now come into Normandy, with disastrous results; that Turenne's Germans—who, said Beauvoir, were intended for those two provinces—would be hopelessly below strength.[48] Smyth, Williams, and de Chatte raised from Dieppe their anguished chorus, invoking schemes and gesturing to skirmishes which, they declaimed, proved how feasible and essential it was to take Rouen. According to Smyth, Henry had already sent letters to Dieppe stating his firm intention to come there for that

45. He wrote to this effect on 19 April to Nevers (*LM*, vol. iii, pp. 377–9), whom he had been assuring since mid-December of his intention to go into Champagne as soon as possible.
46. PRO SP 78/24/97.   47. PRO SP 78/24/190.
48. PRO SP 78/24/105, 107, 114.

purpose.[49] The Spanish ships arriving in Brittany bore only merchandise.[50] Were Rouen captured, 'all this country hereabouts would be in quietness and they would be able to defend all the coast of Brittany'.[51] According to Williams, if 'the Spanish arrive at Le Havre before the King attempt Rouen, he may take his leave of all or the most part of Normandy'. And he appealed to England's pride: 'the enemies boasteth like mountebanks in their market places that England cannot send 5,000 out at once without transporting their troops by handfuls from place to place'.[52]

But colourful expostulations were no substitute for conditions met. There was all too little certainty that Henry, with his journey into Champagne in view, would satisfy Elizabeth on any of them. There was only a measure of hope that he might raise some money. The chorus at Dieppe made what they could of that. Fortified by news that the loyalist *parlement* at Tours had agreed to subscribe towards foreign troops for Henry, Incarville went to Caen to attempt persuasion of its Normandy counterpart to act likewise. On 24 May he laid his proposal before them. The townsmen of Dieppe, he announced in support of it, would supply 10,000 *écus*. The Queen of England was willing to assist Henry in a siege of Rouen, so that her merchants might 'trade with the town as they used to do before the troubles'. Although they welcomed the prospect of returning home, the magistrates' discussions on this proposal lasted for several days.[53] But on the same 24 May Smyth was writing to England from Dieppe, that the magistrates at Caen had agreed to a sum sufficient to maintain the royal army before Rouen for three months; and that most of that sum was already available.[54]

To this exaggerated report Williams was adding another ploy. Two days earlier he had returned to Dieppe. When the Queen's letters directing him to Brittany had reached that town, he had been away inland, busy with a scheme to surprise the enemy-held town of

49. PRO SP 78/24/103.   50. PRO SP 78/24/151.
51. PRO SP 78/24/183.   52. PRO SP 78/24/179.
53. ADSM-B-PRS (Caen), 1589–91, fo. 307. Some weeks earlier Incarville, with Henry's support, had laid before the magistrates at Caen a proposal that they and the Dieppois should jointly equip four ships and put them to sea for six months, to protect royalist vessels and to harass those of the League in general and Le Havre in particular. Incarville himself already had an interest in such a privateering enterprise. The magistrates were unenthusiastic (*LM*, vol. iii, p. 368; PRO SP 78/23/196; d'Estaintot, pp. 172–3).
54. PRO SP 78/24/134.

Louviers, upstream from Rouen on the south bank of the Seine. In that scheme he had been collaborating with de Chatte and with du Raulet, governor of neighbouring Pont de l'Arche who had contacts within Louviers.[55] Now there was a change of plan. By Williams's account he could not take his men to Brittany since Incarvile had commandeered all available shipping to carry himself to Caen. Meanwhile, du Raulet set off towards Henry, still hovering between Chartres and Paris. The governor consulted with the King. Henry swung westwards, sending Biron on ahead. Louviers fell, exactly in accordance with du Raulet's plan, and Henry came peacefully into the town.[56] At once Williams rode to confer with him.[57] Within a few days he was back in Dieppe.[58] By then Henry had finally decided to send de Reau once again to Elizabeth, and had signed the envoy's instructions.[59] They included a specific request that Williams and his troops be allowed to stay. As for Sir Roger, he now lost no time in writing to the Queen and to Burghley, that Henry was actually on his way to Dieppe; that 'our troops and myself was a principal occasion of the King's coming to these parts'; that detailed plans were laid for the coming campaign, which would culminate in the siege of Rouen; and that his own particular friend, La Noue, had been sent by Henry into Brittany.[60]

So the ground was prepared for de Reau's new effort. It seemed that Henry would have at least some money; that he had come himself towards the Normandy coast and had already, as all insisted, struck at Louviers a blow of great relevance to the siege of Rouen; and that

55. PRO SP 78/24/128. Williams was a ready participant in such exploits; a week earlier he and de Chatte had raided Aumale (ibid., 101, 103). The Queen's current frame of mind is evident from her sending him 'hearty thanks' for acting 'to the great honour of her Majesty' (APC, vol. xxi (1591), pp. 167–8).

56. d'Estaintot, pp. 180–2; the attempt upon Louviers may originally have been the idea of one Captain Marin. Grimeston gave a similar account of the exploit (PRO SP 78/24/181).

57. That is, a fortnight after his receipt of the Queen's letters (PRO SP 78/24/177). In the meantime he and de Chatte had again been in action, at St. Saens which 'was the first lodging that [Mr. Devereux] lay in when we came from Portugal' (PRO SP 78/24/153).

58. PRO SP 78/24/217.   59. PRO SP 78/24/210.

60. PRO SP 78/24/217, 219. On La Noue and Essex, see above, p. 33. Williams had written of the former, 'He is known to be one of the worthiest and famous warriors that Europe bred in his days ... the little experience I got was from him' (Discourse, pp. 57–8).

Brittany was not forgotten. These exertions were not in vain. By 25
June de Reau had presented his master's addresses.[61] They included
ample expressions of gratitude and explanation. Hitherto circumstances
had prevented Henry from following Elizabeth's excellent advice regarding the prime importance of the maritime regions. Now he had
sent La Noue with 1,400 harquebusiers and 400 horse into Brittany.
Before de Reau's mission, des Mesnils and others had assured the
Queen that if Parma were delayed Henry would use as she judged
best the additional forces he was seeking. Now he was resolved to do
so. To that end 'the taking of Louviers will prove very helpful. And
for his part, his Majesty is immediately setting about preparing what
he can by way of troops and other commodities, under another guise.'

This was well enough. The Queen's stand had clearly produced
some effect. But explanations and assurances did not come unac-
companied. Henry proceeded to his specific demands. By comparison
with his earlier requirements, these were much inflated. There had
been talk of 4,000 infantry. Henry now wanted 5,000 or 6,000, in
view of the likely stubbornness of the enemy. He wanted 200 or 300
horse, 1,000 sappers, 30 or 40 miners, 12 battery pieces of artillery[62]
with sufficient ammunition to fire 5,000 shot. He wanted 3 sizeable
ships and 3 'pataches ... to guard the Seine estuary during the siege',
as well as additional vessels to carry munitions upstream. He also
wanted licences to transport supplies out of England, and permission
to borrow 200,000 écus from the City of London, recoverable through
exemption of English merchants from dues payable upon their traffic at
Rouen after the town should be taken. Such demands were far in
excess of anything that he had requested before.

And yet there was little delay. On the same 25 June a preliminary
contract was signed between the French ambassadors and Elizabeth's
delegates.[63] There followed some bargaining. While the Queen had agreed
to send 4,000 soldiers,[64] Henry's additional requests were still subject to
negotiation. So was the smouldering question of guarantees. Beauvoir
and de Reau stressed that their principal was acting purely on the
Queen's advice, and that there must be provided 'sufficient means not

61. PRO SP 78/24/210, 244.

62. Henry mentioned thirty-pounders and may therefore be taken to have
meant demi-cannon. For further discussion of guns, see below, p. 164.

63. BM Cotton Titus B VI, fo. 34.

64. That is, either 3,400 infantry to supplement Williams's 600, or 3,150
infantry and 100 horse.

to set at risk their Majesties' honour and reputation'.[65] These considerations drew few concessions from the English side in the articles submitted for ratification. These specified that the entire cost of the expedition should be met by Henry. As security for it, for Norris's force and for the other scheduled advances made to Henry since September 1589, Elizabeth required

a written document authentically sealed under the Great Seal of France before the arrival of the said troops in Normandy, that her Majesty and her commissioners shall receive and shall collect all the profit of all kinds of tolls, taxes, customs and duties payable within and around the towns of Rouen and Havre du Grace by the names of *impositions et domaines forains, gabelles du sel, quatrième des vins,* or any other items or other impositions called new impositions[66] upon imported goods; all of which impositions (by whatever name or names they have formerly been or are now described) shall be freely and actually received by her Majesty through her commissioners, and openly transported from there in cash or in kind, as she should prefer; until by these means she shall have been fully paid and satisfied for all sums of money already expended and for all other charges, past and future.

Payment should commence as soon as either Rouen or Le Havre were taken, and should be subject to no alteration without the Queen's authorization. If any such revenues were in farm, she should at her own choice receive payment either from the farmers or direct from the merchants or their assigns. While Elizabeth would advance pay to her own troops for two months from their arrival, they must then either be paid directly by Henry or be withdrawn. Finally, these articles should be ratified by the *parlement* at Tours and by the *chambre des comptes.*[67]

The Queen was certainly driving a hard bargain. Her proposals about revenue administration in France seemed even to imply a chal-

65. BM Lansdowne 149, fo. 24.

66. According to Smyth, writing in August, the 'new imposition' was 'in part the occasion of the people's rebellion, for the king did take a sou in the franc of all cloth that came into this country and that was made in this country, and a sou upon a franc, which is worth two shillings sterling, upon all "canvys" and other linen cloth made in this country, which came to a great sum of money by the year. At the Estates at Blois all that was put down' (PRO SP 78/25/224). For definitions of the various dues mentioned, see glossary.

67. BM Lansdowne 149, fos. 24–24ᵛ. The last article had required that the whole be consented to by the Estates-General. Upon Beauvoir's objection that this was 'impossible' since the King could not assemble the Estates, this phrase was dropped (PRO SP 78/24/284).

lenge to French sovereignty. Yet Henry had raised his own demands
and could scarcely have expected a soft answer. Despite all bonds and
paper assurances, Elizabeth had seen very little return from her advances to him hitherto, and saw all too little prospect of improve-
ment in the future unless she could put her hand into his very purse.
Moreover, in the arrangement she proposed, which would mean that
her activities in France were formally endorsed by the institutions
of that realm, there were great potential advantages for England's
merchants. Finally, these terms did not constitute an ultimatum. They
were negotiable: if Henry found them unacceptable, he could demur.
At first his representatives did so. The Queen, they objected, was
appropriating everything. Surely Henry in his necessity could be left
'some commodity for his affairs' from the revenues of his ports. They
also objected, predictably enough, that payment of farmed revenues
direct to the Queen's agents would bring 'confusion to the King's
affairs and discontent to his subjects'.[68] Elizabeth deferred to the latter
point, and the relevant clause was modified.[69] She likewise agreed,
on the grounds that the former draft was obscure, that changes in the
revenues in question should require not her authorization but her
consent.[70] If these concessions were significant from the constitutional
standpoint, from the financial, political, and commercial standpoints
they did not seem substantial. In addition, the French pointed out that
to await ratification under the Great Seal before the departure of the
troops would give rise to inconvenient delay. This, too, was accepted.[71]
Having gained as much, the French negotiators did not press whatever
other reservations they may have entertained.

   On 9 July Beauvoir delivered his personal bond for ratification of
the agreed articles.[72] Five days earlier the Privy Council had issued

   68. Beauvoir was to give precision to this objection, by pointing out that 'the
chambres des comptes of France must take cognisance of all the taxes raised
in the kingdom, for which the receivers and officers must render account to the
said *chambres*' (loc. cit.).
   69. She agreed to receive the said revenues via the King's officers or receivers (Rymer, vol. xvi, p. 103).
   70. PRO SP 78/24/284.
   71. With the reservation that until the ratification was received the English
army should not move inland from its port of arrival in France (PRO SP
78/25/70).
   72. PRO SP 78/24/299. The contract for the Rouen customs was signed the
same day. As soon as he heard of it Otwell Smyth, who estimated the income
in question at £100,000 a year, requested for himself the place of Receiver on
the Queen's account (PRO SP 78/25/130).

its orders for levying the troops.[73] On the following day Henry, now back at Mantes, wrote to Beauvoir approving his conduct of the negotiations and agreeing in principle to the reimbursement clauses.[74] Within the week de Reau was taking post horses towards France.[75] While preparations hurried forward there was time, and some occasion, for second thoughts. There were rumours from France that despite his brief excursion into Normandy Henry's intentions were still aimed elsewhere. Elizabeth did allow herself a moment's hesitation. On the morning of 25 July messages were sent to the shires 'for the staying of the forces . . . till there should be a new warning given'.[76] Beauvoir's reaction was instantaneous. The rumours, he protested, were calumnious, put about by Henry's enemies. The English forces must depart as soon as possible, to execute the preliminaries to the main siege, so that all would be ready for the King's arrival with the forces he was himself raising.[77] There was news, too, from Dieppe, that Villars had been made governor of Rouen. If that town were taken Le Havre would fall as well.[78] On the same afternoon, the orders to hold back the English levies were countermanded.[79]

The theatre of England's main military operation for the current season had at last been decided, after months of calculation and of diplomacy. The Flanders plan had proved unworkable; soldiers from Germany had thereby lost their always dubious attraction. With remarkable coolness, Brittany had been weighed against Normandy and had come off second best. The Queen had opted for the latter; already she had mentioned to Norris the possibility of winding up his campaign.[80] Although it was clear that, contrary to her earlier wishes, her forces would be in Normandy before Henry's, this did not deter her from proceeding with all possible speed. Already she had unleashed Williams to accompany the King.[81] She was evidently satisfied that through this operation England could reap important strategic, finan-

73. *APC*, vol. xxi (1591), pp. 220–4.   74. PRO SP 78/24/309.
75. *APC*, vol. xxi (1591), p. 266.   76. ibid., pp. 289–90.
77. PRO SP 78/25/41.   78. PRO SP 78/25/32–6.
79. *APC*, vol. xxi (1591), pp. 292–3.
80. PRO SP 78/25/6. With friends of his own at Court, Norris had realized several weeks before that his operation did not rank first among his government's priorities (PRO SP 78/24/66; cf. Wernham, 'Mission of Thomas Wilkes', op. cit., p. 432).
81. PRO SP 78/24/287; 25/32, 49; cf. Unton, p. 90.

cial, and commercial benefits. Her closest adviser had encouraged her
by every means. Burghley later described himself as 'the principal
furtherer in this voyage'.[82] During Turenne's mission, and in the
months that followed, he had consistently favoured positive action
within the limits of the defensive strategy upon which he and Elizabeth
were always agreed. It was to Burghley that Beauvoir gave credit for
the countermanding orders of 25 July.[83] Palavicino was Burghley's
man. So, too, was Yorke, whose February journey had stimulated
appeals to England from Normandy and fresh demands from Henry.
Often in the analysis of Elizabethan policy it is difficult to distinguish
Burghley's views from those of his mistress. It is apparent enough that
during these months of planning and negotiation there were sharp
differences between them, over immediate priorities, over necessary
preconditions, over tactics. But there is no reason to doubt that despite
such disagreements the Queen had accepted and was acting upon an
important strategic principle. It was the principle of offensive action to
attain a limited object within a defensive war against a superior enemy.
An initiative was to be taken upon the channel littoral, in the form of a
pre-emptive strike to be executed not unilaterally but in co-ordination
with allied forces. This was relatively sophisticated thinking, assimilat-
ing the piecemeal proposals of others[84] into an over-all strategic conception.

Its positive nature rendered Elizabeth and her Lord Treasurer vulnerable to the arguments of those whose appetite for promoting aggressive war was greater and less discriminating than their own. Chief
among these was Essex, pressing his activist ideas either directly
through his personal approaches to the Queen or indirectly through the
foreign envoys with whom he personally dealt. But his was by no
means the only influence at work. There was Williams, content not
merely to rely on argument but even to create the actual circumstances
that would lend conviction to his case. If Williams was Essex's friend,
there were also Smyth and Incarvile with special interests of their own
in what Elizabeth would do. For Smyth, visions of a return to Rouen
were enhanced by hopes of financial gain, from dabbling in the pay
and supply of English soldiers and from a hand in collecting the Rouen
customs.[85] The English paymaster at Dieppe had already noted how
William's little force had been profitable to Smyth; moreover, 'he

82. Unton, p. 60.   83. PRO SP 78/25/47.
84. Such as Williams's arguments, above, pp. 40–2.
85. See below, p. 98, and above, note 72.

covets the applause of the multitude, and because he is gracious in England with the best, and here also, perhaps expecteth a smooth curry-comb.'[86] As for Incarvile, his career and his office were bound up with his King's. But the *intendant*'s was an immediate and personal interest in seeing Normandy speedily reduced to rule of law and subservience to the officers of central government—officers 'only in effigy'[87] as long as present circumstances endured. And of course, there were more—from Turenne to Yorke, from Buzenval in the Provinces to Edmund Palmer at St. Jean de Luz to Nau in Brittany—all disposed in so far as they were able, and from widely differing motives, to insinuate their several views into Elizabeth's deliberations.

It was upon such as these that she had to depend for information. Without information she could not act; and the information laid before her was very often biased, misleading, even false.[88] This might have only a marginal effect upon the broad principles of her strategy. But what it did affect, and very considerably, was the direction and the timing of her actions within the terms of those principles. It affected in one crucial respect her decision to act now in Normandy. She was genuinely persuaded that Henry intended a serious and prompt attempt upon Rouen. She had tested his intentions as far as she could. The terms she had laid down for aiding him were stringent ones. And through his representatives Henry had accepted them with comparatively slight modifications, and had himself confirmed that acceptance. While the divergence was unmistakable between the political circumstances of the two monarchs, and thereby between their strategic aims, Elizabeth had been given ample reason to believe that in the case of Rouen those aims converged. If Henry was anxious to recover Paris, as he clearly was, the Queen was assured that Rouen was relevant to that recovery. If Henry recognized, as in some degree he surely must, his need to control the great towns, the ports, the maritime regions and

86. PRO SP 84/42/9. Among 'the best' there is reason to reckon Burghley himself; he was later at pains to convince Smyth that 'I never used any speech of you to the Queen but to your furtherance and commendment' (PRO SP 78/25/271: September 1592, erroneously endorsed '1591').

87. The phrase is Incarvile's (BN AFF 3619, fo. 122).

88. As she plainly recognized—for example in an anxious note to Henry himself (PRO SP 78/24/195: undated, probably May 1591): 'We have formed our opinion [on the feasibility of recovering Rouen] solely on the basis of advertisements coming from there [and] we beg you, my cousin, to consider the matter carefully and to inquire into the truth of it by the best means that you can.' cf. above, p. 70.

points of access to his realm, Rouen was important on every count. And if Henry wished to confront Parma in France with concentrated forces, Elizabeth was advised that by investing Rouen he could create a situation that must draw the enemy on towards a confrontation at a predetermined location far from base.[89]

Impelled towards such an assessment by a barrage of information and advice, Elizabeth took her decision accordingly and acted on it. Yet she had miscalculated, and overestimated too. Her miscalculation was political, arising partly and ironically out of her great concern to ensure political safeguards and the maintenance of legal forms. Henry had offered, as he had offered before, concessions to her merchants as a means of repaying loans. But she had contrived that he become party to a formal contract by which successfully to besiege a key provincial capital would be to deliver its revenues into England's hands. Such an outcome to the campaign could seriously prejudice the King's efforts to establish his own political credibility—not least in Paris, so intimately connected with Rouen. Elizabeth's overestimate was military. By means of an expeditionary force she was attempting to launch a swift and co-ordinated offensive upon a limited objective of uncertain strength. It was doubtful whether an effective contribution to such an operation lay within England's military capability at this time.

89. cf. N. Machiavelli, *The Discourses* (New York, 1950), bk. ii, ch. xii.

CHAPTER FIVE

ESSEX'S ARMY

ELIZABETH had no army. Nor, after the opening years of the reign, would she have recruited one, if events had not forced war upon her. To imprest soldiers in large numbers and keep them in pay was more than she could ordinarily afford. To have to accommodate such men and their captains out of pay and disorderly within her realm was unwelcome to her.[1] If there should be urgent occasion to raise armed men, she did have the bands of the county militia, the kingdom's military reserve. Only an insensitive monarch would have made incessant demands upon that imperfect instrument. The citizenry might find it pleasant enough to parade in arms from time to time. Their enthusiasm must wane if the pleasure were repeated too often and diluted by discipline and expense. It waned the more rapidly when the drum mustered men[2] to prepare not for the defence of their own localities but for dangerous service overseas. Whether the Queen could require them to take part in such service was questionable. Whenever the need for it arose she took care, through her Privy Council, to stress that it was vital to the defence of the realm. Even so, her subjects objected and evaded whenever they could. And she had other reasons, rooted in the nature of English government and society, for pressing them as little as possible.

Despite appearances of centralization and bureaucratic management,

1. In Essex's army, Williams was to write, 'I see many men that all England could not govern.' The remark was heavily underlined by Burghley (PRO SP 78/25/288).
2. By such procedure as the following: 'On Monday in the morning the drum to give knowledge that all persons appointed to find armour shall have on Thursday in the morning following ready at Mousehold [Heath] all such arms as they are appointed to have to be carried by meet and sufficient men. And also that all other persons from 16 to 60 shall likewise appear there with such furniture as they be appointed or otherwise have ... Item, that like knowledge be given to the Strangers and Aliens to have their men and armour in readiness the same day also as they have appointed themselves. Item, that the Constables in every ward do bring their whole ward with them the said day to the place appointed' (Norfolk and Norwich R.O., Press C, case 13 (Military Documents), shelf a, vol. vi (1590–1), fo. 1).

the government of Elizabethan England depended to a high degree upon co-operation by local potentates. There were obvious dangers in establishing in the shires permanent commands of armed men under their control. Yet to raise men and supplies for unpopular service required local authority and local expertise—qualities to be found only in important local men. Means had to be found of channelling local manpower to the military service of the state without allowing opportunity for its independent exercise. The central government had resorted to judicious use of the office of lord lieutenant. Throughout the earlier years of Elizabeth's reign the office had every appearance of a temporary expedient, exercised only when national emergency made it necessary. With the outbreak of war and the crisis of the later 1580s such an appearance was difficult to sustain. There was now a recurrent need for levies and a constant need to ensure adequacy of military equipment and supplies. When it ordered the lords lieutenant to raise soldiers, the Privy Council was still careful to stress that each occasion was a special one, arising from extraordinary circumstances. It also stressed that through the Council the lords lieutenant were answerable to the Queen and for their deputies. But disaffected persons might all too easily find room for awkward questions. How different in practice were demands for soldiers from demands for revenue?[3] What was the constitutional basis for these demands, and how far could the Council back its alleged authority with penalties? Remote rule, exercised impersonally through bureaucratic means, would have found such appeals to principle difficult to counter. In that respect, Elizabeth's means were limited; in any case, that was not her way. Her government functioned through a cunning admixture of official with personal controls.

The leading officers of the Crown, close personal advisers of the Queen, provided her in many instances with the relevant link between central and local administration. Nine of the twenty shires involved in the levies of July 1591 had privy councillors as their lords lieutenant; and all of these had personal interests in the shires of their lieutenancy. Lord Treasurer Burghley's principal houses were Burghley House at the family seat of Stamford Baron in Lincolnshire, and Theobalds in eastern Hertfordshire close to the Essex border—for all three of which shires he was lord lieutenant. For some years Lord Admiral Howard had been consolidating his landed estate in Surrey, which he had represented in parliament and where he was now lord lieutenant. Although his family estate was centred on Rotherfield Greys in Oxfordshire, Sir

3. cf. below, pp. 90–1.

Francis Knollys held manors in Berkshire, often resided at Reading Abbey, with his sons represented that shire and its borough in successive parliaments, and was himself currently its lord lieutenant. Lord Chancellor Hatton was a native of Northamptonshire and its member in several parliaments. He was at this time its lord lieutenant—and of Middlesex as well, having ready access to the latter from that portion of Ely House in Holborn which he leased and where he resided. In Norfolk, where he was lord lieutenant, Lord Chamberlain Hunsdon could exercise the influence of a close kinsman of the Boleyns.[4] Furthermore, the family of Henry Hastings, third Earl of Huntingdon, President of the Queen's Council in the North and therefore resident in Yorkshire, had long-standing interests in Leicestershire and Rutland; and he was lord lieutenant of those three shires.

But apart from this small, select body of her immediate councillors, Elizabeth had cultivated personal relations with many others who were now her lords lieutenant and were involved in the July levies. In Gloucestershire was Giles Brydges, third Lord Chandos, whose family had long been influential in that shire from its seats of Coberley and Sudeley. The third baron was the shire's parliamentary member before he succeeded to the title; and Elizabeth visited him at Sudeley on three separate occasions.[5] In Buckinghamshire the lieutenancy was held by Arthur, Lord Grey of Wilton, whom Elizabeth twice visited at Whaddon Hall.[6] In Warwickshire was Sir Thomas Lucy, Shakespeare's Justice Shallow, twice the shire's member of parliament, owner of Charlecote and its large estate where in 1565 the Queen knighted him 'in his own house'.[7] Henry, Lord Norris, served in Oxfordshire and resided chiefly at Rycote, near Thame, which he had acquired by marriage, which the Queen had visited on her way to Woodstock as a prisoner before her accession, and where she visited Norris again in happier days.[8] Legend also told of her adventures in Mary's reign, how she had once hidden at Kirtling in Cambridgeshire. Roger, second

4. A nephew of Anne Boleyn, he cultivated the connection, coveted his late maternal grandfather's title of Earl of Wiltshire, and had bought Boleyn lands in Norfolk (*CPR* (1596–72), no. 1464)–though Hunsdon House itself was in Hertfordshire.

5. J. Nichols, *The Progresses and Public Processions of Queen Elizabeth*, vol. i (London, 1823), pp. 391, 552; vol. iii, p. 129.

6. ibid., vol. i, p. 254; vol. iii, p. 660; *VCH Buckinghamshire*, vol. iii (1925), pp. 435–6.

7. *VCH Warwickshire*, vol. v (1949), pp. 34–8.

8. Nichols, op. cit., vol. iii, p. 168.

Lord North, lord lieutenant of Cambridgeshire, had been born at Kirtling and entertained Elizabeth lavishly there in 1578.[9] For the administration of her kingdom in military as in other affairs Elizabeth could rely in great measure upon her personal friends. And the intimate body upon which she relied was itself knit together by family ties. Two more of her lords lieutenant, also concerned in these July levies, were the Earl of Kent in Bedfordshire and Lord St. John of Bletsoe in Huntingdonshire, both of whom shared common ancestry with the Lord Admiral; moreover, St. John's only daughter married the Lord Admiral's eldest son by his wife Catherine, Lord Hunsdon's daughter.[10]

Since she must raise soldiers, Elizabeth put her trust in such proven men as these—men whom she had regularly entrusted with foreign affairs throughout her reign. Apart from her immediate councillors, Lord Norris had served her as ambassador in France, Lord North had been a negotiator in such matters as the renewal of the Treaty of Blois, Lord Grey had fought for her in Ireland, had advised her on measures to resist invasion in 1588,[11] had been a commissioner, with others of this company, for the trial of Mary Stuart. And yet there was always the danger that a governing élite, grown too familiar with power, might become overweening, faction-ridden and injurious to the state. Elizabeth had keen memories of another trusted friend: Leicester, with his gift for polarizing opinion and provoking enmities. Now, with reluctance, she was giving command of the army she was raising to Leicester's successor at Court, the Earl of Essex. Leicester had been no sluggard in building up his own clientele; and Essex was already imitating his example. In the English body politic, relations of the kind the Queen exploited so well might be exploited by others to confound her, if she gave them sufficient cause and opportunity.

At least she might ensure that when the lords lieutenant who enjoyed her patronage raised companies of armed men in their shires, they should not exercise patronage of their own through nominating their own men to captaincies. Once raised, those companies should be

9. ibid., vol. ii, pp. 219–21.

10. G.E.C., *The Complete Peerage*, vol. v (eds. V. Gibbs and H. A. Doubleday, London, 1926), p. 9; vol. vii (eds H. A. Doubleday and Lord Howard de Walden, London, 1929), pp. 170–2; vol ix (eds. H. A. Doubleday and Lord Howard de Walden, London, 1936), pp. 786–7; vol. xi (ed. G. H. White, London, 1949), p. 335.

11. Consulting with him and with others upon that occasion was Sir Roger Williams (*CSPD* (1580–1625, Addenda), p. 248).

delivered to 'such captain as shall be by us sent unto you'.[12] Whatever such arrangements, of amateur recruitment and unfamiliar command, might cost in terms of military efficiency, they were undoubtedly politic in terms of domestic peace. Even so, not all lords lieutenant were prepared to forgo the opportunity of patronage without a murmur. Three months previously, Lords Kent, Grey, and North had each preferred his own nominee to the captaincy of a company for Brittany. The Council's gently worded reprimand had emphasized the need for compliance with 'her Majesty's express pleasure and special choice'.[13] Yet among those who gained command of the companies raised in July were Thomas Acton, captain of the men from Warwickshire, where Lord Lieutenant Lucy's wife was an Acton of Worcestershire; John Shelton, captain of the men of Norfolk and member of one of that shire's leading families;[14] and Thomas Baskerville, captain of the Gloucestershire men, who had married into a prominent family of that shire.

But Baskerville had other claims. He was an experienced and dedicated soldier, had served with distinction in the Netherlands—and, above all, he was an associate of Essex.[15] And having at last persuaded the Queen to grant him his own first major command, Essex meant to make the most of it. Ever since Leicester himself had designated him as his successor to the Mastership of the Queen's Horse, it was in this

12. *APC*, vol. xxi (1591), pp. 220–4. Except where otherwise stated, in what follows all quotations from Privy Council orders to the lords lieutenant are taken from these orders of 4 July 1591.

13. ibid., pp. 28–9.

14. W. Rye (ed.), *The Visitation of Norfolk, 1563, 1589, 1613* (London, 1891), p. 247.

15. The families of Devereux and Baskerville had been neighbours in Herefordshire since at least the thirteenth century. Base-son of Essex's father's receiver-general and trustee Thomas Baskerville was referred to by Essex himself as 'my cousin'. His wife was the daughter of Sir Thomas Throckmorton of Tortworth, Gloucestershire. He had been a 'servant-in-livery' to Leicester and had then worn the blue coat and badge of Essex's own personal followers during the latter's minority. According to Williams, Parma himself said of Baskerville after his gallantry at Sluys in 1587, 'There serves no Prince in Europe a braver man.' A military enthusiast who wrote a knowledgeable treatise on 'the office of the sergeant major' and christened his only son Hannibal, he was in Normandy with Willoughby in 1589, and in 1590 had quarrelled with Norris ferociously enough to warrant Star Chamber intervention. (LD, vol. iv, fo. 307; box ii, no. 40; box xii, roll 17; vol. v, fo. 24. BM Lansdowne 60, fo. 203. Bagot, p. 334. *Gentleman's Magazine*, vol. xcv, pt. ii (1825), p. 315. *Discourse*, p. 58. BM Harleian 5260; ibid. 4762, fo. 53.)

direction that his career had been tending.[16] The 'poorest Earl in England' had been prodigal in equipping himself and his men for service with Leicester in 1585;[17] had furnished at his own expense a larger troop than any other nobleman's for the army at Tilbury in 1588;[18] had sought, vainly, in the Portugal voyage of 1589 to repair by 'mine own adventure' the debts he estimated then at over £20,000.[19] By means of personal action, influence, and patronage he hoped to confirm his claim to a social and political prominence which, in terms of wealth, he could ill afford. When Yorke left on his February mission, Essex's was the name mentioned in Court circles for command of an army for France. Later he was said to have begged for it, on his knees for two hours before the Queen.[20] In July she was still undecided. It was rumoured that Lord Burgh might be sent; it was known that the reluctant Lord Willoughby was in London; it was said that while the French king had specifically asked for Essex, Beauvoir would prefer him to stay at home.[21] But Essex carried his point. The Queen smiled upon him, and his friends, worried by the risks he ran, nevertheless hoped that 'the well managing of this action will further advance him'. It certainly gave him an opportunity to advance some of them.[22]

When Williams was assembling his force in the Spring, he had had to defer unwillingly in the matter of captains to the ruling of the Council.[23] Essex was not so deferential. Once recruitment was under way, he drew up his list of prospective captains. From more than sixty hopefuls now swarming to the Court and the chance of a commission,[24] he listed nineteen names and six more 'gentlemen that desire charge'. Against thirteen of these names and one of the gentlemen's he entered the magic figure '150', to show his recommendation of them for commands of that strength. The list was vetted by Burghley, who added to it the names of three more gentlemen (including Lord North's brother), reviewed the higher command, and carried arrangements one stage further by indicating that every six companies should constitute a regi-

16. Bagot, p. 337.
17. Devereux, p. 178; LD, vol. v, fo. 70.
18. HMC *Fifteenth Report, Appendix V (Foljambe MSS.)*, p. 40.
19. HMC *Salis.*, vol. iii, pp. 458–9.
20. Devereux, pp. 214–15.
21. Lodge, vol. ii, p. 441; HMC *Ancaster*, p. 313; PRO SP 78/24/244.
22. *CSPD* (1591–4), p. 65; HMC *De L'Isle*, vol. ii, p. 120.
23. BM Harleian 6995, fo. 39. He suspected the influence of the lords lieutenant in these appointments, and distrusted their judgement.
24. PRO SP 12/239/33.

ment and that the army would need a provost marshal assisted by corporals.[25] Yet of Essex's thirteen initial recommendations, all save two commanded companies in the army that eventually arrived at Dieppe.[26] Among those captains there were now two more from his original list. Indeed, only two had not been included in it; and both of these had companies from Lincolnshire, one of Burghley's shires of lieutenancy. But these constituted no dilution of Essex's dominance of his army. One was Edward Cromwell, descendant of Henry VIII's Lord Chancellor; he would later follow his present general to the Azores in 1597, to Ireland in 1599, and to the City of London in 1601 as one of his fellow-conspirators. The other was 'little Ned Morgan', who had been to Portugal with the Earl and was one of Sir Roger Williams's particular friends.[27]

In terms of captains, it was very much Essex's army. Hostile observers mocked it, seeing 'so gallant a troop go out of England with so many young and untrained commanders'.[28] Their sarcasm was not altogether deserved. Four of these captains had held similar commands under Willoughby in Normandy;[29] another, Docwra, had seen extensive service under Essex's father in Ireland;[30] at least five had commanded men in the Netherlands.[31] A greater problem than finding adequate captains, for the young general and for the Queen, was finding adequate men for their companies. For three years, since the militia had been mobilized all over the country amid general excitement to resist the Armada, the Privy Council had been struggling to maintain this military reserve in reasonable repair. The winter and spring months of 1589 had passed with 'nothing done for the renewing of the former orders concerning the having of the forces of the country in readiness as were most necessary'. In the summer, although

25. PRO SP 12/239/34.
26. PRO SP 78/25/172; cf. *APC*, vol. xxi (1591), p. 233. These totals of captains do not include members of the higher command, who also held captaincies of companies.
27. HMC *Salis.*, vol. xiii, p. 414. Two other captains, Barton and Poore, were Williams's specific nominees (PRO SP 78/24/236).
28. A. Collins, *Letters and Memorials of State*, vol. i (London, 1746), p. 327.
29. Barton, Hambridge, Mostyn, and Shelton (PRO SP 12/226/31).
30. And won renown there later—the 'founder of the modern city of Derry' (*DNB*).
31. Barton, Cromwell, Goring, Shelton, and Swan; so, too, had several of the volunteers, and all the members of the higher command (*CSPF*, vol. xxii (July–December 1588), p. 410; vol. xxiii (January–July 1589), p. 176; PRO SP 78/25/172).

it was 'very chargeable' to the shires to maintain 'the multitude of the people in training', general musters were ordered once again so that men and equipment might be inspected.[32] In January 1590 it was found necessary to warn all captains and soldiers to 'be always in a readiness to be viewed or otherwise employed as occasion might serve'; necessary also to prod the lords lieutenant with the hint that 'her Majesty might be better satisfied if she should send some special person thither ... to take view of the said forces, that might make true report unto her in what state and sort they were'.[33] But by September the Council was still dissatisfied. General musters were ordered once more, the results to be recorded in 'perfect books as particularly as should be meet, that her Majesty might see the same before the end of the said October, which she very earnestly required for her better satisfaction and for her comfort'.[34] Since then there had been further drains upon the country's manpower. It remained to be seen how the shires would respond to the new demands.

Exactly one half of the English shires were involved. All those of the south coast, and all the south-western shires, were omitted. If it could be avoided the government would not weaken the regions most immediately exposed to invasion. Consistently with its over-all strategy, it was transferring men from further north in a bid to consolidate the line of defence across the Channel. All the Welsh shires, the north-western shires of Lancashire, Westmorland and Cumberland, and Northumberland and Durham in the north, were also omitted. These were the shires facing Ireland and Scotland, liable to commitments and emergencies other than those stemming directly from the continent—and furthest, too, from London-based governmental control. Except for Gloucestershire, all the shires of the Welsh March were omitted as well, as was Staffordshire. Here Essex's personal interest was greatest. Plenty of volunteers might be expected from that region; already Essex had written to his agents to invite 'my friends in all places' to 'send either tall men well horsed, or good horses and geldings'. But apart from such friendly invitations, the Earl's tenants, notably at Chartley, were sternly reminded of how they were obliged to supply 'this service'. Their obligation was expressed in their 'new leases', though if it was 'not expressed in the new it is contained in the general words, to do all former reservations, etc.'. If they 'will not do their duty ... my Lord will use the

32. *APC*, vol. xvii (1588–9), pp. 220–3.
33. *APC*, vol. xviii (1589–90), pp. 294–6.
34. *APC*, vol. xix (1590), pp. 414–16.

extremity of the forfeiture, and of their covenants'.[35] Had the Council sent to this region its own formal demands, the resulting army would have grown more and more to resemble Essex's private force.

So on this occasion the Council's letters were sent to the remaining twenty shires.[36] The orders were precise. They stressed that 'above all things there must be special care had in the choice of men that they be of able bodies and years meet for this employment, and that their armour and furniture be good and serviceable'. In every hundred men[37] there should be 'forty pikes armed with corselets, six halberdiers like-wise armed with corselets, twenty musketeers, and the rest of the ninety to be calivers with their due furniture as hath been accustomed'.[38] The influence of such views as Williams's was evident in this prescription. There were mixed opinions regarding pikemen at this time. Moreover, some commentators held the corselet to be an encumbrance to them: 'their footmen pikers they do allow for very well armed when they wear their burgonets, their collars, their cuirasses, and their backs, without either pauldrons, vambraces, gauntlets, or tasses'.[39] But Williams, an admirer of Spanish practices, believed strongly in pikemen, and that as many of them as possible, as well as halberdiers, ought to wear cor-selets which were proof to caliver shot at twelve score paces. The pike, he held, 'is the chiefest weapon to defend, and to enter a breach';[40] and Essex's army was intended to penetrate the walls of Rouen. Unlike some other commentators, he also judged musketeers 'the best small shot that ever were invented', worth twice their number of calivers.[41]

35. Devereux, pp. 215–16, cf. Bagot, p. 329; Staffordshire R.O. D (W) 1721/3/290, [fo. 60].

36. Though general musters were also ordered elsewhere.

37. That is, on paper; ten 'dead pays' were allowed in every hundred: see below, p. 96.

38. cf. the Council's view in 1589, that 'the ideal company of 100 would contain 60 fire-arms, 30 pikes and 10 halberds or bills' (C. G. Cruickshank, *Elizabeth's Army* (2nd edn., Oxford, 1966), p. 114).

39. Sir John Smythe, *Certain Discourses Military*, ed. J. R. Hale (New York, 1964), p. 42; cf. below, pp. 95–6.

40. *Discourse*, pp. 44–5. Henry himself later wanted 1,000 more pikes for the siege (PRO SP 78/26/178); so did Essex (PRO SP 78/25/121). cf. the Com-mission of Array of 1573, which laid down 'that there be in every one hundred footmen at the least forty harquebusiers and twenty archers' (J. Harland (ed.), *The Lancashire Lieutenancy, under the Tudors and Stuarts*, part i (Chetham Society, vol. xlix (1859)), p. xxix; the editor describes pikemen as 'the most inferior arm of the force').

41. *Discourse*, pp. 41–3.

But for the recipients of the Council's letters, the stipulated propor-
tions were an embarrassment. While diligent lords lieutenant might
lay down regulations for storing and maintaining armour and weapons,
this did not guarantee that adequate quantities of every type would be
available when needed.[42] From the citizens' viewpoint, there was much
to be said for the caliver. At Great Yarmouth, liability to supply a
caliver was rated at only half the burden of either a corselet or a musket;
and while a musket had to be furnished with four pounds of powder,
a caliver needed only two.[43] On the present occasion at prosperous
Norwich, which could muster 300 'trained soldiers', two-thirds of them
were equipped with shot rather than with hand-weapons, and there
were more than twice as many calivers as muskets.[44] From among these,
six pikemen, a halberdier, three musketeers, and five calivers were
eventually sent off for Normandy.[45] The hundreds of Edwinstree and
Odsey in Hertfordshire did rather better, scraping together twenty
corselets and seven muskets for their contingent. But this was not
accomplished from existing stocks. Deficiencies had to be supplied,
which meant raising money.[46] In Norwich it meant a 'general charge,
and taxed upon all the inhabitants of this city and liberties thereof,
except aliens being no denizens, every man to pay fourpence of every
pound after the rate that he is rated and set at in the last subsidy book,
and that would be taxed towards the same, under the value of £3'.[47]

And local expense did not end with the provision of armour and
weapons. Every soldier required a coat costing 14s. 10d. at this time,
the government making a contribution at 'the ancient rate of four

42. Thus in March 1590 Burghley had issued his deputy lieutenants in Hertfordshire with careful instructions for storing and cleaning equipment, without
commenting on how much of every type ought to be kept (Harland, op. cit.,
pp. xxxvii–xliv; HMC Salis., vol. iv, pp. 15–18). His deputies had replied that
the yeomen and farmers of that shire had very little armour or 'warlike
furniture' of any kind (PRO SP 12/231/91). On the present occasion the
Council thought it 'very likely' that local supplies of armour and weapons were
deficient.

43. Norfolk and Norwich R.O., Great Yarmouth Assembly Book (1579–98),
fo. 187. On relative costs of calivers and corselets, see L. Boynton, *The
Elizabethan Militia*, p. 22.

44. Norfolk and Norwich R.O., Press C, case 13 (Military Documents, shelf
a, vol. vi (1590–1), fos. 127–32.

45. Norfolk and Norwich R.O., Norwich Assembly Book (1585–1613), fo. 92.

46. Hertfordshire R.O., vol. 6990, fo. 79.

47. Norfolk and Norwich R.O., Norwich Assembly Book (1585–1613), fo.
92ᵛ.

shillings'.[48] When he arrived to take over his company, each captain would already have been issued with 'a sum of imprest for himself and his officers'. But every soldier was entitled to conduct money. This 'was accustomed to be one halfpenny for a mile', but owing to 'the diversity of their habitations' it was ordered on this occasion that the soldiers be allowed 'their ordinary pay by the day of eight pence sterling from the time they shall be assembled and delivered to the captain ... and for so many days as the said soldiers shall be in marching by reasonable journeys to the place of their embarking, which we hope will not be under twelve miles in a day'. Coat and conduct money might be obtained from local Exchequer officers; failing this, it should be raised 'by some other means' and afterwards recovered in London. In any case, money had to be found locally in the first instance. On the present occasion, owing apparently to an administrative error, there was delay in obtaining the refunds due. Essex's army had already arrived at Dieppe when the treasurer at war, Sir Thomas Sherley, wrote from London to Burghley:

Those men that are now gone with the Earl of Essex enter not into pay until their landing over the other side ... Since your lordship's going from hence the collectors of divers shires have sent unto me their certificates for coat and conduct money ... It shall not do well in me to defer payment unto them for want of warrant. And hard it were for them to stay here at charges until I might send to the Court. Therefore it may please your lordship to send me some kind of general warrant to make payment of such sums of money as shall be demanded for the purpose aforesaid under the hand of the lieutenant, deputy lieutenant or collector of any shire. For those certificates are brought unto me some time under the hand of one and some time of the other.[49]

If matters of recovering money so readily reduced the machinery of state to creaking uncertainty, local prospects for recovering weapons and armour were far less auspicious. The Council ordered that the quantities delivered to the captains be recorded in indentures, to be cancelled when the equipment was returned at the end of the service. It was no better than a pious hope; and sceptical citizens were to have their doubts amply confirmed. Some six months after the army's arrival in France, when a great proportion of the original levies had returned home, the Council noted that hardly any had brought their arms with

48. *APC*, vol. xxi (1591), pp. 222, 308–9.
49. PRO SP 78/25/167.

them. Otwell Smyth was asked to ascertain whether the report was true, that many arms had been left in houses in Dieppe.[50] Smyth made a search. He found only six pikes, and believed that the captains had taken the arms in question away with them to England since no one would buy them at Dieppe.[51] Only a naïve citizen would not have anticipated as much. In such prevailing circumstances, only the most enthusiastic local official would have welcomed the Council's urgent and precise letters. And only the most optimistic Councillor or commander would have felt confident that when the army eventually assembled in France its members would have armour and weapons, coats and money, in accordance with what had been prescribed.

Before it assembled there at all, transport for the sea passages must be found. Predictably, the lion's share of shipping was expected from London; and it was not the south coast ports nearest Normandy but those of the east coast—Hull, Boston, Lynn, Yarmouth, and Harwich —that were called upon for the rest.[52] To carry troops by sea from the ports nearest their homes would ultimately be quicker and cheaper than to march them a greater distance overland at greater risk of desertion *en route*. Moreover, for the east coast ports, as for London, trade to France was important at this time; and in a period of commercial difficulty the prospect of improving facilities in Normandy was an incentive[53] that might produce a willing response. In this same month the borough assembly of Yarmouth was levying a rate of eightpence in the pound towards fitting out an escort vessel for the protection of the

50. *APC*, vol. xxii (1591–2), pp. 292–3; PRO SP 78/27/215.

51. PRO SP 78/27/270. Since Smyth was himself officially authorized to sell much-needed arms and munitions to the French, his report is in no way surprising (PRO SP 78/27/331).

52. London was to furnish eight vessels, Hull five, Harwich two, and the remainder one apiece (PRO SP 12/239/49).

53. For the east coast's and London's trade with France, see N. J. Williams, 'Maritime Trade of the East Anglian Ports', pp. 128–37; L. R. Miller, 'New Evidence on the shipping and imports of London, 1601–2', *Quarterly Journal of Economics*, vol. xli (1927), pp. 740–60; cf. above, p. 6. For the trade of Hull, with its long-standing Normandy connection and where French trade was still important despite the remarkable later sixteenth-century growth in the port's Baltic trade, see *VCH York, East Riding, vol. i: The City of Kingston upon Hull* (London, 1969), pp. 64, 132–8; R. Davis, 'The Trade and Shipping of Hull, 1500–1700', *East Yorkshire Local History Series*, no. 17 (1964), p. 24. There were currently trade difficulties at Bordeaux (for example, PRO SP 78/24/304–8), where English trade was important to both nations and a factor conditioning attitudes towards Henry in that region.

town's merchant shipping against enemy privateers.[54] The same assembly unanimously approved the Council's request for shipping for the Normandy forces, and took immediate steps to arrange it.[55] Even so, there were problems. In London the Lord Admiral had to threaten the merchants whose ships were involved that if they did not promptly unload their vessels to make room for their human cargoes he would order his own officers to do it for them.[56] From Hull the mayor wrote that there were not enough ships available in the port. The Council sent him authority 'for taking up of so many convenient vessels in the other harbours and creeks, with mariners and sailors, as well northward as on Grimsby side towards Lincolnshire'.[57] Yet in the event it was five Hull ships that were found.[58]

Whatever its advantages over land-marches, sea-transport was expensive enough. The government made several advance calculations, based upon estimates of cost per man ranging from 4s. to 6s. 8d.[59] But that covered only the victualling of soldiers by sea. There was also a charge of 2s. per ton for the vessels. There were the wages and victuals of the mariners, generously assessed by the Hull authorities at 12d. each per day for eighty-seven of them.[60] There was expenditure upon casks for beer and biscuits, upon straw, trenchers, lanterns, and candles, upon 'boat-hire to set men aboard', upon ship-alterations to enable men or horses to occupy space normally filled by inanimate cargo.[61] While the soldiers' victualling costs were recoverable out of their wages,[62] the port authorities were entitled to put in claims for

54. Norfolk and Norwich R.O., Great Yarmouth Assembly Book (1579–98), fos. 212–14.
55. ibid., fo. 210ᵛ.
56. APC, vol. xxi (1591), p. 294; cf. HMC Salis., vol xiii, pp. 450–1.
57. APC, vol. xxi (1591), pp. 266–8.
58. Kingston upon Hull Corporation Archives, M94.
59. APC, vol. xxi (1591), p. 229; PRO SP 12/239/49.
60. Hull claimed for transporting eight hundred soldiers (Kingston upon Hull Corporation Archives, M95). cf. Harwich's claim for transporting three hundred in the Great Mary Anne of Ipswich: 'for victuals of 26 men for a month and three days at 6d. the man per day, £20. 3s.; for the wages of the master, 44s. 3d., his mate 22s. 4d., the pilot 22s. 4d., boatswain 19s. 6d., carpenter 19s. 6d., cook 19s. 6d., two quartermasters 39s., the gunners 16s. 9d., and 17 other men at 10s. by the month £9. 11s. 3d.: in all, £59. 16s. 5d.' (PRO E 351/244).
61. Kingston upon Hull Corporation Archives, M95; PRO E 351/244. The Great Mary Anne of Ipswich needed partitions made from deal boards.
62. In accordance with indentures agreed between the port authorities, the ships' captains and the captains of the companies (Kingston upon Hull

their entire outlay. Again, while the duration of the voyage to Normandy was estimated at ten days, ships and sailors were hired by the
month, with payment reducible if they returned home sooner—or at
least if they declared that they had. The Hull shipmasters made sure
of claiming for exactly twenty-eight days. The cost of transporting the
contingent from that port alone amounted to £425, of which the soldiers' victuals accounted for precisely one half. Even so, the government paid up without question.[63]

It was no wonder that Elizabeth so often preferred to pay other
nations to fight on her behalf. Apart from all local charges, she incurred costs in the region of £7,000 merely by assembling an English
army at Dieppe.[64] And in terms of equipment, this was not the army
that had been ordered. At his first general review on 17 August, muster-
master Coningsby found present only 808 pikemen and 139 halberdiers
in the 20 companies of infantry. There were, however, 592 musketeers
and 853 other 'shot' of various kinds. There were also 312 soldiers
doubtfully described as 'armed men'. The army's infantry strength was
thus 2,704. Instead of the 50 per cent proportion of pikemen and
halberdiers that had been required, it could show no more than 35
per cent of these.[65] The infantry companies contained 161 officers.[66]
A further 109 foot-soldiers and six officers were brought from Brielle
by Captain Denton.[67] There were 61 volunteers, gentlemen and pro-

---

Corporation Archives, L97). On the general reliability of the last of these in
money matters, see below, pp. 95–7.

63. Despite Essex's report that the Hull ships had had to be revictualled
at Dover (Kingston upon Hull Corporation Archives, M94, L98; Devereux,
p. 222).

64. That is, for coat and conduct money, transport and one month's pay for
officers and men.

65. Essex had gathered as much before he left England and wrote urgently
from Dover for more pikes, wishing that 'all our halberds were turned into
them' (PRO SP 78/25/121).

66. That is, eight to each company in addition to its listed strength of 150
men (cf. Cruickshank's suggestion of some fifteen 'in the normal company',
op. cit., p. 57). Their composition, as between lieutenants, ensign-bearers,
sergeants, corporals, drummers, surgeons, cannoneers, and preachers, is impossible to estimate from the muster-lists, though the last three groups are rarely
mentioned there. What is certain is that while, as the weeks went by, the
army's strength rapidly diminished in terms of fit soldiers, each company
maintained its full complement of eight officers (cf. PRO SP 78/26/19, 233,
298).

67. 23 musketeers, 44 shot and 42 'armed men'. According to Essex this

fessionals, in Essex's own company, and 58 more such supernumeraries attached to his brother Walter Devereux's band of 154 horse.[68] Thus the maximum effective strength of Essex's army was 3,253 men. To these could be added Williams's little force, now much depleted;[69] and the army's strength seemed greater on paper through the inclusion of the full allowance of 325 'dead pays'.[70] Taking all these into account, Elizabeth could claim that she had kept to the letter of her promise for 4,000 men. But the Gloucestershire contingent had arrived without coats,[71] deserters were already trickling back to England, there were already problems over pay, and tales were already spreading of abuses and of discontent in the ranks—most notably, among the members of the Cambridgeshire company, under Captain Swan.

According to the muster-master, Swan's company was actually four above strength and contained an unusually large number of pikes. But within a week eleven of its members were back in England, 'many with passports made by the captain's clerks of the band, and without one captain's hand to them'. Each told how the money he had had with him, which ranged from several pounds to a few shillings, had been appropriated by the officers on various pretexts, several naming either 'Riggs the sergeant' or even Swan himself. They also told how 'Captain

---

company, of the vaunted veterans, was 'the weakest and the worst in the army' (PRO SP 78/25/170).

68. Nine officers, 126 lances and 19 carabins. The apparent preference for hand-weapons as distinct from firearms is again noteworthy. But though the lance descended directly from the heavily armoured mounted man-at-arms, in Essex's army his equipment was probably that of a light horseman bearing sword, dagger, and pistol as well as the lance itself. In this period of European warfare considerations of expense were not insignificant; the more elaborate and the heavier a cavalryman's armour, the more horses he would need (cf. *Discourse*, p. 32). Although in his requests to Elizabeth by de Reau Henry had asked simply for 'horsemen', his own liking throughout this phase of his career was for light horse, favoured for their mobility. The carabin was a light horseman bearing a heavy pistol of a type that was evidently already displacing the earlier dag and dragon; he also bore sword and staff. Both lance and carabin wore for protection a cuirass 'with a good Spanish morion lined with cheeks and laces to tie under his chin, and doublet sleeves to be striped along downwards with some small chains or plate or a pair of sleeves of mail' (Greater London R.O. (Middlesex Records), Acc. 249/148).

69. On the day of Coningsby's muster, English casualties were reported as 17 killed and 47 seriously wounded in siege-action before Noyon, where Williams and his men were assisting Henry (PRO SP 78/25/181).

70. PRO SP 78/25/172. On 'dead pays', see below, p. 96.

71. PRO SP 78/25/117.

Swan, before his going on ship-board, sold away all the pauldrons, vambraces and tasses that belonged to the corselets which he had delivered unto him in Cambridgeshire to a merchant in London'.[72] Here was an early warning that Essex's army would be no freer than its predecessors of dishonest dealing on the part of captains—and especially in respect of pay. Despite the system of dead pays, whereby every captain of a company was entitled to the pay of ten men in every hundred,[73] few were content with that allowance. It was the captain who received all the money due weekly to his company by way of lendings and issued it to his men. Only serving soldiers were entitled to pay; and so the captain had every financial incentive for making his company appear to contain more of them than in fact it did, ignoring casualties and deserters. In theory, his certificate of his company's strength was subject to correction by the muster-master and his agents, viewing the men themselves. In fact, even if these inspectors were honest their task was impossible. There were too many opportunities and too many motives for fraud.

During service in the field, no muster-master could hope to assemble the entire army and count its numbers. He might try to count each company in turn. Before Rouen 'we have no place that is out of the view and danger of the artillery of the enemy but one only, the which is [so] small and strait that it would hardly contain above one company at a time. In the which I was constrained to take the musters. And so ... it is not to be wondered if the captains took their advantage to deceive me.'[74] By mutual agreement between captains, the same men might appear time and again to be counted. While the army might be viewed 'upon the next march, for then by counting of their number by ranks and comparing the same with the former muster it will manifestly appear where any fraud hath been',[75] companies might still be augmented for the occasion by including 'passevolant boys and stragglers'.[76] Officials had harsh words for the corruption of captains, and were loud in their advocacy of the benefits to be derived from payment by the poll rather than by companies.[77] But this was rather an

72. PRO SP 12/239/141; cf. above, p. 89, for the view that the items allegedly sold were superfluous.

73. Which meant that every company listed as 150 strong in fact never consisted of more than 135 men.

74. PRO SP 78/27/142, cf. 308.

75. PRO SP 78/26/22.

76. PRO SP 78/26/31.

77. PRO SP 78/26/121, 282; 27/30, 180.

empty excuse for their failure to operate the existing system than a realistic alternative to it. Payment by the poll would have needed no less careful a count of soldiers' heads than was in any case confessed to be impossible. The government was ready enough to believe that the fault lay always with the captains. Indeed, it went to the length of inviting soldiers to give evidence and enter pleas against their company-commanders.[78] Obviously, ignorance of the precise strength of every unit could have serious consequences for the army's efficiency as a fighting machine. But in spite of abuses, the existing system was not without redeeming features. The responsibility of captains for their companies might be exploited by the general as an aid in enforcing discipline.[79] Moreover, a captain who could lay his hands on a greater supply of money than that to which his men were strictly entitled might use at least some of it to obtain for them food that would otherwise have been beyond their means.

Essex himself was fully aware of the importance of ensuring suffici-ent supplies of victuals. Before leaving the Court he had sought Burghley's aid: 'How much we may be distressed for want of such provision, and how many impediments may happen through variety of wind or otherwise, if the transportation be too much restrained, your lordship's wisdom may well consider.'[80] But in Normandy the army was dependent on local supplies. While its general estimated its food requirements at 4,000 loaves and twenty cattle a day,[81] in addition to drink for men and fodder for horses, it was a diet of bread and some fish that proved forthcoming[82]—and little enough of that. Reckless

78. PRO SP 78/27/215.

79. See below, p. 125.

80. PRO SP 12/239/106. One of Henry's requests by de Reau had been that victuals be allowed to 'pass freely' from England (BM Lansdowne 149, fo. 50v).

81. BN AFF 3645, fo. 15. For his Brittany force Norris had thought, with more hope than realism, of shipping from England supplies of biscuit and beer with 'beef for four days in the week' and 'butter, cheese or fish for the other three days in the week' (PRO SP 12/238/15). cf. what the Queen allegedly 'doth allow her mariners, 4 quarts of beer a day ... also she doth allow every man 2lbs. of beef a day, 1lb. of bread, half a pound of butter to a meal and half a fish a meal to four men' (PRO SP 78/27/281). In many respects Elizabethan seamen fared a good deal better than soldiers (cf. relative wages, above, pp. 91, 93 and note 60)—a consideration that may well in some measure account for the relative degrees of success and failure achieved by either service in this period.

82. PRO SP 78/25/316; 26/22, 29.

soldiers tried to supplement and vary such a diet and 'died not of
the plague but of the flux and agues through eating fruit and drinking
milk and cider'.[83] Food prices rocketed upwards. By the end of the
siege they stood at '12*d*. a halfpenny loaf, a pot of beer 18*d*., for a pot
of wine 2*s*., for a pound of cheese 12*d*.';[84] and fermented liquor was
essential at the siege, 'for that there is no water: the wells are all spoilt
by the League'.[85] Even for officers the situation was bad enough.[86] For
men subsisting on 8*d*. a day it was desperate; and for a time they
would have received nothing at all had not Essex himself found it for
them.[87] At one point Burghley, following an earlier suggestion, recommended that the troops receive a proportion of what was due to them
in the form of food and clothing.[88] But even this placed them at the
mercy of competing merchants. Otwell Smyth, self-advertisingly the
soldiers' friend, complained of importers of shoes and stockings, 'I
do buy them here better cheap than I can do in England by them that
brings them over to sell here without licence.'[89]

Indeed, for all its concern over matters of trade, the government
seemed not much disposed to rely upon the services of merchants in
matters either of supply or of pay. Excited by the prospect of the army's
coming, Smyth had volunteered his own services to raise money for it
locally, and argued that the favourable exchange rate would be advan-
tageous to all concerned.[90] No doubt the knowledge spurred him on
that for some time his fellow-merchants had been involved in paying

83. PRO SP 78/26/74.   84. PRO SP 78/27/353, cf. 369.
85. HMC *Salis.*, vol. iv, p. 167. cf. the besiegers' immediate tactic of diverting
streams flowing into Rouen, below, p. 150.
86. Among the higher command, the marshal received 40*s*. per day, the
sergeant-major and the trenchmaster 20*s*. apiece, the provost marshal, muster
master and head corporal 6*s*. 8*d*. each. Each colonel received 10*s*. per day in
addition to his allowance of 4*s*. as captain of 100 men. In each foot company
the lieutenant had 2*s*. per day, the ensign 18*d*. A captain of 100 lances had 8*s*.
per day, his lieutenant 4*s*., his ensign 2*s*., trumpet, clerk and surgeon 20*d*.
apiece, and every lance 18*d*.—a reflection both of the greater expenses incurred
and of the superior status enjoyed by cavalry over infantry, notwithstanding
tactical considerations. Skilled posts enjoyed special rates, such as the master
gunner's at 2*s*. per day (PRO E 351/244; cf. the rates of pay estimated by the
Council, *APC*, vol. xxi (1591), pp. 228–9).
87. See below, p. 123.
88. PRO SP 78/26/22, 296. Earlier suggestions from the French for payment in kind had been spurned, in favour of that more easily reckonable but
less nutritious commodity, cash.
89. PRO SP 78/25/250.
90. PRO SP 78/24/103, 151. Incarvile later recommended Smyth as one

the Netherlands forces, issuing abroad at the best rates they could get
the amounts credited to them in London. But Smyth was disappointed.
Treasurer-at-war Sherley shipped to Dieppe the cash that would be
needed, where his paymaster and his assistant took charge of it and
placed it under a guard of ten of the general's company, each receiving
an extra allowance of 4d. a day to steel him against temptation.[91]
During this campaign 'portage of treasure', at a charge of £10 for
every thousand, cost the government over £600.[92] It did not save the
army from great suffering. Indeed, the injection of so much currency
into the local economy at a time of dearth no doubt contributed
significantly to the inflation of food prices. Meanwhile the soldiers
were driven to scour the countryside for food, in a manner that exposed
them to enemy attacks and fostered disorder at the expense of discipline.[93]

Discipline was ultimately Essex's responsibility as general. To
assist him in controlling the four regiments into which his army was
divided, he had Williams as marshal, Arthur Bourchier as provost
marshal,[94] and Baskerville as sergeant-major with his four field-
corporals. The Queen had instructed her general to 'cause such ordinances as were devised by the late Earl of Leicester in the Low
Countries for the discipline of the Army there to be considered and to
cause an extract to be made out of the same, or out of the like, that
have been published by the Duke of Parma, selecting so many articles
as shall be thought meet for the time and place where you shall serve
and for the companies whom you shall govern'.[95] Essex acted accord-

---

well qualified to make such arrangements for paying the Brittany force (PRO
SP 78/26/150). In fact, the latter's advice was wildly misleading; on the
scarcity of money in Normandy in general and Rouen in particular, cf. above,
p. 7, and below pp. 135, 143.

91. PRO SP 12/239/16 (i).

92. PRO E 351/244. It covered transport of £57,000 to Normandy and a
further sum to the Netherlands. According to Norris in Brittany, value for
money was virtually unobtainable whatever method was adopted: 'for if you
should send over English money the loss will be great to the soldiers; and if
you should trust to bills of exchange here we shall be disappointed' (PRO SP
78/25/322).

93. PRO SP 78/26/29.

94. A kinsman of Essex's, Bourchier had recently been in danger of imprisonment for debt. Essex had interceded for him, and now did so again 'in respect
of his present employment in her Majesty's service, and the rather for my sake
under whom he is employed' (HMC Salis., vol. xiii, p. 459).

95. PRO SP 78/25/70.

ingly, but his articles of discipline showed significant differences from those published by his stepfather.[96] Both designated numerous capital offences, though not invariably the same ones.[97] Both penalized immoral and disorderly conduct, such as blasphemy, drunkenness, unlawful games, womanizing, rape, and affrays. Both would punish with death any mutiny or any threat to a superior officer, and with lesser penalties any failure to obey orders or to co-operate with the provost marshal in his disciplinary endeavours. Treasonable conduct of any kind, dealings with the enemy, desertion to or in face of the enemy, absence from sentry-post, betrayal of password, and raising false alarms, were serious offences in both codes. Both laid down stern regulations against defiling the camp—a matter of great consequence, owing to the decimating effects of infection and disease. But while Leicester had issued orders for attendance at divine service, Essex's articles included none to that purpose, although the Queen had directed him 'to serve God daily both yourself for example and to direct all our people under you to do the same at all times and places usual'.[98] Yet, unlike Leicester he threatened with death all persons convicted of atheism, heresy, or spoliation of churches; and with imprisonment, all who entered churches during mass.

Perhaps this amounted to no more than a difference in emphasis and expression, or derived from anticipation of problems likely to arise during service in a Catholic country. But other differences sprang from other considerations. Leicester had published several articles against stealing food, exceeding rations, and independent foraging by his men. Essex published none, apart from ordering, like Leicester, that recognized victuallers should not be robbed. He did prohibit unauthorized pillaging in any captured town; but while Leicester had made several regulations to the effect that all prisoners must be declared and none ransomed without the general's licence, such articles did not figure in Essex's code. He did order, unlike Leicester, that his men should exercise daily with their weapons.[99] Moreover, he was much more severe than Leicester upon offences stemming from

96. For Essex's disciplinary articles, BM Harleian 7018, fos. 77–8; Leicester's are printed in Cruickshank, op. cit., pp. 296–303. What follows is based on a close analyisis of the two codes; cf. Cruickshank, op. cit., p. 163.

97. Thus, Essex was harsher than Leicester on fraud at muster, Leicester than Essex on quarrelling with friendly foreigners.

98. PRO SP 78/25/70.

99. Article 36. Leicester had ordered his men to learn the signals of command by drum, fife and trumpet (article 43).

cowardice, penalizing any dereliction of duty by sentry or by scout, any failure to try to recover a captured officer or ensign, any discarding of weapons during retreat. Yet by his ruling, again unlike Leicester's, failure to obey the order to retreat was an offence, and punishable by death. Leicester declared against breaking ranks in the field; Essex, against breaking ranks on the march. While Leicester required from all his men an oath that they would obey his code of discipline, Essex did not ask them so to swear.[100] But the principal difference between their respective codes was one less of severity than of circumstance. Leicester's was a long-term role in the Netherlands, as much political as military; and he was instructed to avoid military engagements wherever possible. Essex was in Normandy on a brief, offensive mission. He must march his army through hostile territory, and looked forward to some engagements and to a siege; hence his concern that his scouts be alert[101] and that his men be ready for action. Even so, the rigours they would face were in a manner anticipated in what their general omitted to say on the question of foraging.

This was Essex's army. As its general, he seemed presented with a great opportunity. He was in France by his own wish and by the King's express invitation.[102] He had his own men as field officers, his own nominees as captains; even the muster-master, Coningsby, had been a follower of Leicester's.[103] Although Elizabeth had saddled him with two overseers, he had every reason to expect kind dealing from them. One, Henry Killigrew, had been a loyal protégé of Leicester's throughout his career;[104] the other, Sir Thomas Leighton, was Essex's uncle and had recently been a beneficiary of his patronage.[105] Even the newly appointed English ambassador to France, Sir Henry Unton, son

100. He may later have regretted his not having included Leicester's injunction against unauthorized fires in the camp; see below, p. 116.

101. For Essex's use of scouts, see below, p. 115.

102. BM Lansdowne 149, fo. 50v.

103. LD, vol. v, fo. 25. A Herefordshire gentleman and a prominent figure in the Welsh Marches, Coningsby had also been a friend of Sidney's, accompanying him in Vienna and in Venice in 1573 (Buxton, op. cit., pp. 63, 66).

104. See Amos C. Miller, *Sir Henry Killigrew* (Leicester, 1963). Both Killigrew and Leighton had served in Normandy in 1562.

105. In an Admiralty lawsuit (BM Add. 12506, fo. 245). Leighton had married one of the daughters of Sir Francis Knollys, Essex's grandfather; other members of the Leighton family, of Wattlesborough, Shropshire, married into the Devereux family itself (LD, vol. iv, fo. 325; G. Grazebrook and J. P. Rylands (eds.), *The Visitation of Shropshire taken in the year 1623*, pt. ii (London, 1889), p. 324).

of another of Elizabeth's friends, was to prove no less of a friend to Essex.[106] All these would give favourable accounts of the young general's ability as a commander of men: 'I cannot see,' wrote Leighton, 'that any other shall be able to bring them unto any order.'[107] In performing that task, Essex could rely not only on such formal machinery as the court martial,[108] but also on the authority of his noble rank. With his contemporaries he believed that 'where good men lead [soldiers] they will all follow, but when all shall lie upon their hands that were peasants two months ago her Majesty must not look for honour nor service from her army.'[109] In designating the service intended the Earl had had his say, and seemed to have been given every chance of winning honour.

Yet none knew better than Essex the hazards that awaited him. He was aware of the imperfections of the military instrument he commanded. There were serious logistic problems, evident from the very outset. His men's equipment was not what he had hoped for. They lacked skill, they 'beggar themselves and fall to disorder' he noted, during the first week in France.[110] His government had raised the army with extraordinary speed. This had not been accomplished without taxing the administration and modest resources of the kingdom. It was Essex's interference in politics, as critics could fairly claim, that had occasioned such an effort, with all that it implied; and it was he, with his friends, who were now in charge. All this heightened his responsibility and increased his vulnerability to censure without improving the means at his disposal. Nor could he employ those means without

106. He was the son of Sir Edward Unton of Wadley, near Farringdon, in Berkshire, and Anne, widow of John Dudley, Earl of Warwick. Sir Edward gave Elizabeth an extravagant gift on her visit to Wadley in 1574. Henry Unton may have been on the Portugal voyage, and certainly met Turenne at York House during the latter's mission. While he currently regarded Lord Chancellor Hatton as his patron, Unton was loyal to Essex throughout the present campaign, during which time Hatton died. Later, an opinionated member of parliament, Unton was to act as Essex's agent in the management of property in Berkshire and Oxfordshire, and enjoyed cordial—indeed, familiar—relations with the Earl (Nichols, op. cit, vol. i, pp. 379, 391, and vol. iii, p. 85; Camden, *History*, pp. 430–1; Rymer, vol. xvi, p. 134; Unton, *passim;* Neale, *Parliaments,* vol. ii, p. 306; LD, vol. i, fo. 131; W. Murdin, *A Collection of State Papers relating to affairs in the reign of Queen Elizabeth* (London, 1759), p. 655).
107. PRO SP 78/26/27.
108. For example, HMC *Salis.*, vol. iv, p. 150.
109. PRO SP 78/25/365.
110. PRO SP 78/25/170.

first consulting with King Henry. If nothing were done, the blame would be his. Whatever he might attempt would be watched from England, by the Queen and by his rivals. Her prestige and her personal interest were engaged, to a degree as great as her general's. The strategy governing the campaign was ultimately hers; and she was unlikely to leave tactics to his discretion. It remained to be seen how far he would be able to conduct himself and his army to her satisfaction.

CHAPTER SIX

MARKING TIME

BETWEEN Essex's arrival at Dieppe in August 1591 and the commencement of the siege of Rouen, three months elapsed. During that time Elizabeth plumbed depths of frustration and annoyance. Savagely, she censured her general in the field for betraying her trust, for irresponsibility and mismanagement, for frittering away time and resources on futile exercises. According to her, Essex 'idly spent one month and odd days' upon 'a voluntary action of your own', namely a 'private' and 'unadvised journey' to visit the King at Noyon, 'leaving the army without any head or marshal, and none else but a sergeant major'. Attempting to rejoin his main force, he would have been cut off 'if they had not adventured to have come to you'. He then made 'a bravado' before Rouen, where 'as a reward of your unadvisedness you lost your only brother'. As general, he was thus guilty on the one hand of 'wasting of her people without any service'; on the other, of having 'hazarded' them on 'desperate attempts'. His personal behaviour was an 'absurdity'. Before the town of Gournay he demeaned himself 'by trailing of a pike to approach the place like a common soldier'. Elsewhere he went 'with a few horses a-hawking, being forced to come away from the field by pursuit of some number bigger than yourself who proved in the end to be of the King's party'.[1] No words were too harsh either for what he had done or for what he had failed to do.

In historical terms, Elizabeth's strictures have had damaging effects upon Essex's military reputation. Her heated and contemptuous allegations are mirrored in the judgements of many subsequent commentators. Under Essex, 'the best equipped and most prompt of all her expeditions accomplished least: at one point he went caracoling with most of his officers, only a troop of horse, through enemy country to meet Henry IV'. Following this 'jaunt' or 'escapade' to Noyon, he indulged in 'a somewhat unnecessary bravado under the walls of Rouen'. He joined in the siege of Gournay because he was 'determined to see some action before he left'. During these months he 'won the admira-

1. Unton, pp. 73–5; PRO SP 78/26/3.

tion and affection of his followers by his constant activity, his bravery and his amiable manner, but it cannot be said that he had shown any special gifts of generalship'. What has been said is that 'Essex, for all his popularity with his soldiers, was rash, impetuous, and often unable to follow orders; and it has yet to be shown that he really understood all the aspects of military science set forth by contemporary writers on the subject'. Indeed, far from seeking such understanding he 'had no sense of the responsibilities of command, but played at war as the most glorious of field sports'.[2] After Rouen, the Earl was involved in a number of key campaigns by land and sea. He was a central figure in Elizabethan affairs during the remaining years of the Spanish War. His quality as a general is thus a significant matter; and so it is important to establish whether or not the opinion which the Queen expressed of him in the course of his first major command was a well-founded one.

Moreover, Elizabeth was hardly less critical of her ally, the French king. Far from hastening to join in the intended operation in Normandy, 'when our army was ready landed, the King was so far off in the furthest part of Picardy as neither our general nor any of the King's ministers where our army was could tell where very well he was'. Careless of his agreement with her, he wasted precious time in besieging Noyon. Then he disappeared into Champagne, 'which made her feel abused and contemptuously treated', and dissipated the aid she had sent him.[3] With his subsequent political achievements to sustain it, Henry's historical reputation, unlike Essex's, has escaped the worst consequences of Elizabeth's censure. While some romantic minds have ascribed his siege of Noyon, like that of Chartres, to his desire to gratify his mistress, Gabrielle d'Estrées,[4] more sober judgements have recognized his 'resourcefulness and political acumen', his 'grasp of political realities' and 'sense of opportunity'.[5] Even so, the specific

2. A. L. Rowse, *The Expansion of Elizabethan England* (London, 1955), pp. 396–7; R. Lacey, *Robert, Earl of Essex* (New York, 1971), p. 85; R. B. Wernham, 'Queen Elizabeth and the Siege of Rouen, 1591', *Transactions of the Royal Historical Society*, Ser. iv, vol. xv (1932), pp. 169–70; E. P. Cheyney, *History of England: from the defeat of the Armada to the death of Elizabeth*, vol. i (New York, 1948), p. 273; H. K. Webb, *Elizabethan Military Science* (London, 1965), p. 63; J. E. Neale, *Queen Elizabeth I* (Harmondsworth, 1960), p. 327.

3. Unton, pp. 89–90; *MM*, vol. v, p. 155; PRO SP 78/26/142.

4. P. de Vaissière, *Henri IV* (Paris, 1925), pp. 401–4; R. Ritter, *Charmante Gabrielle* (Paris, 1947), pp. 81, 102.

5. J. H. Elliott, *Europe Divided, 1559–1598* (London, 1968), p. 342; H. G.

allegation remains, that for the delay in commencing the siege of Rouen, Henry's 'exaggerated nervousness concerning Parma must be blamed'. He stayed 'deep in Champagne, besieging small towns and waiting for the Germans', and so infuriated Elizabeth by his 'duplicity'. As in other campaigns, his movements reveal an 'astonishing inconsequence', characteristic of this 'most inconsequent' of generals.[6]

Now if general assessments of the conduct of war during the later sixteenth century are sound, astonishment is misplaced and inconsequence only to be expected. While Parma's stature remains by and large unshaken, he was, it seems, a giant among pygmies, employing tried instruments in a manner that compelled respect. He enjoyed the advantage of commanding the Spanish army, could call upon Spanish military engineers, and had at his disposal Spain's military organization. Among his contemporaries, only Maurice of Nassau proved capable of some fresh thinking, such as reducing the size of infantry units to good tactical effect, increasing the proportion within them of pikes to muskets, and moving the units with extraordinary speed in related offensives. For the rest, strategic thinking 'withered away' as 'theorists, rationalizing their own impotence, extolled the superior science of the war of manoeuvre, and condemned battle as the last resort of the inept or unfortunate commander'.[7] Problems of maintaining discipline, finance, and supply over an extended term seemed insurmountable; and so armies were left with a random role. They engaged in small sieges, coalescing 'round the first obstacles they encountered'. Perhaps they helped to speed up negotiations; but they were 'not expected to settle everything by a glorious victory, or a precise programme of raids on vital spots'.[8] If Henry eschewed such ambitions, he was merely a man of his time. Yet the Rouen campaign furnishes some grounds for believing that, like Essex's his conduct has been misjudged.

On 29 July Essex paraded his cavalry before the Queen at Burgh-

---

Koenigsberger, 'Western Europe and the power of Spain', *The New Cambridge Modern History*, vol. iii, ed. R. B. Wernham (Cambridge, 1968), p. 303.

6. Wernham, 'Siege of Rouen', op. cit., p. 171; Stone, *An Elizabethan*, p. 175; C. Oman, *A History of the Art of War in the Sixteenth Century* (London, 1937), pp. 469, 505.

7. M. Roberts, *The Military Revolution, 1560–1660* (Belfast, 1956), pp. 6–7.

8. J. R. Hale, 'Armies, Navies and the Art of War', *The New Cambridge Modern History*, vol. iii, pp. 200–1.

ley's house in Westminister.[9] Three days later she addressed his
captains at Greenwich, and signed his commission and his instructions.[10] Another five days elapsed before the Earl left for Dover.[11] On
the day of his departure Elizabeth wrote apprehensively to Henry,
making several warning points. While she recommended her general
for his fearlessness, she felt that he was 'in greater need of the bridle
than the spur'. She warned of the likelihood of friction between French
and English troops. She also warned of the need for Henry, when he
joined the latter, to 'stop up every route' by which Parma might come.[12]
There had been some talk that she would accompany Essex to his port
of departure.[13] This mark of honour did not materialize. He went off
to Dover, she to Nonsuch in Surrey.[14] At Dover Essex waited in
frustration, prevented by bad weather and contrary winds from reaching his transports riding at the Downs.[15] At last he boarded them, but
the crossing to Dieppe took three days, owing now to lack of wind.
De Chatte welcomed him and his party warmly enough, but there
was no one from the King to greet them. The busy Incarvile was
there, however, and promptly introduced himself with assurances that
all would be well.[16]

A week went by. The English army steadily consumed the food
available locally.[17] In the interests of good order, Essex moved the
camp some four miles inland, to Arques.[18] There was ample time for
him to peruse his instructions and to compare notes with Unton, who
was equipped with a copy of the articles agreed between the English
and French negotiators six weeks previously. Neither document left
room for doubt that Elizabeth intended to advance pay to her army
for two months only, and that she was eager to lay hands on the profits
of the Rouen customs. Yet neither document was immediately very
helpful. The articles spoke of sending troops into Normandy without
specifying what should be undertaken once they were there.[19] The
instructions advised Essex to urge Henry 'at your first access to the
French king' that he ought to feel 'most thankful' towards Elizabeth,
and that the English army should be 'joined with his great forces': so

9. BM Cotton Titus B VI, fo. 34.
10. PRO SP 78/26/3; LD, Box v, no. 74; PRO SP 78/25/70.
11. PRO SP 78/25/101.   12. PRO SP 78/25/94.
13. *CSPD* (1591–4), p. 74.   14. BM Cotton Titus B VI, fo. 34.
15. PRO SP 78/25/121.   16. Unton, pp. 21–3; PRO SP 78/25/163.
17. Unton, pp. 27–8.   18. PRO SP 78/25/170.
19. Unton, p. 8. cf. Henry's requests by de Reau, which implied, without
explicitly stating, that Rouen would be besieged (above, pp. 74–5).

that 'you may be speedily informed of the purpose intended by him in what sort you and your forces shall be employed'. The Earl should then consult with his own advisers 'and shall in honourable and discreet manner take exceptions to any such part of the service propounded to you as shall appear inconvenient or over-desperate'.[20] Quite clearly, until Henry became accessible and made his purpose known, no such exceptions could be taken, and indeed nothing could be done.

Perhaps messengers had gone astray. Perhaps Henry had been caught unprepared by so quick an arrival on the part of the English. The army waited, restlessly; rumours spread of enemy raids in the offing.[21] At last, on 23 August Sir Roger Williams rode in from Noyon. That town had fallen to Henry four days before.[22] He had immediately sent Williams 'with a letter of credit to believe him as himself, and his message is to cause me to leave the forces under my charge in surety and to come to him to Compiègne whither he will come of purpose to communicate unto me his whole purpose for this year's war'. The route was reported 'very safe' for a body of fifty horse; Essex proposed to take six times that number with him. The ratification which the Queen expected 'is done 15 days ago'; and Essex would be back 'within 6 or 7 days'. Henry had plans for meeting his German army on the French frontier, and for Biron to bring the main French army first to Gournay and so to Rouen. Parma, however, was expected to enter France within sixteen days.[23] However eager for action Essex may have become, however tedious the waiting at Dieppe and inconvenient the fact that Unton, ill with yellow jaundice, could not go,[24] there was good reason for as prompt a conference as possible with the King.

Leaving the rest of the army in Baskerville's experienced charge, Essex ordered his troop to travel as light as possible, 'that none should carry baggage, but merely a shirt'.[25] In August weather, to travel in arms, even on horseback, would be tiring enough; and the proximity

20. PRO SP 78/25/70.
21. PRO SP 78/25/170, 163; Coningsby, p. 13.
22. HMC *Salis.*, vol. iv, p. 133.
23. PRO SP 78/25/200, 202, 204. There is little doubt that the King had in fact already signed the ratification (cf. below, p. 111); the estimate of Essex's travelling time—wildly over-optimistic, in the event—was presumably based on Williams's report; cf. below, note 27.
24. Unton, p. 31.
25. Except where otherwise stated, this account of the journey to Noyon is based on Coningsby, pp. 13–18.

of enemy forces dictated that a state of constant vigilance and combat-readiness must be maintained. So, despite the need for haste, baggage was carried in carts and included some provisions. The troop was ordered by Williams, as marshal and as one familiar with the country. First went a body of French hargulutiers, as outriders; next, Essex himself accompanied by his gentlemen-volunteers; then a squadron of lances headed by Williams, then the baggage-train, with the remainder of the lances under Walter Devereux in the rear. So compact a body had few stragglers although a hot pace was maintained. They tried to keep to open country, so that movement might be brisk and the danger of ambush reduced—a danger intensified whenever the company passed near woodland. In the Normandy countryside, 'planted with more forests, bushes and brush than any other part of our kingdom',[26] such considerations dictated a circuitous route and reliance upon guides pre-arranged by Henry. Even so, Essex and his men covered the distance from Dieppe to Compiègne via Gisors and Clermont in four travelling days with a day's rest on the way, which meant maintaining an average speed more than twice the best that would normally have been expected of a sixteenth-century army on the march.[27]

At Compiègne the Earl held a reception for local dignitaries and their ladies. The King had sent the Marquis d'O and the Marquis de Pisany[28] to greet him, and these accompanied the English party the remaining distance to Attichy. Henry made the gesture of coming himself to meet Essex there, from Pierrefonds where he had just laid siege to the castle.[29] Elizabeth's general managed to arrive with a

26. According to the surveyor Louis de Saint-Yon, quoted in M. Devèze, *La Vie de la forêt française au XVIe siècle*, vol. i (Paris, 1961), p. 238.

27. cf. Cruickshank, op. cit., 61; and above, p. 91. For comparative estimates of speeds achieved by couriers and by private travellers, see C. Samaran (ed.), *L'Histoire et ses méthodes* (Paris, 1961), pp. 113–14.

28. On the colourful Jean de Vivonne, Marquis de Pisany, frequently employed as an ambassador by both Henry III and Henry IV, notably at Rome, see G. de Bremond d'Ars, *Jean de Vivonne* (Paris, 1884); for his presence at Compiègne, HMC *Salis.*, vol. iv, p. 134. François, Marquis d'O, had been appointed to the office of *surintendant des finances* by Henry III, and had aligned himself promptly with his successor in August 1589. In terms of status and of office, these were both highly suitable representatives for the King to send to Essex at this time—especially in view of the question of paying the English army.

29. Bagot, p. 338; PRO SP 78/25/230. Attichy lay to the east of Compiègne, well off the route to Noyon. It is at least possible that the initiative for inspecting the latter, where Biron lay, sprang from Essex rather than from Henry;

splendour befitting the Queen's representative, preceded by six mounted pages in gold-embroidered orange velvet to match his own jewel-encrusted apparel.[30] Henry received him 'with all the contentment that might be'.[31] There was a banquet, and 'a preaching' in the King's chamber—a timely advertisement of the allies' religious bond. Noyon was inspected and found to have been severely distressed by the siege, 'the countenance and face of all things showing desolation'. In this dismal setting, with Biron present and sick through gout, the conference between Earl and monarch at last took place. How had Henry been spending his time? Why had he besieged Noyon? What did he propose to do now? How was Essex to employ his own army?

Throughout 1591 Henry had patrolled the environs of Paris, to north, west and south, never straying very far from the city except for his brief excursion towards Dieppe. By taking Noyon he strengthened his partial blockade of the capital, never entirely relaxed since the siege of the previous year. Again, Noyon, lying in effect between Compiègne and St. Quentin, was on the direct route from Paris to Brussels, and 'being much better provided with horse than foot, infested all the roads round about it, and greatly incommoded those places that adhered to him in that country'.[32] These places would be immensely important when, as everyone expected, Parma re-entered France. The King had established control over numerous strongpoints in this region and had more in view. This was hardly inconsequential behaviour. It was wholly consistent with his strategic priorities: to gain control over his kingdom by dominating its capital, and to prepare to resist the greatest single challenge to that control, in the shape of Parma. Moreover, Noyon offered at least temporary alleviation of another of his major difficulties. Its terms of surrender had included an indemnity to the King of 40,000 écus, which would go some way towards enabling him to pay his soldiers and notably his Swiss mercenaries.

If money were the only consideration, Rouen offered a great deal more. But the situation was far too fluid and far too complex to allow Henry simply to vacate his position in the Île de France and fling himself into an effort deep in Normandy on Elizabeth's terms. For all

there is reason for believing the Marshal to have been more sympathetic than the King towards the Rouen enterprise. cf. above, p. 66, note 22.

30. Palma Cayet, vol. i, pp. 464ᵛ–465.
31. PRO SP 78/25/230.
32. Davila, p. 227.

his efforts to control the Parisian approaches, Mayenne still held court at Ham, unwilling to do battle and yet within thirteen miles of St. Quentin. The King's own loose confederation of supporters was restive. Already that summer he had had to issue three proclamations, one giving fresh concessions to Protestants, another reaffirming his concern for Gallican Catholicism, a third protesting against recent bulls published against him by the new pope. But opinion was in a state of flux on the League's side no less than on the King's. Against the background of earlier exchanges between moderates of both parties,[33] it was known that Pierre Jeannin of the Dijon *parlement*, a close friend of Mayenne's and yet a committed advocate of firm monarchy in France,[34] had been taking soundings in Spain. What he had gathered there was not known; how it might affect developments was unpredictable. Problems within the League, and especially the question of its leadership, were further complicated at this very time by the escape of the young Duke of Guise from captivity in the castle of Tours. Rarely can the balance of political opinion within France have seemed more delicately poised. Meanwhile, Parma's movements and intentions were tantalizingly uncertain. Between mid-August and mid-September Henry advised his own supporters that the Spanish governor was delayed by events in the Netherlands, that he was 'coming soon', that he could not come 'for three months', that he would arrive within a fortnight.[35]

Beset by uncertainties, Henry was pressed from all sides for decisions. There was Essex, with his Queen's instructions. There was Turenne with his Germans, expecting at Metz 'to receive his Majesty's commandments as to what we are to do'.[36] There was Nevers, whom Henry had been promising for some time to come into Champagne and who had been threatening to quit his command if the promise were not kept.[37] Each represented support of a kind that Henry could not afford to lose. The agreement with Elizabeth seemed to allow room for manoeuvre. He had signed the document she required and had sent off de Reau with copies of it, to Mantes for sealing by the

33. See above, p. 18.
34. On Jeannin, one of the authors of the *Articles et mémoires* of May 1591 condemning republican elements in the League, see H. Drouot, *Mayenne et la Bourgogne*, vol. ii (Paris, 1937), pp. 210–13. The *Articles* are printed in *CM*, vol. ii, pp. 90–103.
35. *LM*, vol. iii, pp. 463–86.
36. BN AFF 3618, fo. 103.
37. *LM*, vol. iii, p. 451.

Chancellor, to Tours for ratification by the *parlement*, and so to England.[38] On 22 August, before Essex left Arques, the King sent letters after his envoy.[39] Parma's coming was reported imminent. In that case, Henry must amass his forces and tackle his adversary without delay, for otherwise Parma would divide and conquer them piecemeal. In accordance with what he regarded as the spirit of his agreement with the Queen,[40] Henry asked that the Earl be authorized to join him with his army. He also spoke of Parma's advancing into Normandy and of his own intention, given time, of concentrating forces about Rouen. Evidently, Henry was thinking in terms of a decisive battle and envisaging that in certain circumstances this might take place upon the north-western littoral.

Meanwhile, there were Nevers and Turenne. In the case of the former something might be made of the fact that the powerful Duke had a claim upon revenues payable at Rouen, amounting annually to 1,700 *livres tournois* and denied him as long as the town remained under enemy control.[41] But Turenne and his Germans raised further, urgent problems which also involved Nevers. Four years previously another German army raised for France with English backing had rendezvoused on the French frontier with French troops under William de La Marck, Duke of Bouillon. The result had been disastrous, owing partly to shortage of money and partly to failure to establish a unified command. Within the year Bouillon had died, survived by his sister Charlotte, heiress to the great inheritance of Sedan and lacking a husband. The possibility had then been aired of her marrying Christian of Anhalt,[42] now sharing command with Turenne. But there were several other noble aspirants to her hand, their gallantry enhanced by the attraction of those strategically important hereditary lands upon France's north-eastern frontier. The leaders of the house of Lorraine were keenly interested in who should emerge as their neighbour. Nevers proposed his son, Rethelois, whose lands lay adjacent to the La Marck inheritance. Montpensier had in mind his own, the Prince of Dombes, Henry's cousin, currently struggling in Brittany. Yet all

38. Unton, pp. 46–7, the English ambassador declaring at Dieppe on 3 September that he had himself seen the relevant copies.

39. PRO SP 78/25/192.   40. If not its letter: see above, pp. 107–8.

41. It was Incarvile, once more, who explained the matter to Nevers in these terms and stressed the need for besieging Rouen (BN AFF 3619, fos. 106, 122, 129).

42. Patry, p. 136.

of these were Catholic by faith. Bouillon's will had stipulated a
Protestant match for his sister; and the question was still unsettled. A
qualified suitor was now at hand, in the shape of Turenne himself,
whose power and ambitions had hitherto lain elsewhere,[43] who would
require some reward for his services, and who now commanded the
means of getting it for himself. The situation was one that Henry could
not ignore. It involved the competing dynastic interests of prominent
adherents to his own cause, and that of his enemies. It bore upon the
religious issue, upon the abiding problem of the kingdom's north-
eastern frontier, upon the fate of his painfully raised army. And he
himself was heavily indebted to the house of La Marck.[44]

So if Henry was to move at all out of the île de France, there
were excellent reasons for an excursion eastwards, to mollify Nevers, to
satisfy Turenne, to bring the Germans on. Uncemented by the King,
the situation in north-eastern France would in all likelihood disinte-
grate, and Parma, Mayenne, and the rest would be left to reassemble it
among themselves. Eager to go, he had waited for Essex. At the Noyon
conference the Earl was 'much troubled', speaking his mind 'plainly',[45]
insisting on immediate action and yet unwilling to march his army
inland without his Queen's authority. A plan of campaign emerged.
Henry would go to deal with the situation in Champagne. He would
leave some of the Germans there, send some into Brittany for Dombes,
and bring most of them with him towards Rouen. If Parma arrived in
the meantime, he would have to be attended to. But to content Elizabeth, 'and to shew he hath no intent but the siege of Rouen', he was
sending Biron and the army from Noyon into Normandy. The English
were to prepare the ground for the siege, and the King would join them
as soon as possible. This plan was accepted by Essex for reasons 'which,
though I dare neither censure nor allow, yet I assure your lordships
[of the Privy Council] I cannot impugn'.[46] Certainly it was more in
harmony with the Queen's wishes than was the sequence of movements
which Henry indicated in his letter by de Reau.

But Elizabeth was too far out of temper to weigh the merits of any
such reasons. Already, while Essex was *en route* for Compiègne, she
had written from Sussex to Henry, expressing amazement and dismay

43. See above, p. 32.   44. PRO SP 78/26/11, 74.
45. Devereux, p. 226; PRO SP 78/25/230.
46. Devereux, p. 226. cf. Turenne's report to Burghley that while Normandy
was relatively secure, Champagne was 'greatly infected by the League' (PRO
SP 78/26/347–9).

at the news from France.[47] As the passing weeks brought fresh reports and explanations, her anger mounted with her feeling that she had been hoodwinked. Neither the French king nor his ambassadors, the English general nor his advisers, enjoyed any indulgence on her part, nor any verbal mercy. De Reau was received insultingly, and told that unless Henry brought all his forces at once to Rouen she would withdraw her army forthwith.[48] Beauvoir was so discomfited that for weeks afterwards he 'never came near the Court'.[49] Essex, his 'reasons' notwithstanding, was denounced for a fool, in terms which, when they reached him, 'put his honour in such an extreme agony and passion that he sounded often and did so swell that, casting himself upon his bed, all his buttons of his doublet broke away as that they had been cut with a knife'.[50] Surely his passion was understandable; surely he had interpreted his instructions and dealt with Henry as carefully and effectively as could have been contrived. But the Queen's passion was no less understandable. What was taking place was not her conception of the Rouen campaign. For her own excellent reasons, not least logistical ones, she had planned a swift operation; and she was given merely words. She had insisted upon constitutional safeguards, and upon Henry's presence to license that of her forces; and he was not there. The initiative seemed lost. Despite all calculations, she lay once more at the mercy of events, to be dictated as before by Parma. She might as well cut her losses. Before the expiry of the two months for which she had contracted to pay her army, a public declaration was prepared of her intention to withdraw them out of hand.[51]

But for all her bluster, Elizabeth proved placable. It was not arguments that placated her, though there was plenty of these, pressed by Burghley himself and by all and sundry from Dieppe.[52] It was action, taken eventually by Essex in accordance with the plan he had agreed with Henry.[53] After the Noyon conference, he and his company retraced their path to Gisors.[54] Their outward journey had taken them past Gournay, which they had judged to be strongly garrisoned by the

47. Unton, pp. 40–1.
48. PRO SP 78/25/252, 259.
49. Unton, p. 87.
50. PRO SP 78/25/294.
51. Unton, pp. 88–93.
52. PRO SP 78/25/290–350 *passim*.
53. Unton, pp. 104–5.
54. Except where otherwise stated, this account of the return journey is based on Coningsby, pp. 19–23; Carey, pp. 12–15; Bagot, p. 338.

enemy, lying in 'country very apt, being somewhat close and upon straits betwixt hills, for ambushes'.[55] Now intelligence reached them that Villars had reinforced the garrison there, and was lying in wait with a strong contingent of horse and foot.[56] Reconnaissance confirmed this; clearly the direct route to Dieppe was blocked. Essex made a wide detour, crossed the Seine downstream from Vernon, reached the safety of Pont de l'Arche with its friendly governor du Raulet, and sent to Baskerville for substantial reinforcements.[57] Rumour spread at Dieppe that he must have some immediate enterprise in view.[58] But the general was content to collect intelligence regarding enemy movements and to rest his company, first at Pont de l'Arche and then at Louviers; for 'this journey was so hard that it has discouraged divers young soldiers'.[59]

Essex was moving with extreme caution, making extensive use of scouts and to good purpose. Learning that Baskerville was on his way, he returned to Pont de l'Arche and sent riders to check upon this information. Two days later, written reports arrived of the sergeant-major's approach. Again horsemen were sent to ascertain the positions of Villars and his men before Essex would move from the place of safety. Villars was reported to have put troops in readiness at Blainville-Crevon, barring the passage across the Rouen–Gournay line. Essex arranged to cross that line *en masse*. The rendezvous with Baskerville was effected at Ry. A detachment of cavalry was sent back to Pont de l'Arche for the baggage that had been left there until the junction was made. Meanwhile, the infantry was stationed in open country behind pickets of seasoned soldiers.[60] Scouts brought word that enemy horsemen were making their expected approach. At once the general positioned his main army on high ground, and sent well-mounted skirmishers to engage the enemy until his own cavalry should be available for a counter-attack in strength. Before this manoeuvre was completed, the opposition withdrew towards Rouen, inviting pursuit. But there was none. Essex marched his entire force across the Rouen–

55. Coningsby, p. 15.

56. Earlier information, that Gournay was only lightly defended, stimulated notions of attempting the town. No such attempt was made; and the army's preparations for leaving Gisors, baggage and all, do not suggest that any was seriously intended.

57. PRO SP 78/25/246.

58. PRO SP 78/25/248; HMC *Salis.*, vol. iv, p. 134; Unton, pp. 52–3.

59. Bagot, p. 338.

60. Devereux, p. 229; for arrangements in writing between Baskerville and Essex, HMC *Salis.*, vol. iv, p. 167 (misdated).

Gournay line to comparative safety at the village of Cailly, well on the road towards Dieppe. Despite a severe bout of ague, he was anxious to victual his men. After some argument with the French, bread, beef, and mutton were made available at Pavilly. The army encamped there, and Essex held a council of war.[61]

Already, one month had elapsed of the two to which Elizabeth had agreed. Already, in letters that had reached Dieppe before Baskerville's departure, she had commented on the 'uselessness' of her army in Normandy and had talked of its recall.[62] Knowing this, and with a skilfully executed journey behind him, Villars outmanoeuvred, the soldiers rested and fed, Essex and his officers were disposed for some action, although the general himself was too weak to sit his horse. The campaign might be furthered, the tables turned upon Villars, if the governor, reported absent from Rouen, were now to be cut off from his town and its communications with Le Havre also severed. Perhaps Le Havre itself might be surprised—a *coup* that would certainly please Burghley.[63] The operation misfired, and in the event pleased nobody. It was begun by sending a large detachment of horse and foot to worry the Rouen garrison. With it went young Walter Devereux. There were exchanges of gunfire. Over-enthusiastic, Devereux was drawn forward with a few companions, ran into an ambush of shot behind a hedge and was hit in the cheek by a ball that penetrated his brain. His body was recovered. Chastened, everyone returned to Pavilly, where at dinner-time the next afternoon fire broke out near a munitions store and destroyed the entire village, the soldiers barely escaping in time. Without further ado, the army retired to base at Arques, where Essex found the Queen's irate letters awaiting him.[64]

No development hitherto—least of all the Earl's grief and his advisers' good opinion—was likely to dissuade her from calling off the entire campaign. Never did Essex stand more in need of a positive

61. Poole, p. 530.

62. Unton, pp. 43–5, cf. pp. 48–9.

63. For the discussion at Pavilly, PRO SP 78/25/277, 288, 338; HMC *Salis.*, vol. iv, p. 148.

64. Poole, pp. 530–1; PRO SP 78/25/285, 287. Inside Rouen, the activity of the English before the town was explained in terms of their desire to win a prize offered by Elizabeth for the first cannon shot upon it; and the fire at Pavilly, in terms of their spite for the loss of Devereux (Valdory, p. 15). The circumstances of Devereux's death were immortalized in Latin verse by the epigrammatist Thomas Campion, probably an eye-witness (P. Vivian (ed.), *Campion's Works* (Oxford, 1909), p. 272).

military success. Within two days the opportunity arose. Biron had
come into Normandy. Following Essex's departure from Noyon the
Marshal had tried to bring the siege of Pierrefonds to a swift conclusion. Faced by unexpectedly strong resistance, he had abandoned it and
had marched westwards in accordance with the agreed plan, sending
repeatedly ahead to Essex to join him in besieging Gournay.[65] As everyone agreed, and as the Earl had good reason to know, that town was 'a
place in the judgement of all men of service both French and of our
own nation most necessary towards the siege of Rouen. For, being
in the passage from Picardy to Rouen, it may be a dangerous harbour
to receive the forces of the Duke of Parma or any other, and also a
continual means to spoil our victuals and thereby to annoy us at the
siege, so as that being left behind our backs, instead of besieging Rouen
we shall be in a manner besieged ourselves.'[66] Even so, the English
general did not respond at once to his ally's summons. Acting strictly
in accordance with his instructions, he consulted with his advisers at
Dieppe. It was agreed that Biron be asked to come forward to Neufchâtel, accessible with reasonable safety from Dieppe; and that Essex,
Unton, and Leighton meet him there and hear what he had to say,
leaving the English army to be mustered meanwhile at Arques.[67]

At Neufchâtel the English party showed considerable diplomatic
skill. Already convinced of the need to take Gournay, they nevertheless
expressed to Biron unwillingness to participate in any such siege. As he
afterwards recounted to the King, the Marshal had to recapitulate all
the reasons why Henry had gone into Champagne and had to summon
maps and every argument he could think of to satisfy them that what he
proposed was relevant to Rouen. Simulated reluctance on the part of
the English persuaded him that Henry must come promptly and, despite other claims upon him, must take responsibility for paying their
army. This must be in cash, since the English demanded such enormous quantities of meat and bread; and Biron took it upon himself to
advise Beauvoir of what was taking place, and why.[68] Essex had thus
taken steps to provide for his army, to safeguard his own position
vis-à-vis the Queen and to add to the pressure upon Henry to join him
in Normandy. Only then, and with his advisers' unanimous support,
did he agree to attempt Gournay. As he had already written to

65. Unton, pp. 76–8; HMC Salis., vol. iv, p. 136; Poole, p. 531; PRO SP
78/25/292, 312.
66. PRO SP 78/25/290.   67. PRO SP 78/25/340.
68. BN AFF 3645, fo. 15; cf. PRO SP 78/25/330.

Burghley, 'to do nothing but besiege Rouen may hinder the siege of
Rouen very much; for a man must first take the porte that would lodge
in the market-place.' If the places about the Norman capital were left
in enemy hands, 'there shall not a tittle of bread come to our army
without a wonderful great convoy'.[69]

Apart from the Queen, food was by now Essex's most serious problem. Leaving Biron to go on ahead to Gournay, he returned to his
army and spent two days in scouring the countryside about Dieppe
for carriages and provisions. All too little of the latter was found, and
during the siege the army had to live on what it could get by foraging.
Abandoning hope of conveying supplies from Dieppe, Essex effected
the march to Gournay at high speed.[70] He agreed with Biron, already
arrived there, that the town must be taken quickly. The townsmen were
reported to be strengthening its defences. Like Elizabeth's patience, the
weather was breaking; three days and nights of continual rain followed
the English arrival. Since Gournay stood upon marshy ground, the
besiegers were sadly inconvenienced and Biron himself much troubled
by his gouty foot. The surrounding country was infested by the enemy.
Hostile garrisons at Beauvais and Pontoise threatened raids; League
commanders with itinerant forces were said to be in the neighbourhood; rumours flourished that the Rouennais were preparing great
numbers of white scarves—the identifying mark of Henry's supporters
—and would wear them in order to penetrate the besiegers' lines and
take them by surprise. There was thus every stimulus to hasty and pre-
cipitate action. Yet the siege was carried through with professional
deliberation; and despite his accustomed antipathy to sharing a command,[71] the afflicted Biron was warm in his praise of Essex's conduct
and of his judgement.[72]

His own activity, before the English arrival, was desultory. Discouraged by his experience before Pierrefonds, he had concluded that
he now had with him insufficient artillery to mount an effective bom-

69. Devereux, pp. 238–9.

70. Covering a distance of over forty miles in two and a half days.

71. See Biron's *Maximes et bref avis pour le maniment de la Guerre*, BN
fonds français, Ancien St. Germain français, no. 16988, fo. 8; cf. Williams's
view that 'it is impossible for two Chiefs to agree, having equal authority'
(*Discourse*, p. 20). cf. also Machiavelli, *Discourses*, bk. iii, ch. xv.

72. BN AFF 3645, fo. 33. For descriptions of the siege of Gournay, Poole,
pp. 532–5 (Coningsby); BN AFF 3956, fos. 24–33 (Biron to Henry); PRO SP
78/25/365 (Essex), 367 (Leighton), 369, 371 (Yorke), 393 (Biron to Beauvoir);
Unton, pp. 96–100.

bardment. He had lodged his men in scattered buildings and villages about the town. Like the English, they lacked supplies; time and energy were expended in capturing small châteaux in search of food. The coming of the English army raised the Marshal's spirits; never, he exclaimed, had he seen a more handsome sight than their infantry. He conferred with Essex. Additional guns were promptly summoned from Dieppe. Essex's soldiers, on the night of their arrival, set about preparing gabions. Next morning the two commanders reconnoitred the town. At nightfall Essex put his men to work on entrenchments, opposite one of the gates. While the French had so far accomplished little in that respect and, owing to their scattered disposition, were experiencing difficulty in maintaining an adequate watch at night, Essex was acting in accordance with Williams's precept, that 'None besiegeth any place but entrencheth himself and troops in such sort, that 5,000 will defend trenches, against thrice their number: wherefore the succours are ill conducted to force trenches, and may fight better cheap'.[73] Gunfire from Gournay wounded some soldiers, but by daybreak the trenches were deep enough to be occupied with reasonable safety.

With these approaches so quickly completed, the besiegers endured a three days' wait for artillery. Essex sent a party of one hundred horse to chivvy along the three pieces coming from Dieppe to supplement the six already brought by Biron. He himself, with Biron, Williams, and a French engineer, carried out, under cover of darkness and within range of the Gournay guns, a close survey of the ground to determine the best position for the battery. On the night before it commenced, two English volunteers braved shooting by the light of blazing straw thrown down by the garrison, and discovered the depth of water in the town ditch at the point of the intended breach—essential information, if matters should come to an assault. Meanwhile, in heavy rain, the guns were manhandled into position. There were three emplacements. One unit of four cannon,[74] and another of three, were aimed at two points of the selected bastion; an eighth cannon and a culverin were positioned at longer range to batter its flank and the adjoining curtain wall.[75] Two breaches were hoped for, one for each assailing nation, to prevent dissension.[76] At seven o'clock in the morning the battery com-

73. *Discourse*, p. 52.

74. In view of the rate of fire achieved, it seems doubtful whether these were full cannon; cf. below, p. 164.

75. cf. *Discourse*, p. 22.

76. cf. Elizabeth's comment, above, p. 107.

menced.[77] After one and a half hours of exceptionally rapid fire, both breaches had been effected and the governor of Gournay called for a parley. His case was now hopeless; he had, after all, only 300 soldiers in the town. He proposed terms to Biron, but Essex insisted upon unconditional surrender, and brought up his infantry to menace the breach. Capitulation followed at once. The governor, with all his captains, officers, and gentlemen were 'to be prisoners not of war but at discretion, so as the Marshal may hang them if he will'. Mercenary-fashion, he handed them over to his own officers to be ransomed. The soldiers were to leave their arms and to depart with white staffs in their hands. Care was taken to preserve the townsmen from pillage and rapine; they were to be dealt with by Biron as subjects of the King. Essex claimed jurisdiction over any English subject found in the town. There was only one—an Irish soldier, whom he summarily hanged.

The siege of Gournay was a model of its kind. It was carried through unhurriedly, with minimum losses and with maximum psychological effect. Gournay's capitulation induced the immediate surrender of a number of other strongpoints in the vicinity, hitherto held for the League. More important still was its effect upon Elizabeth, adamant in her displeasure until now. On his way back from Noyon Essex had sent to Burghley a personal representative, Francis Darcy, to explain the situation.[78] The result had been condemnatory letters from the Privy Council.[79] More news, of the meeting at Neufchâtel, drew from the Queen orders to Essex to deliver his command to Leighton and return home.[80] These orders reached Essex before Gournay. At once he sent back Darcy 'to desire longer stay'.[81] As the Earl was completing his survey of the Gournay approaches, and before Darcy had reached the Court, Burghley was reviewing her general's case with the Queen, as favourably as he could. She took exception to every point.[82] The Lord Treasurer was tenacious enough to continue the argument over four days, but Elizabeth would make only one concession. In the unlikely event of Henry's actually beginning to pay her army, some of it might stay, exclusively in order to take Rouen.[83] At least her claim upon the customs would thereby be kept alive. But she can scarcely have considered this more than a token gesture. All the signs from France were that Henry had as yet issued his officials with

77. Eight o'clock, if Coningsby is preferred to Leighton.
78. Devereux, p. 230.   79. Unton, pp. 72–6.
80. Unton, p. 85; PRO SP 78/25/388.   81. Carey, p. 15.
82. PRO SP 78/25/352.   83. PRO SP 78/25/378.

no authority to pay her forces, and had in any case no money for that purpose.[84] Whether he did or not, Essex must come away, and must not be told that there was any possibility of his army's staying. For an earl to loiter in Normandy, commanding a dwindling and inactive force, was patently absurd—the more so when the force in Brittany was simultaneously wasting away. In all this, Burghley could detect only one glint of hope: 'if by the coming of the forces thither Gournay may be recovered, that her Majesty will change her opinion and allow of [it] if [it] is done'.[85] But to all appearances, even that practical success would modify only her displeasure, not her decision.

Unaware of these latest developments at Court, as soon as Gournay fell Essex sent off another gentleman, Robert Carey, with the request, ironical enough, that if the Queen should still insist on withdrawing her army the Earl himself might be permitted to stay with half a dozen gentlemen, 'to see this German army for a month'.[86] Meanwhile, Biron was talking of investing Rouen without delay, or at least of taking Caudebec as the next preliminary to the main siege. But Essex had no heart for either project. Whatever might come from England, news had arrived from Henry and it was dismal.[87] His resolution to join them before Rouen, never very firm, seemed to have dissolved altogether. After Essex had left him at Noyon, over a month before, he had moved eastwards a mere dozen miles and had spent a fortnight in collecting intelligence and in further deliberation. He had admitted to Grimeston his continuing preference for having Essex join him in northern France where, in his view, battle with Parma ought to take place.[88] All his own preparations had been geared to this end, and he still entertained hopes of persuading Elizabeth to agree.[89] Spanish reinforcements from Naples were *en route* through Lorraine to join Parma. A papal army of unknown strength was approaching by a similar route to reinforce Mayenne. Turenne's Germans required pay; the problem of the La Marck inheritance required solution. Judged against the potential cauldron in the north-east, the Normandy pot could surely be left to simmer for a while, protests from Essex and Elizabeth notwithstanding. So Henry at last concluded, and swept away towards the frontier. His achievement there was considerable. Battle was offered Mayenne before Verdun; he declined, and lost contact with the Neapolitan Spaniards who marched on for the Netherlands. Money for the

84. PRO SP 78/25/316, 340.   85. PRO SP 78/25/352.
86. PRO SP 78/25/365.   87. BN AFF 3645, fo. 33.
88. PRO SP 78/25/263.   89. PRO SP 78/25/279.

Germans was scraped together, thanks mainly to the capture of the richly stocked town of Attigny. Turenne was married, and Nevers, among others, reconciled to the fact—'not without some difficulties, but the King's presence and the young lady's good disposition surmounted all'.[90] Yet all this took time. Time was what Essex could least afford; it seemed that Henry would never come, however excellent his reasons. His messenger, hurrying into the Gournay camp, rode roughshod over all the Earl's hopes.

Removing his army to relative safety at Bellencombre, Essex waited, conferring daily, anxiously, with Biron. Ambassador Unton had been persuaded to travel to the King, but his meagre influence was unlikely to affect Henry nor the course of events very far.[91] Everything depended upon other emissaries, upon the messengers chasing each other across the Channel—above all, on Elizabeth's reaction to the news of Gournay. But by the time Robert Carey brought it to her at Oatlands, having completed the passage in four days, his predecessor Darcy had left with Essex's final recall. His arrival left the Earl with one forlorn chance of completing his mission, through exploiting local knowledge. The ingenious du Raulet of Pont de l'Arche had in hand a scheme identical with his successful ruse at Louviers four months previously. A local gentleman and acquaintance of his, Captain Graveron, commanded the Beauvoisin gate at Rouen and had quarrelled with the governor. He had agreed to let the royalists into the town. In the small hours of 17 October Essex and Biron, both rakish

90. *LM*, vol. ii, pp. 485–501; Davila, pp. 238–41; PRO SP 78/26/11.
91. Unton had been two months in France without setting eyes on the Court to which he was accredited and where, to his increasing irritation, Grimeston continued to discharge his office. Before the Neufchâtel conference with Biron he had thought of proceeding from there to meet the King's Council. Elizabeth insisted that he wait for Henry to come to Rouen; and he still had every intention of complying with her orders after Gournay fell. But on 11 October he left the camp with Henry's returning emissary, to go to the King, defying the Queen's command that her ambassador ought not to wear armour. After a ten days' journey he made contact with Henry at Vervins in Picardy, still striving to master the northern approaches. The King sent him back to Noyon, joined him there briefly, then left him again to deal with a threatened mass desertion to the enemy by his unpaid German mercenaries. Unton found some reason to report that the King 'hasteneth now to the siege of Rouen'. But all the ambassador's exertions had little influence upon developments. It was Gournay's capture that conditioned Elizabeth's attitude; and financial need, news of Parma and Sir Roger Williams's persuasions that ultimately drew Henry into Normandy (Unton, pp. 68–125).

for the occasion in white-plumed hats, assembled their armies and waited for the signal. None came. While the various captains were rolling dice for the honour of leading the entry into Rouen, Captain Graveron was disclosing the plot to Villars, and he was preparing a warm reception. The army was warned and, disappointed, fell instead to sacking Darnétal.

It had been an adventurer's throw, contrasting with the cool professionalism of the Gournay siege, and marked a significant alteration in Essex's behaviour. He had taken the earlier notice of recall very hard. The Queen's anger brought him 'ruin and disgrace' and would 'utterly overthrow my poor reputation'; for 'to go out of action when all other men come into action, were to wear a note of perpetual infamy'.[92] Now it seemed that she was set upon his disgrace. But the Earl was not without means of reply. The army he commanded was now even more firmly his than before. On 12 October Elizabeth's undertaking to pay it expired. Essex promptly took personal responsibility for the army's pay.[93] It meant heavy expense for him, hard commons for the troops, as supplies forthcoming from Dieppe fell sharply away.[94] But despite privations and subsequent disorders, the soldiers remained notably loyal to their general. On the day of his departure he addressed them, within sight of Rouen,[95] 'and said he was very sorry that no opportunity was offered him to have led them into a place where they might have gained honour, but the fault was not his, neither yet in them; for he had received a great goodwill in all, and thereof was determined to give notes of honour to some, and there made 24 knights'. His commission empowered him to do so, though the Queen had warned him not to bestow

92. Devereux, pp. 241–2.
93. The fact is beyond doubt, though the evidence leaves some ambiguity over dates. Sherley's account indicates 3 October (Old Style: PRO E 351/244); another note reads: 'The 14 days ending 10 October [O.S.] the pay was prolonged by the Lord General 14 days more to the 24 [O.S.]. Then the French king 14 days ended the 7 of November [O.S.]. Note the Earl sayeth that the Queen's checks should begin only from the 20 of November [O.S.]' (PRO SP 78/26/233). According to Sherley's agent Maurice Kyffin, the money received from Henry was merely 'lent to my Lord General upon a bill of his hand for repayment' (PRO SP 78/27/30). Such an arrangement was by no means unique at this time; Parma himself borrowed 1,000,000 écus on the security of his personal revenues to pay his army in 1591 (van der Essen, vol. v, p. 313). It explains the enormous expenditure incurred by Essex during this campaign; see below, p. 190, and cf. above, p. 25; also cf. L. Stone, *The Crisis of the Aristocracy, 1558–1641* (Oxford, 1965), p. 456, and Lacey, op. cit., p. 83.
94. PRO SP 78/26/22.   95. Coningsby, p. 27.

the honour of knighthood 'rather of favour or mediation by friendship than by desert', and to reserve all doubtful cases for her ruling.[96] She would hardly take kindly to such a gesture at this time—nor be blind to its implications.

In fact, she had already agreed to one month's extension of the Earl's and the army's stay in Normandy. Better than words and promises, Gournay was positive evidence that the Rouen campaign might after all prove worthwhile. Carey had tarried at Oatlands long enough only to collect letters giving the revised orders. Despite his haste, he missed Essex at Dieppe by two hours.[97] The Earl himself reached Rye, and went no further. Pleading travel-weariness, he sent yet another messenger 'to bring me the desired news of your Majesty's welfare, and to present my humble duty'. Evidently, the Queen did not fare well enough to encourage him in his duty of reporting to her. He wrote again, briefly and apparently submissively: 'I see your Majesty is constant to ruin me; I do humbly and patiently yield to your Majesty's will.' But the remainder of the note hinted that Essex was neither entirely without friends nor entirely resigned to explaining himself and enduring Elizabeth's censure: 'I appeal to all men that saw my parting from France, or the manner of my coming hither, whether I deserved such a welcome or not. To be full of words when a man is in affliction is for him that is not resolved what to do with himself.'[98] Reconciliation followed. Essex saw the Queen and in less than a week was on his way back to Normandy, assuring her of his unshakeable devotion.[99] Advice and mild admonition continued afterwards

---

96. PRO SP 78/25/70. Such cases would include men 'not being descended in blood of either noble or gentlemen'. In fact, nearly all of Essex's knights dubbed at Rouen are identifiable as men of gentle birth, and several were younger sons of noblemen. The disparaging comment that there were 'many of them hardly good gentlemen' is more valid in respect of the 150 knights made by the Earl in subsequent campaigns than of those made at Rouen. According to Burghley, news of these was kept from the Queen for several weeks (Coningsby, p. 71; Poole, pp. 536–7; T. Wilson, 'The State of England, Anno Dom. 1600', *The Camden Miscellany*, vol. xvi (1936), p. 23; Stone, op. cit., pp. 72–4; HMC *Salis.*, vol. iv, p. 151).

97. Carey's account naturally stresses the importance of his own rhetoric in persuading Elizabeth to permit Essex to stay: having heard him, she wrote the same day to the Earl, and Carey bore the letter triumphantly away with him. But the Privy Council had already written the previous day to the same purpose (Carey, pp. 16–19; HMC *Salis.*, vol. iv, pp. 143–4; PRO SP 78/26/3).

98. BM Loan 23 (Hulton MSS.), fo. 34.   99. Devereux, pp. 246–7.

to reach him from the Court. But never again during this campaign did Elizabeth subject her general to abuse and peremptory commands; and his earlier 'fault ... we are not disposed to rehearse or further to remember'.[100]

Yet Elizabeth's attitude was conditioned not merely by apprehension of what might follow if Essex were not tolerated and indulged. Back at Dieppe he found his army, their morale dwindling with their victuals and their pay, so disordered that 'they would have mutinied if my lord general had not come over'.[101] Disease and desertion had reduced them to less than half their former number.[102] Essex held a court martial, and invoked the principle that every captain was fully responsible for his men and must answer for any misdemeanour committed by them.[103] Within a week Incarvile obtained the long-promised money from Caen, and the French at last took over responsibility for pay.[104] On his own initiative Biron had captured Caudebec, overcoming resistance enhanced by news of Essex's departure.[105] He now proposed to attempt Harfleur and after it, perhaps, Le Havre.[106] But Essex would not move. There were assurances from every quarter that Henry was on his way. But Essex had sent Williams to the King himself, with an ultimatum.[107] Thus adjured, Henry finally gave way. On the day of Williams's return with this news, Essex began to move his army towards Rouen. But Williams also brought fresh requests, which Henry wanted him to convey personally to the Queen: for a further 1,000 soldiers and 450 sappers. In the light of Elizabeth's earlier attitude, towards Henry and towards Williams himself, it seemed a preposterous errand. Certainly, the gallants at Court found it so, ready as always with rumours of the Queen's foul temper, when the irrepressible

---

100. Devereux, p. 261. For the moderate tone of subsequent letters to Essex from Elizabeth, Burghley and the Privy Council, ibid., pp. 260–2, 267–9; PRO SP 78/26/290; HMC *Salis.*, vol. iv, pp. 150–1.

101. PRO SP 78/26/58.

102. The muster lists notwithstanding (PRO SP 78/26/19, cf. 31).

103. PRO SP 78/26/121; Coningsby, p. 29; cf. above, p. 97.

104. PRO SP 78/26/74, 233; Coningsby, p. 30. Pay was soon sadly in arrears; cf. Smyth's assurance in May, above, p. 72.

105. 'They of Caudebec call out of the town to those of the camp and say, "Where be your Englishmen?"; where they answered, "You shall hear of them shortly". "No, no", quod they, "they and the Earl be gone into England" ' (PRO SP 78/26/54).

106. HMC *Salis.*, vol. iv, pp. 148–9.

107. PRO SP 78/26/50.

veteran arrived. But without delay, she agreed to send the reinforcements.[108]

For all the delays, the strategic principle upon which she had acted over four months before[109] might still prove valid. For all the dangers of putting an army into Essex's hands, he seemed set upon the objective she had held firmly in view. Williams declared, on the evidence of his own eyes, that an army amounting to 30,000 men was assembling in Normandy.[110] Henry was coming: marching through Picardy, denuding the countryside of supplies, creating as many obstacles as possible for Parma. If time had been wasted in France, the Spanish governor had lost time too, distracted by Maurice of Nassau's incessant attacks, suddenly upon Hulst in September and now back at Nijmegen. Perhaps Parma might not be able to come at all. Perhaps, when he did come, Rouen would have succumbed. He might not be able to advance very far, owing to Henry's preparations. He might come only to relieve Rouen, and there would be 'a great battle in France'. Recriminations died down, old calculations revived, as November opened and the English army appeared purposefully before Rouen.

108. *LM*, vol. iii, p. 506; HMC *Salis.*, vol. iv, pp. 152–3; Bagot, p. 336; PRO SP 78/26/142. In Elizabeth's earlier strictures Williams had been singled out for special mention, and Essex condemned for listening to his 'glorious windy discourses'. But the Queen was often less irascible and her moods less wayward than Court gossip and the vigour of Elizabethan language made her appear. The present reinforcements were to be taken from the Provinces: a decision made, according to Bodley, at the worst possible time since 'the Deputies are in their provinces and there is no Assembly' (HMC *De L'Isle*, vol. ii, p. 124).

109. See above, p. 78.

110. PRO SP 78/26/130. In December Williams was much more explicit regarding the distribution of these forces among various of the King's supporters, many of whom were in fact not present at the siege (PRO SP 78/26/315; cf. below, p. 151).

CHAPTER SEVEN

THE BESIEGED

At midday on Tuesday 7 February 1589,[1] the town clerk of Rouen was summoned to the *hôtel de ville*. There he found a tumultuous gathering of townspeople, together with clerics and officials of various kinds. Their spokesman, *maître des requêtes* du Bourdeny of the *parlement*,[2] ordered him to take his place and to do his duty as clerk. Complying, he observed that the *échevins* of the town were not seated in their accustomed *bureau*, but had joined the other councillors upon the latter's benches. A list of names was given him, with the order that he announce them to the multitude. There were twelve names, including du Bourdeny and his brother, and consisting in equal numbers of clerics, lawyers, and *bourgeois*. It was these who were now charged with directing the affairs of the town. They would do so in company with the existing *échevins*, of whom five were present and whose request for release from their responsibilities was overruled. By popular demand, the *parlement*'s ratification of these Conciliar nominations was to be sought, and with it a formal pronouncement that Rouen was now held for the League. All pledged themselves 'to live and die for the Catholic, Apostolic and Roman religion'. Three days later a public oath was extracted from the *bailli*, that he would conduct matters 'in accordance with the arrangements made at Paris'; and a promise, that he would send representatives to all local administrative bodies 'to advise them of the people's demands, so that the said bodies might be brought to swear allegiance to the League'.[3]

In the normal hierarchy of Rouen government, executive responsibility was vested in six elected *échevins*, who ran the town's affairs in consultation with the *bailli*. These were answerable in principle, through the Council of Twenty-Four, to the General Assembly of the town. In fact that Assembly consisted of a select body of substantial

1. Following the events of the previous Sunday; see above, p. 8.
2. Son of the former *premier président* Jacques de Bauquemare du Bourdeny; cf. the opposition to the royal appointment of his successor, Claude Groulart, in 1585, above, p. 4.
3. RD vol. 20, fos. 405–6.

bourgeois and ecclesiastical and secular officials.[4] While those involved in the events of February 1589 were concerned to maintain, together with religion, a measure of administrative continuity and observance of constitutional forms, their actions struck at the oligarchic character of this governmental structure. They also appeared to challenge the social foundation of government itself. Was not as much implied in the predominance of clerical and lawyer elements in the Conciliar nominations; in the fraternity avowed with a Paris in the grip of the revolutionary Sixteen; above all, in the insistent emphasis upon what 'the people' required? Such an implication was not lost upon the *bailli*, the moderate but vacillating Count of Carrouges. Within a few days, preachers had pronounced his treachery to 'the people', his residence was seized and he himself imprisoned. Nor was it lost upon the Duke of Montpensier, responsible under the King for the province's government. He recognized in these developments a 'popular confusion' that would 'obliterate the privileges and dignities of all the noblemen of the realm'.[5]

That view proved to be exaggerated. Certainly the revolt at Rouen brought to fresh intensity the unrest, rural and urban, that had been seething in Normandy. In the countryside were operating companies of marauding soldiery, associations of rebellious villagers, bands of insurgent peasants such as the *gauthiers*, striking at officials and at landed proprietors, and now relieved of Rouen-based attacks upon them by government forces.[6] Now, too, with the sole exception of Pont de l'Arche, the towns of the Seine valley aligned themselves with the provincial capital and recognized its leadership. Royal government was collapsing. At Caen the fugitive members of the *parlement*, having received letters patent from Henry III, nervously waited upon events.[7] Promises from the King to reduce taxation were gestures of impotence, hardly relevant in these disordered circumstances. But while anarchy

4. For the thirteenth-century origins of this system, see A. Giry, *Les Établissements de Rouen* (Paris, 1883), pp. 14–15.

5. cf. Unton's conviction that 'The common people in most of these towns are Leaguers' (p. 363). Montpensier had succeeded Épernon as governor in Normandy in 1588. The latter had held the office for a mere ten days (Floquet, pp. 251, 257; d'Estaintot, pp. 11, 20); for his subsequent unreliability, see below, p. 159.

6. While the *gauthiers*, or brigands of the woods, were cut to pieces by Montpensier at Argentan in April 1589, their variously appellated counterparts multiplied apace in the months that followed.

7. The letters were received in February; formal sessions opened in June.

threatened and confusion was real enough, there was to be no popular revolution. The situation at Rouen was stabilized by the intervention of Mayenne.

By the end of February he had arrived in person in the town, accompanied by armed forces and by deputies from the *parlement* at Paris. He was authorized by the General Council of the League at Paris to arrange matters at Rouen 'for the good of all the towns of the League'. In his presence the rump of the Rouen *parlement*, which for three weeks had refrained from endorsing the actions taken on 7 February, was presented with an ultimatum in the form of the oath of the League, on the one hand affirming steadfast adherence to the Catholic faith, on the other condemning the author of the murders at Blois—the King himself. Several of the members balked at such a denial of their allegiance to the fountainhead of law. But Mayenne's control of the situation did not immediately depend on his ability to coerce the members of the *parlement*, however important their formal support in the long term. More immediately significant was the attitude towards him of the municipality itself. On 4 March, the day that the General Council of the League designated him Lieutenant-General of the kingdom until the Estates-General should meet,[8] the Duke was present at a meeting of the Rouen General Assembly. His welcome was enthusiastic; and important measures were carried through.

Two delegates from Rouen were appointed to serve upon the General Council of the League. Its authority was recognized in all matters affecting the welfare of the state, pending what should be decided by the Estates-General to be summoned by that same Council. The condition of the kingdom was to be advertised to the Pope, and his confirmation sought for the Sorbonne's decree absolving all Frenchmen from their allegiance to the tyrant, Henry III. In the name of 'the people' Mayenne was urged to accept the governorship of the province. This he declined, on the grounds of 'the resolution taken by all princes and lords of the Catholic League not to take any such charge except by direction of the Estates'. What he did seek, and what transpired, was the effective absorption of the rebellious Rouen Council into a provincial council of the League. The latter was to consist of all those elected to the Council of 7 February, together with two additional representatives of the *parlement* and two noblemen, committed supporters of the house of Lorraine. Three more Lorraine *protégés*—

8. E. Maugis, *Histoire du Parlement de Paris* (Paris, 1914), vol. ii, p. 66; Mayenne took the oath of office at Paris on 13 March.

Villars of Le Havre and two *lieutenants* of the province, the brothers de la Mailleraie and de Pierrecourt—were authorized to attend and to speak at the council's sessions. Finally, the formal alliance and confederation of Rouen and Paris was proclaimed, in the presence of representatives of both towns.[9]

So the Rouen uprising was assimilated into a centralized organization, carefully steered by Mayenne between the Scylla of conservative institutionalism and the Charybdis of populist extremism. Its object was political: specifically, displacement of the royal head of state, the alleged abuser of monarchy, coupled with redirection rather than overthrow of existing institutions. Steadily affirming the ultimate authority of the Estates-General, the General and provincial councils of the League endeavoured on the one hand to seduce or browbeat the members of the sovereign courts and, on the other, to hold in check revolutionary tendencies such as those exhibited by the Parisian Sixteen. But the success of Mayenne's policy of conciliar management was short-lived. At Rouen, as elsewhere, the *parlement* remained hesitant and often obstructive, despite a fresh purge carried out in May to compel its docility and its recognition of the Duke as Lieutenant-General.[10] Popular unrest persisted, to be exploited from time to time by competing factions in which clerics and lawyers were prominently involved and by which sectional and municipal rights and interests were strenuously invoked. If such difficulties were inherent in the disturbed political situation, they were exacerbated by personal rivalries and, above all, by military setbacks. Thus impeded, it was in vain that Mayenne and his adherents explored avenues of ultramontanism, federalism, and elective monarchy, in search of a novel constitutional solution to the predicament of France.

Military control of Normandy eluded them. Early in April Montpensier arrived at Caen and set about the reconquest of the southern region of the province. Towns fell before him in rapid succession; by June he had entered Honfleur.[11] In August the royalist recovery was

9. RD vol. 20, fos. 408–11ᵛ. The Pope was also to be warned of the danger of a change of religion in the state (ibid., fo. 412).

10. The record of these events, in ADSM—B—PRS (Caen) for July 1589, in all likelihood exaggerates the degree of violence involved; cf. Floquet, vol. iii, pp. 314–16.

11. Among his successes was the capture of 400,000 *aunes* of linen belonging to Spanish and Flemish merchants at Rouen (Lapeyre, *Famille de marchands*, p. 430); cf. below, p. 134 for the Leaguer sympathies of cloth merchant

interrupted and complicated by the King's assassination. Like the *parlement* at Caen, which he had been instrumental in convening, Montpensier considered his position.[12] Eventually both declared for Henry IV who, with his depleted army, came from the environs of Paris into Normandy, captured Gisors and a number of other towns *en route*, and arrived at Dieppe. His manoeuvres about Rouen[13] brought Mayenne from Paris in anxious pursuit. Battle was joined at Arques in September, and Henry won a brilliant victory from an entrenched position against a greatly superior force. Losses on both sides were comparatively light, but Henry was reinforced by Willoughby from England, and Mayenne withdrew towards the Somme. The King returned to Paris at speed, occupied the south-western suburbs and attempted to storm the city walls. The attempt failed, and Mayenne brought his army to relieve and reinforce the capital.

In the meantime the League had consolidated its hold upon the towns of the lower Seine. Now Henry swept back through lower Normandy, seized town after town, and appeared once more at the Seine estuary. Again Mayenne followed him westwards. Again battle took place, this time at Ivry, where the League army suffered a crushing defeat. And again the King returned to Paris, with the revised intention of starving the capital into submission by blockade. For this purpose he took Corbeil, Melun, and Montereau on the upper Seine, and so dominated river access to the city. During the summer months the royal grip was tightened upon the suburbs. Paris was reduced to great distress, with Mayenne this time incapable of intervention.[14] But Parma marched from the Netherlands, and the siege was raised. Yet in Normandy, in the winter of 1590–1, Montpensier and Biron went far, with little difficulty, towards restoring the royalist position, which had suffered afresh in the absence of royalist leaders and forces during the summer.

Dupont, and p. 143 for the subsequent impecuniosity of two of the Spaniards involved.

12. ADSM—B—PRS (Caen), 1589–91, fos. 1–3^v, 31^v–34.

13. On this campaign, see d'Estaintot, *La première campagne de Henri IV en Normandie* (Rouen, 1878). League propaganda described the activity before Rouen as a full-scale siege, and claimed that the King was beaten off by some Walloon captains (*Vray Discours et Defence des Catholiques de la ville de Rouen contre le siege et force du Roy de Navarre, lequel fut contraint de se retyrer ayant perdu de ses hommes au fort de Saincte Catherine* (Paris, 1589); cf. Mornay's version, above, p. 37, note 37.

14. de Croze, vol. ii, pp. 408–9.

No more than Mayennne had Henry neglected Normandy. He had twice campaigned there in person. On both occasions he had exploited victories over the League leader as a springboard for investing the French capital. Evidently, Paris was his principal objective; by comparison, the small and weakly fortified Norman towns, repeatedly won and lost by either party, were temporarily expendable. But care was taken to preserve Dieppe and Caen, to counterbalance League control of Le Havre and Rouen and to ensure that the military situation in the disordered province should not deteriorate beyond stalemate. Such a stalemate might appear to be duplicated in political terms. Both parties summoned meetings of the Estates of Normandy.[15] Both conducted a vigorous pamphlet war. Both, parading the authority of *parlement* and *chambre des comptes*, ordered sequestration of opponents' property. Whether or not those orders could be enforced, such punitive measures, administered at Caen by a newly created *chambre du domaine* under Groulart's direction,[16] were in many ways counter-productive, alienating offended officials and landlords, and bringing law further into disrepute. But in important respects advantage accrued to the royalists, despite their own divisions. If at Caen there was friction between the uprooted members of the *parlement* and of the *chambre des comptes*, at Rouen the authority of the League counterpart of the former was eroded by the defections of key officials;[17] while by 1591 Mayenne had to recognize how 'most of the *maîtres des comptes* in the said chamber have absented themselves, adhering to the opposing party', and to declare that seven remaining officers were sufficient to discharge its functions.[18] Such marks of deterioration in the League's position were matched by indications of its disintegration within Rouen itself. In August 1590, as Paris seemed about to fall, there were reports that in Rouen 'they are in great division, having three factions in the town, but none for the King in open show. One is for Monsieur de la Mailleraie, who holds the Castle and the Old Palace. Another is for

15. In November 1589 rival meetings were summoned by the League and by the King (RD vol. 20, fo. 421; d'Estaintot, p. 115).
16. Floquet, vol. iii, p. 509. For examples of its awards, see 'Tables des registres mémoriaux de la Chambre des Comptes de Normandie', *Mémoires de la société des antiquaires de Normandie*, Ser. 2, vol. 8 (1951), p. 17; and cf. below, p. 185.
17. Floquet, pp. 585, 328. Apart from the *premier président* Groulart, the defectors included all three *présidents à mortier*, the king's advocates and the registrars.
18. ADSM II B 53/9/7–8ᵛ.

the Viscount of Tavannes, and the third for the governor of [Le Havre], so as they say they are barricaded one against another and their gates shut.'[19]

The hostility between these three was indicative of the breakdown during the preceding months of the provincial council of the League. From the outset its efforts had been vitiated by friction between two of its members, Guillaume Pericard and Michel de Monchy, both clerical lawyers: the one, a son of a former *procureur-général* of the *parlement*,[20] the other a scion of one of the province's leading families. Its policy, of forcefully suspending dissident officials of the *parlement* and of the municipality and encouraging informers against religious backsliders, had failed to ensure the co-operation of the townspeople or the security of the town itself. In May 1589 de la Mailleraie, leading figure upon the council, had announced that the League required a contribution from the town of forty thousand *écus* towards the costs of war. The money was not forthcoming.[21] In June, with Montpensier at Honfleur, only the interception of conspiratorial letters prevented the delivery of Rouen to him in a plot organized by an officer of the *chambre des comptes*.[22] In August flagging spirits were revived by processions and sermons to celebrate the death of the Valois tyrant and to condemn his heretic successor. But not until December, in the presence of Mayenne's first cousin the Duke of Aumale who had led its autumn offensive from Rouen into lower Normandy, was the League's own candidate for the throne proclaimed as Charles X, by a *parlement* fresh from its own decree that a councillor must be appointed to discharge the vacant office of *bailli* in the town.[23]

In that same month Aumale's hopes proved abortive for an initiative, funded by subsidies to be furnished by the town and to be administered by members of the council of the League, against Pont de l'Arche and the castle of Blainville-Crevon.[24] The initiative came instead from the

19. HMC *Finch*, vol. i, p. 32.
20. cf. the conduct of du Bourdeny, above, p. 127.
21. RD vol. 20, fo. 413; cf. below, p. 135.
22. *La thraison descouverte des politiques de la ville de Rouen, contenant un discours veritable de ce qui s'est faict et passé en ladicte ville, le mercredy 7 et jeudy 8 de ce present mois de juin* (Paris, 1589), pp. 7, 10: Montpensier and his men would enter the town from the west when a signal, in the form of 'a great tuft of wool of many colours of the circumference of a small cask', was displayed upon the fourteenth-century belfry of the Great Clock.
23. Floquet, p. 345; RD vol. 20, fo. 422.
24. RD vol. 20, fo. 427ᵛ.

master of Blainville himself, who in February 1590 seized the castle of Rouen in the name of the King and was narrowly prevented from seizing the town as well.[25] Alarmed by the support accorded him, the municipal Council now agreed that all stocks of weapons held by armourers or merchants within Rouen be sequestered and stored in a central magazine. But a week later it rejected as 'very pernicious and injurious' fresh proposals for levying taxes to pay for fortifications and munitions.[26] There followed Mayenne's defeat at Ivry, and the League's position at Rouen became critical. Recognizing the weaknesses of existing arrangements there, the Duke sent Tavannes not only to command League forces in Normandy but also to take charge of the province's capital.[27] The summer's rift between him and de la Mailleraie confirmed the collapse of Mayenne's conciliar experiment, the failure of which was manifest in July when armed *bourgeois* invaded a meeting of the council of the League at de la Mailleraie's house and threatened the lives of the members present.[28]

If Tavannes's appointment was intended to harmonize relations within Rouen through assertion of aristocratic leadership, no such harmony resulted. Arrogant in his attitudes, authoritarian in his approach, the Viscount was no conciliator. In July he was instructed by Mayenne that the customary elections to the major municipal offices were due and must be held. For Tavannes, here was an opportunity to ensure the emergence of compliant and co-operative *aides*. At a meeting of the Council of Twenty-Four he delivered a harangue, warning that he would tolerate the election of no one who was not a man of substance, Catholic, and adherent of the League. But while the attendant councillors wanted no renewal of the disorderly proceedings of February 1589, they were insistent that time-honoured procedures must be followed. As much was retorted to Tavannes by the acting *bailli* and by the principal *échevin* Dupont, cloth merchant and a member of the

25. A. de Bouis (ed.), *Discours véritable de l'execution faicte de plusieurs traystres et sédicieux de la ville de Rouen, faict par le commandement de Monseigneur le chevallier d'Aumale, faict le vendredy 23 de février 1590* (Société rouennaise de bibliophiles, 1878). As a result of this affair the castle was seriously damaged and weakened; cf. below, pp. 139, 152.

26. RD vol. 20, fos. 431–431v. On earlier attempts to restrict possession of arms, see above, p. 6.

27. RD vol. 20, fo. 435v.

28. Floquet, pp. 363–4. De la Mailleraie seems subsequently to have defected to the King: see PRO SP 78/27/363.

provincial council of the League.[29] The customary General Assembly was convened. Most of its *bourgeois* members failed to appear; they were summoned again, under penalty. The retiring *échevins* made their report to the Assembly, in apologetic terms. Subjected though they had been to commands from the *parlement* and from the General Council of the League, they had done what they could for the good of the town. But the municipality was gravely impoverished. The increased imposition on wine had had no effect, for no one had taken the farm. They had themselves suppressed the new impositions on cloth. Work had been continued on repairing the bridge,[30] but the League authorities had directed that these efforts be diverted to the town walls. They had, however, obtained relief from the subsidy of 40,000 *écus* demanded of the town. Elections ensued and six *échevins* were chosen, two of whom attempted unsuccessfully to excuse themselves.[31] And on the following day the dissatisfied Tavannes, for all his anti-populist enthusiasm,[32] announced to a further meeting of the Council of Twenty-Four that two others of those elected 'were not agreeable to the people'. Amid protestations from the *échevins*, they were replaced.[33]

Such developments were eloquent of the profound administrative disorientation within the town. As circumstances deteriorated still further local bitterness increased and focused upon Mayenne's aristocratic representative. It was fomented and exploited by his rival Villars, to the point of violence. In August Tavannes attempted to rid himself of a particular critic by expelling from Rouen one of its councillors, Charles Guéroult, a *bourgeois* member of the provincial council of the League and former notary in the royal household. Villars sent letters opposing the expulsion. In Tavannes's absence the municipal Council resolved to thank the governor of Le Havre for his interest in the

29. RD vol. 20, fo. 440[v].

30. These repairs had been in hand since before 1587; cf. the *échevins*' report of that year (Félix, p. 84). In England it was reported in July 1591 that the bridge at Rouen 'is so broken that it can hardly be repaired' (PRO SP 78/25/51).

31. Félix, pp. 85–92.

32. 'Cruelty is necessary against popular enterprises, it is the only remedy ... the people live upon the ruin of the rich, for which they care nothing as long as they profit from it' (Jean de Saulx, vicomte de Tavannes, 'Mémoires de Gaspard de Saulx-Tavannes', *Mémoires pour servir à l'histoire de France*, ed. J. F. Michaud et J. J. F. Poujoulat, vol. viii (Paris, 1838), p. 152).

33. RD vol. 20, fos. 449[v]–50; Félix, pp. 93–4. In 1594 the elections of these replacements were declared void by the *parlement*.

town's welfare. Within two days Villars was threatening to intervene with armed force unless Guéroult were justly treated; and Mayenne himself wrote to assure the latter of his goodwill. Repeatedly the Duke urged the two main rivals to compose their differences which, if they continued, were bound to bring decisive advantage to the enemy. Repeatedly Tavannes protested to the municipal Council against refusal to accept his leadership, against failure to find money for his troops, against slanders that he was a 'stranger' whose object was to subject Rouen to a garrison of 'strangers'. The councillors continued alive enough to such issues as related directly to their several interests: the movement of commerce along the Seine, appointments to municipal offices, titles to vacant ecclesiastical benefices. But they remained antipathetic towards an intruder whose large pretensions and assertiveness of manner were unwarranted and unredeemed by military success.

Falling back upon the *parlement*, Tavannes extracted from it a measure of support, but found this insufficient for his needs and further tainted the court's authority with his own discredit. It gave urgent orders, as Chartres fell to the King in April 1591, for labourers to be recruited from the surrounding villages to attend to the town's defences, for a fifteen-days' suspension of work on private buildings in order that craftsmen be released for this task, for an inventory to be made of available supplies of victuals and munitions, for fund-raising through fresh impositions upon fish, salt, and cloth. To these essential requirements the town responded with objections, its Council with forecasts that unrest and allegations of corruption must grow unless Tavannes would manage affairs in consultation with three elected councillors. In June the cloth merchants demanded repeal of the impositions. In July the municipal Council resisted the *parlement*'s call for appointment of a receiver of revenues accruing from the goods of those absent townspeople who opposed the League. With Villars implementing positive measures to overthrow his rival by force, Mayenne again intervened in person. His other stratagems for governing Rouen having failed, there now remained to him only one alternative beyond abandoning town and province to their own devices. Tavannes was packed off to Picardy; and the governor of Le Havre was at last given command of the Normandy capital.[34]

34. RD vol. 20, fos. 454 sqq.; vol. 21, fos. 1–10. *CM*, vol. i, pp. 124, 170–4, 322; vol. ii, pp. 118, 123. ADSM PRS (Ligue), 6 March–11 May 1591, fos. 67–90. A. Desjardins, 'Les parlements du roi, 1589–96', *Séances et travaux de l'Académie des sciences morales et politiques*, vol. cxii (1879), p. 620. In return

Unlike that of Tavannes, Villars's reputation in Normandy stood high. He also enjoyed substantial support within Rouen itself among merchants and councillors. Related as he was to the governors of Dieppe and Caen, his potential was considerable as a local leader capable of rehabilitating and perhaps of enlarging the League within the province.[35] What remained doubtful was whether the League's general interests were his principal concern. From the standpoint of its leader, Villars's potential in the province was offset by his political unreliability. Although it was Guise patronage that had earlier gained him his governorship of Le Havre, he was reported by the Spanish ambassador to have endeavoured in 1589 'to prevent the Rouennais from declaring in favour of those of Paris'.[36] Mayenne did what he could to guarantee his loyalty. Villars was to exercise his governorship at Rouen in the name of the Duke's own thirteen-year-old son, and took his oath of office between Mayenne's own hands.[37] His designated deputy, de La Londe, had attended the Estates-General at Blois in 1588, had held key office at Rouen throughout the period of the League's ascendancy, and was consistently favoured by Mayenne.[38] Command of the Old Palace was held by du Mesnil, another of Mayenne's own *protégés* and a member, with his brother du Bourdeny, of the provincial council of the League.[39] Yet these men were loyal enough to Villars himself, and constituted no impediment to his exercise of power: 'such absolute power', in one commentator's view, 'that the town of Rouen was promptly reduced to his will'.[40]

Nevertheless, whatever Mayenne's misgivings, and whatever local

for repeal of the impositions the cloth merchants offered a subsidy of 8,000 écus. For Tavannes's embittered comments upon the ungrateful reception accorded those who came to the aid of afflicted provinces, see 'Mémoires de Gaspard de Saulx-Tavannes', p. 259.

35. For overtures by Villars to de Chatte, see above, pp. 65, 67. In August 1589 Pélet de La Vérune of Caen, hitherto royalist but a staunch Catholic, came close to aligning himself with the League (C. Groulart, 'Mémoires ... ou voyages par lui faits en cour', *Nouvelle collection des mémoires pour servir à l'histoire de France*, ed. J. F. Michaud et J. J. F. Poujoulat, Ser. i, vol. xi (Paris, 1838), p. 556).

36. de Croze, vol. ii, p. 395.

37. G. de Bouteiller, *Relation des funérailles de l'amiral de Villars, faictes à Rouen le 5 septembre 1595* (Rouen, 1879), pp. viii–ix.

38. de La Londe's Ms. 'Mémoires' are extant in BN fonds français, ancien petits fonds français, no. 20152, fos. 511 sqq.

39. *CM*, vol. i, pp. 7–8, 11; Valdory, p. 2; see above, p. 127.

40. Palma Cayet, vol. i, p. 501^v.

advantages Villars might enjoy in terms of his military reputation, his power base at neighbouring Le Havre and his relative acceptability within Rouen itself, his authority there was by no means absolute. Like his predecessor, he faced three pressing and essential tasks. Fortifications must be strengthened; money must be raised, for munitions and for soldiers' pay; and food supplies must be conserved. In all three, the governor encountered reluctance, criticism, and outright opposition. Retrospectively he was credited with such 'success, that during the whole time of the siege, there neither happened any disorder, nor did anyone suffer from want of victuals'.[41] But he owed that success far less to arbitrary assertion of the force that he commanded than to his care and ability in winning the active connivance of the urban militia and in working through the *police* organization closely associated with it. Villars recruited to his support not only the *bourgeois* captains[42] but also the leaders and their subordinates of every *quartier* and its subdivisions—the *quarteniers*, *centeniers*, and *cinquanteniers*. Thereby, he gained a degree of control over the populace and a means of mobilizing the town's resources markedly greater than had proved possible hitherto.

The town's fortifications remained deficient despite all proposals and piecemeal measures of recent years. The Rouennais had an impressive record of dilatoriness in this regard. After the siege of 1562 the fort on St. Catherine's Mount had been demolished on royal orders. It remained indefensible, and the defensibility of the Martainville *quartier* in particular was therefore much reduced. In 1569 orders were issued for a ravelin to be constructed beyond the Martainville gate, to cover that *quartier*. The construction was still not complete.[43] On the north

41. Davila, pp. 259–60.

42. One of Villars's first actions was to interview the *bourgeois* captains at his lodging in the archbishop's palace (Valdory, p. 2ᵛ). Only one of the twelve captains had figured in the elections of February 1589: Jean de La Faye who, with the elections apparently concluded, gained the important *police* post of *lieutenant-criminel* 'through the clamour of the people and especially of those of the Beauvoisin *quartier*' (RD vol. 20, fo. 407ᵛ). For a discussion of the development of the urban militia in Paris and its significance in the period of the League, see P. Robiquet, *Histoire municipale de Paris* (Paris, 1880), pp. 536–41, 660.

43. C. Richard, *Recherches historiques sur Rouen: fortifications, Porte Martainville* (Rouen, 1844), pp. 116–19. Despite Richard's view, on the evidence of the *échevins'* reports, that the ravelin was completed in the mid-1580s, the *échevins* who reported in 1587 claimed only to have begun the laying of pile-foundations—especially necessary in sandy or marshy ground—

side of the town, the castle was in serious disrepair following the events of February 1590. In general, walls and ditches needed urgent attention. Villars judged that the readiest remedy lay in earthworks, which would require recruitment of a labour force of 800 men from the various parishes to work for twelve hours each day with picks, shovels, and great baskets. Costs should be met by means of contributions from the *bourgeois* of every parish, to be assessed by the *échevins* in accordance with a precedent of 1567. On 27 July 1591 proposals to this purpose were put to a meeting of the Council of Twenty-Four. During the next two days objections multiplied not merely against the assessed rates of contribution but against the very legality of such a levy. Villars promptly held another meeting, to decide upon 'the most suitable and least injurious means of working on the ditches and fortifications'. It was agreed that 'the parishes should be divided by the *quarteniers*, each one attending to his own *quartier* in association with the *centeniers* and *cinquanteniers*: that is, each parish in six parts from which one sixth shall go to the ditches each day under the supervision of two men from each of the said parishes appointed by the said *quarteniers*, *centeniers* and *cinquanteniers*'. Only fit men should be employed; and tasks should be allotted according to ability.[44]

On this basis, work on the fortifications at last went forward to appreciable effect—and not a moment too soon. Within a fortnight Villars was reporting to Mayenne that there were 6,000 Englishmen in Dieppe, sent by their Queen to 'besiege Rouen with forty cannons, to the which she is instantly moved by her subjects to the end they may open up that trade'.[45] But neither the materialization of this threat nor the measures adopted in July to deal with defence works disposed of the problem of dissidents within the town. While in the interests of defence the governor insisted on the demolition of buildings especially in the suburbs, the municipal Council endorsed *bourgeois* unwillingness to destroy *bourgeois* dwellings, and itself declined to demolish houses abutting on the marshland of the *Lieu de Santé*,[46] below the Cauchoise gate. In the suburb of St. Sever members of the Dominican Order resisted attempts to demolish their house; and at the com-

---

and the covering of the accompanying earthworks with ashlar (Félix, p. 84; cf. the 1590 report cited above, p. 135.

44. RD vol. 21, fos. 12–15.

45. PRO SP 78/25/156 (English translated copy of Villars's letter to Mayenne, 11 August 1591).

46. Valdory, p. 4ᵛ; RD vol. 21, fo. 25.

mencement of the siege in November they so abused a *bourgeois* captain and his men at work upon the adjacent fortifications that the latter were compelled to withdraw.[47] During the siege itself, *bourgeois* enthusiasm for such work evaporated still further; increasingly 'they excused themselves owing to their inability, and their lack of means, and the necessity to which they were by then reduced'.[48] Yet even at a moment of extreme crisis in February, with the besiegers poised to break through at St. Catherine's,[49] Villars resorted not to coercion but to the *parlement* for an order to the citizens for work parties to repair breaches.[50]

In these circumstances, what Villars achieved in terms of fortifications was limited: more than had earlier seemed likely, less than he could have hoped. The town walls were reinforced with earth, and at selected points, especially adjacent to each gate, platforms were erected as gun-emplacements. But these developments took shape upon and behind the walls, without projecting beyond them in the form of bulwarks or bastions such as would have enabled the ditches to be covered and raked with cross-fire. While the ditches themselves were deepened, they remained for the most part dry,[51] as did the ditch lying a mere seven feet deep before the newly thrown-up earthen wall upon St. Catherine's Mount.[52] That wall, 600 paces in over-all length, followed the line of the old fort and, thanks to efforts led principally by Tavannes's former anatagonist, Guéroult, reached some eighteen feet in height. The curtain was flanked by bulwarks: yet these lacked epaulement, orillion, or embrasure, the refinements of true bastions. As the siege got under way Villars recognized how, owing to these deficiencies, garrison and guns upon St. Catherine's were seriously exposed to enemy fire. He took what steps he could to remedy these lacks, and also to promote construction of ravelins and counter-trenches beyond the walls of both fort and town.[53] But if such measures con-

47. ADSM PRS (Ligue), 12 October 1591–6 November 1592, entry for 23 November 1591 (no volume nor folio numbers).

48. Valdory, p. 3ᵛ.

49. See below, p. 161.

50. ADSM PRS (Ligue), 12 October 1591–6 November 1592: entry for 20 February 1592.

51. cf. *Discourse*, p. 50: 'no dry ditch can be compared for strength unto a wet ditch'.

52. cf. ibid., p. 49: 'The best dry ditch is to have the ditch 100 paces broad and fifty foot deep'; according to d'Aubigné (p. 252) the St. Catherine's ditch was thirty feet broad.

53. d'Aubigné, p. 252; Davila, pp. 259–62; Valdory, pp. 3–4, 16ᵛ–17: the sources conflict in detail and are inconsistent in terms of technicalities.

formed to principles of static counter-attack so dear to the hearts of contemporary theorists, the piecemeal works that belatedly materialized at Rouen were scarcely consistent with their elaborate schemes. All this had a determining effect upon the tactics employed by the governor throughout the siege. With the morale of the townspeople doubtful and the fortifications imperfect, it was more than usually important to keep the enemy at a distance. Earthen walls might be expected to absorb the impact of long-range artillery bombardment. But it was unlikely that resistance would prove prolonged if the besiegers should succeed in pushing approaches forward to the point of establishing themselves upon the counterscarp before fort or town.

To prevent this, Villars relied mainly upon the guns and professional soldiers at his disposal—and especially the latter. He had brought from Le Havre forty pieces of artillery together with shot and thirty-six *milliers* of powder.[54] He had also reinforced the garrison with 500 light horse, 200 hargulutiers and 1,200 French infantry in four regiments. One of these, under the Chevalier Picard, was permanently stationed in the St. Catherine's fort; another, under Captain Jacques, at the priory of St. Paul on the riverside, to cover the important terrain between the Mount and the Martainville *quartier*. With 300 German infantry also available to supplement existing resources within the town, the governor could draw upon a total fighting strength of some 6,000. But his principal arm consisted in his units of cavalry and his regiments of French infantry: the former distributed among ten commanders, the latter composed of companies of fifty men.[55] Relatively small though they might seem by normal contemporary standards, such mobile units were tactically well conceived. While guns firing directly towards the besiegers might accomplish something by way of distressing them and keeping them at bay, it was upon continual harassment through sortie and skirmish that Villars meant to hinder their advances. His defence of Rouen was primarily conducted in terms of dynamic counter-attack.

But reliance on professional soldiers entailed raising money for their pay; and the Rouennais, living largely by trade and provoked to rebel-

54. RD vol. 21, fo. 27.
55. cf. Davila, pp. 258–62; de Thou, vol. xi, p. 453 (vol. v, p. 111). The names noted by Palma Cayet, p. 501ᵛ, are confirmed in Valdory, pp. 6–12, who lists the captains without stating the total number of foot-soldiers. cf. Coningsby, p. 44: 'The garrison is not above 1800 men, horse and foot.'

lion at least partly by monarchical taxation, had not responded readily to the financial demands of their subsequent masters. Under Villars those demands swelled rapidly, from 5,000 *écus* at the beginning of August to 30,000 by the end of that same month. Further sums were required to pay for the munitions he himself had supplied. Faced with objections from the municipal Council, the governor resorted as before to direct dealing with representatives of the *quartiers*. But agreement was difficult to obtain. Proposals for selective indirect taxation offended parties whose commercial transactions had already suffered severely from the effects of war. Alternative proposals to tax the sale of salt, regardless of customary exemptions, offended still more. In September the municipal receiver, elected eleven months previously, reported that there were no funds and tendered his resignation. Early in October the *parlement* proposed a levy of one *écu* above existing rates on every flagon of wine conveyed in or out of the town, payable by natives and strangers alike. The Council called for a meeting of the General Assembly before such a levy could be authorized; and despite eventual nominal agreement, objections persisted on the part of those engaged in the wine trade. The situation was exacerbated by disorderly conduct on the part of the soldiers themselves. While the General Assembly gave favourable consideration at the end of the month to revived proposals for raising their pay through indiscriminate taxing of salt, alarming rumours followed that soldiers were to be quartered in private houses with the same disregard for customary immunities as such a tax itself implied.[56]

The rumours, coinciding with the opening of the siege, stimulated agreement from the Council that military personnel would be maintained by the *bourgeois* by means either of direct victualling or of cash contributions, at the contributor's choice. This flexible arrangement did not endure, not least because the sums of money involved were dauntingly large; for Villars's soldiers required pay amounting monthly to 14,000 *écus*. In December, *parlement* and Council tortuously settled upon detailed provisions for assessing rates of contribution from each parish. They also insisted that the governor respond in kind by drawing up a 'bill or roll of his soldiers both horse and foot, by name and surname, and how much each captain or lieutenant ought to receive by way of pay each month'.[57] In these belated provisions, garrison and

56. RD vol. 21, fos. 16–28; ADSM PRS (Ligue), 12 October 1591–6 November 1592: entries for 15 October to 16 November 1591.
57. RD vol. 21, fos. 28ᵛ–34; ADSM PRS (Ligue), entry for 7 December

townspeople found for a while an uneasy *modus vivendi*. But in March the *quarteniers* reported that payment could no longer be made. At the same time, Spanish merchants resident at Rouen, and named in a bill of exchange for 30,000 *écus* newly arrived from the Duke of Parma, declared their inability to advance the necessary sum.[58] Hoarding and the disruption of normal intercourse had taken their toll; there was not enough currency left in the town. Villars and the municipal authorities debated the relative merits of manufacturing a supply of debased coins, or of marking up the face value of existing coins for the duration of the siege. They decided upon the latter course. Within a month, unpaid soldiers were raiding bakeries for food.[59]

The problem of victuals was closely related to the problem of money, and drew comparable responses from the authorities. The attitudes that dictated maintenance of Villars's soldiers along mercenary lines also dictated the continuance of commercial practices in relation to food distribution. Yet in view of the policy pursued by the authorities, food supplies lasted remarkably well. In October, on the eve of the siege, the governor favoured institution of a central commissariat, and sought the support of the *parlement* for a house-to-house search for stocks of food. What transpired was a general directive 'to all the *bourgeois* of this town to furnish themselves with victuals and munitions of war for six months, and to the labourers and countrymen to bring such wheat and other grain, wine, cider and other drink as they can ... into this town'.[60] As the siege commenced, the municipal Council issued regulations restricting the grinding of grain to appointed windmills under a general supervisor who, with two assistants from each *quartier*, should keep a register to limit the quantities ground.[61] Despite endorsement by the *parlement*, such regulations

1591. cf. the problems of musters and pay in the English army, above, pp. 96–7. Villars declared monthly rates of pay at twelve *écus* for a cavalryman, five for a hargulutier and four for a footsoldier: figures which furnish an additional basis for calculating the numerical strength of the garrison.

58. Two of them—Antoine Delrye (*alias* Antonio del Rio) and Charles de Rebouillède (*alias* Carlos de Rebolledo)—were among those who had suffered losses of linen to Montpensier's men three years earlier (see above, p. 130, note 10).

59. RD vol. 21, fos. 46–50ᵛ; ADSM PRS (Ligue), entries for 10–11 March and 11 April 1592. Money had been scarce for several years; cf. above, p. 7.

60. ADSM PRS (Ligue), entry for 29 October 1591.

61. RD vol. 21, fos. 28ᵛ–29.

were far from effective. Not surprisingly, they drew immediate objections from the bakers, whose conduct was in turn quickly criticized by the soldiers of the garrison; and within a month complaints were general against profiteering by dealers in grain. On 13 December, after consultation with four non-commercial representatives from each *quartier*, the *parlement* issued a decree stipulating maximum prices: that best-quality wheat must not exceed seven *livres* per *mine*,[62] mixtures of wheat and rye six *livres*, oats four *livres*. Moreover, purchase of grain with a view to its resale was prohibited; and grain merchants were enjoined either to bring supplies promptly into the market or to open their granaries for direct selling to the townspeople. Within five days reports indicated serious infringement of these regulations;[63] yet for the time being they represented the limit of the authorities' disposition to intervene.

In mid-January 1592 intensified complaints against hoarders produced orders for a search of suspects' houses. These were followed by allegations that the bakers had unilaterally raised the price of bread, the latter responding with counter-allegations against merchants for failing to sell their grain on the open market. By 1 February the general supervisor himself was reporting that the market was collapsing and that certain merchants were selling at nearly twice the authorized price. Accordingly, official prices were raised; by the end of the month vendors were demanding fresh increases.[64] Thenceforward the situation deteriorated apace, and controls tightened. The cargo of a boat that arrived at the quayside on 4 March, laden with grain,[65] was requisitioned by the *parlement* for direct distribution in accordance with the needs of the people. The next day, all beggars were ejected from the town in order to conserve food.[66] Yet the municipal authorities still

62. Dry measure, approximately equivalent in the case of grain to four English bushels (see Lewes Roberts, *The Merchants Mappe of Commerce* (London, 1638), pp. 248, 251; Gerard Malynes, *Consuetudo vel Lex Mercatoria* (London, 1629), pp. 45–6).

63. ADSM PRS (Ligue), entries for 2, 13, and 18 December 1591.

64. ADSM PRS (Ligue), entries for 21–27 January, 1, 3, and 5 February, 2 March 1592.

65. ADSM PRS (Ligue), entry for 4 March 1592. Villars had taken early steps to commander river-craft and appoint captains to them; and until mid-March supplies continued to enter the town by these means (Valdory, pp. 9ᵛ, 20, 25, 29, 51, 52; cf. below, p. 150.

66. ADSM PRS (Ligue), entry for 5 March 1592. On 19 March Unton reported that forty or fifty women were daily being ejected from the town, and that beer-brewing there was prohibited owing to its consumption of edible

refused to surrender the keys of the granaries to Villars; and during
the following weeks, beyond appointing a baker in each *quartier* to
cater for the poor and another for the soldiers, the *parlement* still relied
in effect upon regular adjustment of existing orders governing the price
and quality of bread and the hours for its sale. The price of wheat
reached twenty *livres* the *mine* and oats nine *livres* on 4 April.[67] Even
so, circumstances were not yet desperate. The rate of inflation of grain
prices in terms of money of account was deceptive. It derived at least
partly from shortage of real money and from adjustment of currency
values, not simply from diminution of grain reserves. Meat was still
available; in March the soldiers could still threaten to slaughter all
cattle within the town unless fodder were supplied for their horses. But
by 16 April distress had at last become acute. On that day, thousands of
townspeople took part in a mass riot at the *hôtel de ville* and in the
courtyard of the *palais de justice*.[68]

For five winter months the resources of the capital of the rich
province of Normandy had enabled it to stave off serious scarcity, and
so to escape its political consequences. But the eventual onset of dearth
devastated the town's morale. Throughout the siege that morale had
been uncertain. It had been diligently sustained by processions, by
sermons and other propaganda, by incessant public affirmations of
commitment to the service of a deity that had intervened with re-

---

grain (PRO SP 78/27/244). Since Normans generally had a liking for cider,
the latter deprivation was perhaps less burdensome than might be supposed;
cf. BM Cotton Caligula E VI, fo. 326.

67. ADSM PRS (Ligue), entries for 11, 24 March, 4 April 1592. cf. the
situation in Paris during the 1590 siege, where the price of wheat was held
at 24 *livres tournois* the *setier* until the end of May when market-supplies
were exhausted, and oats rose from 7.50 *livres* in May to 10.50 at the end of
July, none being available in August. In September, with the siege raised,
wheat opened in the range of 54 to 90 *livres* the *setier*, oats at 16 (M. Baulant
and J. Meuvret, *Prix des céréales extraits de la Mercuriale de Paris*, vol. i
(1520–1620) (Paris, 1960), pp. 228–9). Variation in weights and measures in
terms both of places and of commodities was extreme in sixteenth-century
France, but for purposes of broad comparison it is noteworthy that by the
measure of Paris a *setier* was reckoned as twice a *mine* in the case of grain (Y.
Bezard, *La Vie rurale dans le sud de la région parisienne de 1450 à 1560*
(Paris, 1929), p. 36).

68. ADSM PRS (Ligue), entries for 5 March, 16 April 1592; Valdory, p.
66. Slaughter of cattle would have denied the town of, *inter alia*, milk as a
beverage. On prices, cf. Valdory, p. 69ᵛ; his claims regarding available supplies
are to some extent contradicted by his own representations to the *parlement*
in 7 March (ADSM PRS (Ligue)).

assuring frequency on the side of the besieged. Much capital had been made of 'miraculous' escapes from enemy fire; of the consequences that must befall those misguided Catholics who, from materialistic motives and regardless of their souls' welfare, fought for King Henry; of such feats as that of the *bourgeois* musketeer whose divinely guided bullet struck down an enemy thrower of stones at a cross in the churchyard at St. Gervais. Plainly, heaven's mercy towards Rouen exceeded even the perfidy of the King, whose letters to procure the assassination of Villars had been published for all to see.[69] And what inspiration lacked was supplied by fear, stalking the street corners in the shape of gibbets.[70] Until mid-March such measures, mixed with the more delicate management of the authorities, had been enough to stiffen resolve within the town. Now that resolve was fast disappearing. 'Give us peace or bread!' clamoured the April rioters about the *hôtel de ville* and the *palais*. Villars and his horsemen had to disperse them by force. The governor was quick to disseminate the view that such disturbances were not warranted by the real facts of Rouen's situation, and had merely been fomented by fifth-columnists. But in that case, King Henry's agents had been ominously successful in bringing the Rouen rebellion close at last to breaking-point. It could not be concealed that the uneasy combination of municipal, *parlement*ary, and gubernatorial authorities was now facing mass popular opposition within the town. Surely what must shortly follow was Rouen's long-deferred delivery into the hands of the besiegers.

69. Valdory, pp. 57ᵛ–60ᵛ, and *passim*.
70. C. Lormier (ed.), 'Arrest de la court de parlement de Rouen du 7 janvier 1592', *Miscellanées de la société des bibliophiles normands*, Ser. i, vol. v (1887), p. 4.

CHAPTER EIGHT

THE BESIEGERS

ESSEX and Biron had agreed that Rouen should be invested early on
11 November, 1591 when the besieging armies would establish themselves in the surrounding villages under cover of darkness. The English
were to head the march towards the town, and were to be the first to
occupy their appointed quarters. At two o'clock in the morning Essex
and his troops came to the rendezvous, three miles from the objective.
But two hours elapsed before Biron made his appearance; and the
besiegers' eventual arrival upon the northern hills above Rouen took
place in bright sunshine. They were immediately observed by watchers
upon the walls. Throughout the day Villars subjected them to severe
harassment, beginning with an attack to the north-east upon Biron's
division and switching westwards when François de Montmorency
de Hallot[1] descended with his contingent towards his intended station
on the fluvial plain. With the support of some English musketeers, de
Hallot managed to recover much of the ground he initially lost. Now
Villars turned upon the English quarter. At first, firearms supported by
pikes repelled the Rouennais's attempts to advance uphill *en masse*,
and Essex was able to hold his cavalry in reserve. A mounted counter-
attack became necessary as the English infantry grew increasingly
distressed under fire from snipers. But once the ground had been
cleared of these, the position was held comfortably enough until nightfall.[2]

After the initial loss of time, the besiegers had maintained co-
ordination throughout the day, and had completed their operation successfully in testing circumstances. The English were lodged at Mont
aux Malades, overlooking the Cauchoise gate, and had covered de
Hallot's installation at Croisset, downstream from Rouen on the north
bank. On Essex's left, de Chatte had occupied Bois-Guillaume; and
Biron, having kept his division in battle formation on high ground

1. Great-grandson by direct male descent of a first cousin of the Constable
Anne de Montmorency (see above, p. 5), de Hallot had been chamberlain in
Alençon's household, had seen extensive service with Montpensier, and had
fought at Ivry.
2. BM Lansdowne 149, fos. 39ᵛ–41ᵛ.

while these dispositions were completed, finally descended to his quarters at Darnétal. From there he sent up a detachment of French and Swiss mercenaries to Blosseville, alongside St. Catherine's fort. Only two additional measures would be needed to complete encirclement of the objective. The first, planned in fact for this same day, was seizure of the suburb of St. Sever across the river, which was to have been effected by the Count of Soissons, approaching from the south. However, nine days passed before Soissons arrived.[3] By then Villars had overridden *bourgeois* protestations and had burned the suburb, robbing the dilatory besiegers in that quarter not only of cover against counter-attack but also of shelter against winter weather. The second measure was far longer delayed, and still more significant in its implications. It was the task of establishing mastery over the river itself. This was why Edmund Yorke had come.

Following the unfortunate outcome of his February mission, Yorke's best hope of furthering his career had seemed to lie in a speedy return to Ireland.[4] But early in July he was still at Stratford and was *persona grata* at Beauvoir's house, where the happy completion of negotiations had stimulated lively discussions on how to capture Rouen. Knowledgeable on matters of fortification, Yorke had declared that special measures would be needed to mount an effective battery against that town: 'whereupon in this idle time I made a draft of the town with a fantasy for a battery with a ruse to defend it from fire, with a sort of booth to go to the assault, and how her Majesty's troops should be lodged for the guard of it and for their own safety'.[5] He had sent this to Burghley. Within a fortnight he had had consultations with Essex and Beauvoir, and had devised a more elaborate scheme. The platform should be built at Pont de l'Arche, floated downstream to Rouen and incorporated into a timber construction, or 'staccado', to be erected in

3. His arrival was reported by Killigrew from Dieppe on 20 November (PRO SP 78/26/164). Charles, Count of Soissons, was a son of Louis, Prince of Condé (see above, p. 5) by his second wife, and was thus half-brother of Charles of Bourbon, cardinal archbishop of Rouen.

4. cf. above, p. 59. Arrangements had been made in May to send him there to take charge of Duncannon fort (*APC*, vol. xxi (1591), pp. 134–5).

5. BM Lansdowne 167, fo. 114. Enthusiastic but untrained amateur that he was, in sharp contrast to the professionalism of Spanish military engineers, the prominence of Yorke at this time as a technical adviser in English military affairs is eloquent of England's military limitations. His drawings for the Rouen device and for others are extant: BM Cotton Augustus I, vol. ii, nos. 87–91.

readiness athwart the river.[6] This would facilitate pounding of the weakest section of the town walls, on the riverside. Yorke assumed the presence of English troops on the south bank to execute this operation, and of English ships to patrol the lower reaches of the river and to 'defend the platform from fireworks and boats artificial'. Above all, he had insisted that sufficient 'ordnance, munitions, miners and pioneers' must be provided to enable the besiegers 'furiously to beat Rouen'.[7] On the strength of these proposals he had accompanied the army to France, though not at first in an official capacity.[8] Shortly after Soisson's arrival at the siege, he was hard at work upon a survey of the river.[9]

Like so many contemporary siege-engines and other military schemes, Yorke's 'fantasy for a battery' was rather more remarkable for ingenuity than for realism. He also found at first that the location best suited for construction of his 'staccado' lay a mile distant from the town. But whatever the practical obstacles in the way of implementing his proposals, there was perfect realism in the view that if the town were to be effectively blockaded the river must be closed to the Rouennais. De Reau's June specifications had included a request for shipping that was urgently repeated by Henry, Biron, and Incarvile within four days of the opening of the siege.[10] Moreover, any such project as Yorke's depended on availability not only of river craft and other materials but also of labourers and craftsmen to shift earth, to join timber, and generally to perform skilled and unskilled tasks which soldiers considered beneath their dignity. None of these became available for some time. A month had elapsed before some 300 pioneers were delivered to Yorke at Dieppe and sent on by him to Rouen with shovels, axes, pickaxes, baskets, and bills. Among them were 'many old

6. The artificial bridge, of linked boats, rafts, and platforms, 'is an instrument very much used amongst great armies in the wars at these days' (William Garrard, *The Art of Warre* (London, 1591), p. 276). In Garrard's view materials for such constructions were among the first necessities for any besieging army; his book was in fact published by Thomas Garrard, who was present at the siege of Rouen. cf. below, p. 187.

7. PRO SP 78/25/51.

8. Yorke was appointed trenchmaster at the end of November, made master of the ordnance, commissary of musters and captain of an infantry company in the following March, and died at the end of May, his company being taken over by his son (PRO E351/244; *APC*, vol. xxii (1591–2), pp. 275–6, 477–8). Throughout these months he kept up a steady correspondence with Burghley.

9. Coningsby, pp. 43–4.

10. See above, p. 74; PRO SP 78/26/123; Unton, pp. 129–33.

soldiers which will never work'; and those who would were at once employed elsewhere than upon the river. At the same time four pinnaces to patrol the lower Seine in association with crumsters and other vessels expected from the Provinces were ordered from Chatham under Captain Thomas Grove, whose instructions included tempting mention of 'great wealth that is to come down the river from Rouen to avoid the danger to ensue from the siege'. But it was in January that Grove arrived before Rouen, to pass the next three months in desultory activity no less dissatisfying to Henry than to himself.[11] In mid-March a boat-borne structure not dissimilar from Yorke's brain-child, and built of materials carried downstream from Pont de l'Arche as he had planned, did at last take shape close to the town. It was immediately effective in barring the river to the Rouennais, and instrumental in reducing them to extremity.[12] But in the meantime, as Yorke had remarked four months earlier, it was doubtful 'if that may be termed a siege that hath a river at liberty to go'.[13]

In these circumstances there was little likelihood of starving Rouen into submission by blockade. Nor was more than a token blockade seriously attempted, despite the initial deployment of forces in partial encirclement of the town, and Biron's immediate tactic of diverting the stream Robec to deprive its water-mills of their motive force. As was soon evident to Baskerville's practised eye, the necessary steps were not taken either on the river or on land to cut off supplies for the town. Townspeople continued to forage and even to tend gardens beyond the walls, venturing close to the besiegers' encampments.[14] These encampments, scattered over a distance of many miles, were linked by no lines in any technical sense apart from occasional *corps de garde*.[15] Between the several encampments, of French, Swiss, Dutch, Germans,

11. PRO SP 78/26/229, 223; 27/155.
12. Valdory, p. 52^v; see above, pp. 144-5.
13. PRO SP 78/26/193. As soon as he heard of their arrival in Normandy, Villars expressed to Mayenne his alarm at reports that the English meant to bar the river by means of chains (PRO SP 78/25/156).
14. PRO SP 78/26/235; 27/180; Valdory, pp. 33, 52^v.
15. *Corps de garde*, or outlying sentry-posts where small bodies of soldiers covered main entrenched positions, are mentioned by Coningsby in connection with besiegers and besieged alike (cf. Garrard, op. cit., p. 300). Williams recommended that besiegers ought always 'to make ways round about the place assieged to march with horse and foot' (*Discourse*, p. 20). But the variations in the routes followed by Essex, Henry and others in travelling between Mont aux Malades and St. Catherine's Mount do not suggest that this was done before Rouen.

English, the Rouennais and their allies passed to and fro virtually at will. The besiegers lacked both organization and numbers sufficient to make possible constant surveillance over such a distance. While there was some truth in Williams's estimate that Henry might call upon some 30,000 men to come to Rouen if he chose, no more than 10,000 were at any one time available for the siege itself.[16] No doubt this tallied with Williams's view that only one half of an army ought to be employed in besieging a well-protected town, the rest refreshing themselves in safety until the moment came for assault.[17] In fact, the King had other reasons for avoiding premature summonses to the various commanders by whom so much of his potential support was controlled and upon whose allegiance he so heavily relied.[18] Meanwhile, the English were so few that, as Essex remarked, 'when we must make our approaches to the town we shall not be able to keep our guards'.[19]

Failing a blockade, the besiegers were left with two alternative ways of pressing the siege. Attack could be concentrated either upon St. Catherine's fort or upon the town itself. Essex's remark indicated a preference for the latter: and in view of the need for quick results, historical precedent suggested likewise. In his famous siege of 1418 Henry V had taken St. Catherine's and had then relied upon blockade, barring the river and stationing his troops about the five gates. Though greatly distressed, the Rouennais had held out for a further four months.[20] The besiegers of 1562 had again concentrated their initial attack upon St. Catherine's. But when the fort was taken the town had refused to yield until its own walls were breached and penetrated. No doubt the converse was possible: that the fort would continue to resist even if the town should fall. In that event, St. Catherine's could be surrounded with relative ease and blockaded at leisure. But *ville prise, château rendu* predicted many of the commanders now on the spot.

---

16. See above, p. 126. Contemporary estimates of troop numbers are notoriously unreliable. Mine are based upon indications given by eyewitnesses: d'Aubigné (p. 251), Sully (p. 281), Zerotin (p. 70), Mornay (PRO SP 78/26/342) and Williams (PRO SP 78/26/130, 315), critically evaluated in the light of eye-witness accounts of the besiegers' numerical weakness (for example, Yorke, PRO SP 78/26/191).

17. Though not with his prior condition that in such circumstances 'they will block it up with forts' (*Discourse*, p. 21)—absence of which was noted by Baskerville (PRO SP 78/26/235).

18. See below, p. 182.

19. BM Lansdowne 149, fo. 49ᵛ.

20. H. F. Hutchison, *Henry V* (London, 1967), pp. 160–8, 231–50.

Even so, the distinction itself implied the desirability of isolating the one from the other, by occupying the intervening terrain. In due course this was attempted—by Essex, who, lacking support, found the position untenable.[21] Yet the most immediately hopeful direction for positive measures against the town did not lie upon that eastern side, where walls and gate had evidently been strengthened and where concentrations of attackers, with the Mount held by the enemy at their backs, would have to make their approaches over marshy ground. Nor did it lie towards the north, where the ground lay open between the walls and the besiegers' encampments, offering little cover. But urban overspill, which Villars had been unable to burn in time, afforded valuable cover for approaches from the north-west and west towards the walls running from the castle to the Old Palace. Guns had been installed in the former, though its defences remained weak and were under repair throughout the first month of the siege; and alongside the latter, running through marshy ground, a tributary of the Seine presented an additional obstacle. It was between these points that Rouen was most vulnerable, and especially around the Cauchoise gate, approachable from Mont aux Malades: where Essex lay, with de Hallot on his right to whom Henry had promised the governorship of the town.

The opening days of the siege saw frequent consultations between these two eager commanders. De Hallot made several attempts to occupy the ruined St. Gervais church, lying within 200 yards of the Cauchoise gate itself and on the direct line towards Mont aux Malades.[22] He was beaten off by sorties from the town, where work was furiously in hand upon the castle, upon a ravelin to cover the gate, and upon a cavalier to mount artillery against the English approaches. Meanwhile, Essex had lost no time in entrenching his position. It was inspected by Biron, who offered immediate assistance and encouragement for 'our barricado to be advanced nearer the town than we made the first day by 220 score'. A few days later 'we received 80 pioneers from the marshal Biron to draw the trench down to the hill somewhat nearer the town than our lodgings'.[23] A culverin was brought to bear, and urgent appeals sent to England for more powder and shot.[24] Four months later the relevance of this line of attack was to be amply confirmed when a sixty-two-pace section of the wall collapsed at this

21. PRO SP 78/26/333; cf. above, p. 141.
22. Valdory, p. 18; Coningsby, p. 41.
23. Coningsby, pp. 34, 39.
24. PRO SP 78/26/144, 146, 159.

very point.[25] But on 23 November Henry arrived at Rouen; and guns, pioneers, and the besiegers' main energies were redirected elsewhere.

With the Germans reluctant and mutinous through lack of pay, Henry's army had pillaged its way through Picardy, inconsistent in its pace and in its direction. Informed that Rue, on the Somme estuary, was about to fall to his supporters, Henry had dashed to the coast in order to supervise its capture. There was now hope, wrote Unton, that Montreuil-sur-mer to the north of Rue and Abbeville to its south would also succumb. In the same region useful employment was found for Nevers, who had followed Henry out of Champagne, publicly complaining over his treatment by the King. The Duke was left behind to see to the capture of St. Valery-sur-Somme, a task that proved within his limited abilities as a commander.[26] Authorized by the King to pay his army by levying funds from the neighbouring villages,[27] Nevers took the town within a fortnight, assisted by three English guns and their cannoniers. By Henry's orders these were sent to St. Valery from Dieppe and did not return there until mid-December, to be brought at last to Rouen with the four other pieces which had remained inactive in Normandy since their dispatch from England in September.[28] Meanwhile, the King had talked of approaching Rouen via Dieppe, had changed his mind and had come eventually by the more direct route towards Neufchâtel, sending to England along the way for ships and pikes. Without these he would not be able to take the Normandy capital. Without a further loan of 200,000 écus upon the City of London he would not be able to meet the Germans' demands. Without mastering the Somme towns he would not be able either to deal with enemy shipping operating from bases there on the Seine, or to bar the northern approaches to Rouen against Parma's coming. So Henry accounted for his consumption of time, and of resources greatly needed by the besiegers.

He stationed himself at Darnétal, where Biron had prepared quarters and commissariat with his customary diligence. Relaxed and bonhomous as ever, the King inspected troops and encampments and then

25. Valdory, p. 51.

26. Unton, pp. 128–40, 146–50; PRO SP 78/26/168. For a scathing account of Nevers in action, see Sully, pp. 298–300. During the following months Henry repeatedly tried to persuade him to return to Champagne. For his particular interest in Rouen see above, p. 112; for the relevance to the campaign of the Somme towns, below, p. 177.

27. BN AFF 3619, fo. 116.

28. PRO SP 78/26/156, 201, 237, 252–3.

conferred with his commanders. The decision was taken to concentrate the attack upon St. Catherine's fort. Objections were raised, with Essex and others[29] affirming the vulnerability of the town, the desirability of multiple approaches from several directions to stretch Villars's resources,[30] the inadvisability of a single approach upon a narrow front towards the strongest line of defence. But from Henry's standpoint there were good political reasons against subjecting Rouen to storm, pillage, and English occupation, and good strategic ones against precipitating events too soon. While activity continued about the town, including abortive attempts to seize and hold St. Gervais, the English trenches were not developed as had earlier been envisaged. It was upon the Mount that Yorke got his chance to exercise his talents; and there too that Essex and his officers increasingly spent their time.[31]

Six days after Henry's arrival the Earl again left for England, accompanied by Leighton. He won from the somewhat mollified though still sceptical Queen agreement in the matters of ships, powder, and renewal of the army's pay. Unton was in high favour, Williams commended for his plain dealing, Essex himself chided rather than censured for having issued a chivalrous challenge to Villars.[32] During his absence Henry published the conventional address to an invested town, drawing the Rouennais's attention to his fair treatment of other Catho-

29. Including Sully, whose opinion that Biron was responsible for Henry's decision has gained wide currency. Allegedly, the Marshal was embittered because Rouen's governorship was promised elsewhere, was perversely determined to demonstrate his ascendancy over the King, had hopes of getting for himself the office of Lieutenant-General appropriated by Mayenne, and sought by prolonging the wars to avoid having 'to return to plant cabbages at Biron' (see Sully, p. 283; Davila, p. 313; A. Poirson, *Histoire du règne de Henri IV*, vol. i (Paris, 1864), p. 315). To some extent such motives are mutually cancellatory; more important, cf. Biron's co-operativeness over the projected line of attack upon the Cauchoise *quartier*, above, p. 152. For Essex's opinion, Carey, p. 22; although no satisfactory authority exists for the discussion at this council of war—and some of his advisers may well have chosen subsequently to dissociate themselves from Henry's decision—such opinions were undoubtedly current among Essex's associates.

30. PRO SP 78/26/235.

31. PRO SP 78/26/191.

32. Essex had offered to maintain in combat with Villars, 'on horse or on foot, armed or *en pourpoinct*', that 'the King's cause is more just than the League's, that I am better than you, and that my mistress is fairer than yours'. In Elizabeth's view, such terms were inappropriate for 'a noble man and a peer of this realm by birth' in dealing with one who was 'neither a lawful Captain nor a soldier but a mere rebel' (PRO SP 78/26/194).

lics within his realm and promising as much to them in return for submission and obedience to their lawful king. The offer was formally
rejected, and the King's strictures on the rebels' reliance upon Spain
countered with the reminder that he had 'himself filled the kingdom
with German and English heretics'.[33] Meanwhile, approaches went forward upon St. Catherine's Mount—slowly, despite Henry's energetic
supervision and his extraordinary wish to 'take his own turn at guard-
duty in the trenches every fourth night'.[34] Royal enthusiasm and amateur engineers were poor substitutes for skilled technicians, carpenters,
smiths, miners.[35] Yet the King's eye was surely practised enough to
recognize the limitations of Villars's defensive preparations. Owing to
the deficiencies of the fortifications there seemed every promise of success through determined attack: by artillery bombardment, by trench
and mine, by storm.

Two weeks after his arrival Henry had brought batteries to bear
upon the curtain and upon the bulwark on the besiegers' left that
looked towards the Thuringe wood on the mountainside above the
Seine. The latter battery consisted of four culverin positioned within
100 yards of their target—a reasonable distance for wall-pounding,
according to theorists of the day.[36] Its proximity provoked the garrison
to a powerful sortie in an attempt to spike the guns. The attempt failed.
A week later the English pioneers arrived and were promptly put to
work upon the St. Catherine's approaches, pushing trenches forward
to 'within a butt's length of the castle ditch'.[37] They were temporarily
transferred to the English encampment to reinforce defences there following a vigorous engagement one week before Essex's return. There
was some talk of renewing approaches towards the Cauchoise *quartier*,
but the King's decision remained firm. He had successfully besieged
Chartres by taking his approaches to within a yard of a massive earthen
bastion, which had then been sapped.[38] There was no reason to sup-

33. *ML*, vol. v, pp. 107–8.
34. According, at least, to Sully, p. 284.
35. cf. above, p. 148, note 5. Even Yorke was unwilling to be rated a captain
of pioneers after having been a captain of soldiers (PRO SP 78/26/191).
36. PRO SP 78/26/206; H. J. Webb, *Elizabethan Military Science: the books
and the practice* (London, 1965), p. 132. Strictly, the range in question was
stated by Yorke as 'v score', which may refer not to yards but to paces, perhaps
of five feet (the Roman *passus*) but perhaps of some other, lesser length,
such as the *passus simplex* (2 ft.): see Malynes, *Lex Mercatoria*, p. 52; cf. M.
Lewis, *Armada Guns* (London, 1961), p. 37.
37. Coningsby, pp. 51–2, 56.   38. HMC *Salis.*, vol. iv, p. 97.

pose that similar tactics would not eventually prevail at Rouen. Nor did
the English general's return, with fresh instructions indicating continued misgivings on Elizabeth's part, result in any alteration in the
line of attack. It did, however, produce intensified efforts on the part of
the besiegers, further stimulated by news that Parma was at last on
his way.

On 21 December, the day of Essex's third and last arrival at Dieppe,
Parma completed his preparations at Landrecies in Hainault and
crossed the frontier. Two days later Elizabeth warned her general
that if Henry should now seek to raise the siege in order to move against
the Spaniard, her army was to be withdrawn at once.[39] In accordance
with her instructions Essex reorganized the company distribution of
the men under his command,[40] and reviewed the situation. Six weeks'
effort had produced disappointing results; indeed, as Unton had written, in the Earl's absence from the siege things had gone 'backward
rather than forward'.[41] While the besiegers had gradually brought some
twenty pieces of field artillery into play, marksmanship was poor and
neither the angle nor the weight of fire gave much promise of a breach.
Moreover, Yorke and his fellow-engineers had been maladroit in their
direction of the trench works approaching the Thuringe bulwark.
They lacked depth, were too narrow, had too few redoubts, and followed so ill-chosen a line that enemy guns were able to fire along them
with devastating consequences.[42] Alive to every opportunity for counter-
measures, the defenders were advancing trenches of their own beyond
the glacis to intercept the besiegers' approaches. The weather, formerly
spring-like, had become extremely cold.[43] With the besiegers' wants increasing, disease spreading, Parma looming in the north, and the
Queen's impatience mounting with every augmentation of her invest-

---

39. PRO SP 78/26/280, 290; van der Essen, vol. v, p. 337.

40. They now consisted of 380 survivors from the original force, 336
pioneers and 638 new arrivals from Flushing (PRO SP 78/26/261). The
object of the redistribution was to economize, on pay, part of which was now to
be made in the form of victuals and clothing (PRO SP 78/26/282, 296); cf.
attempts to persuade Anhalt to accept in the form of cloth a proportion of the
pay due to the Germans (Unton, p. 170). In fact, the seven companies from
the Netherlands remained distinct, eight companies each consisting of ninety
men being formed from the remainder.

41. Unton, p. 183.

42. d'Aubigné, p. 253; Davila, pp. 263–4.

43. Devereux, p. 270; Zerotin, p. 74; Pierre de l'Estoile, *Mémoires-journaux*,
eds. G. Brunet, A. Champollion, etc., vol. v (1589–93) (Paris, 1878), p. 317.

ment in the campaign, it was plain that gradual and half-hearted measures would no longer do.

At the end of December Essex transferred most of his Netherlands veterans to the Charterhouse on the north side of St. Catherine's Mount.[44] Two days later, after a period of comparative respite during which the guns' elevation was improved by raising them upon cavaliers, the besiegers' battery recommenced with new vigour.[45] On the night of 3 January King and Earl joined forces in a drive upon the enemy counterscarp.[46] Once there, the English pressed forward into the ditch itself. Fierce resistance compelled a partial withdrawal, but only to an entrenched position in the immediate vicinity of the counterscarp and with occupation maintained of a bastile and casemate newly constructed by the defenders themselves. Gabions were raised; briefly it seemed that success was imminent, either through a final direct assault or through prompt mining operations. But the position was too lightly and incompetently manned. It was held for about twelve hours until, in Essex's temporary absence, a powerful sortie swept away the gabions and exposed the besiegers to missiles from above. While Baskerville distinguished himself by counter-attacking virtually single-handed, the English soldiers attempted a stand with their pikes,[47] found this impossible and took to their heels, seconded by their French supporters under Biron's son. In Unton's view this setback 'killeth our hope of Rouen'.

Essex himself was profoundly disappointed and discouraged. The Queen herself and friends of his own at Court were urging his return. To Burghley he confessed that 'I desire for private respects to be rid of this French action'.[48] It was Williams who contrived a second

44. Devereux, p. 270; Coningsby, pp. 63–4; BM Harleian 4762, fo. 125; PRO SP 78/27/308. It was at the Charterhouse that Henry V had sat to receive the surrender of Rouen (Hutchison, op. cit., p. 249).

45. Davila, p. 264; Valdory, p. 22ᵛ.

46. From the conflicting accounts of Coningsby (pp. 64–5); d'Aubigné (pp. 252–3); Davila (p. 264); Essex (Devereux, pp. 270–1); and Unton (pp. 233–4, 240), it seems clear that the order for this assault came from Henry who, for all his willingness to consult, never delegated his authority as commander-in-chief and determiner of tactics and strategy after he had arrived at Rouen. He may nevertheless have been prodded by Essex; and, while the French are unlikely to have yielded first place to the English in this, the first major assault of the siege, it was the latter who subsequently played the leading role. Carey's account (pp. 22–4) confuses a number of separate incidents.

47. cf. above, p. 89.

48. HMC *Salis.*, vol. iv, pp. 164, 166; Unton, pp. 211–12, 230; Devereux, pp. 271–2. Essex's current 'private' concerns included the Chancellorship of

chance.[49] Three days later he persuaded the King to authorize another assault by the English, not only to recover the lost ground but to scale the fort's walls in a single surge by means of ladders supplied by the French.[50] Diversions were arranged about the town. With Essex again participating in person the assault was made, the ditch gained, the ladders raised—and found to be too short by the length of a halberd. Nevertheless, the counterscarp was held, and reinforced despite strenuous attempts by missile and by sortie to dislodge the besiegers. Covered by heavy artillery fire, they set about sapping the wall.[51] And at this promising juncture Henry decided to depart, taking with him the German *reiters* with whom, after prolonged negotiations, he had at last reached agreement over pay. He left his infantry at the siege, and indeed sent more to join them. But the inexpert pioneers made slow progress there and were firmly repulsed once more in a sortie on 13 January. For Essex the game had gone cold. Five days later a letter to him from the Queen, secretly sent by Cecil to Unton, fell into the Earl's hands by chance. It was to have been delivered only if his own judgement and the arguments of others, including the King himself, should fail to persuade him finally to come away. In fact he had already resolved upon withdrawal, had delivered his army to Williams, had followed Henry to Gournay to take his leave, and now made for home, drawing his sword and kissing it in a theatrical gesture of farewell as he sailed from Dieppe, never to return.[52]

Among those who had urged him to depart was Mornay, currently at Dover awaiting fair winds for France. On 2 January he had arrived in England, sent by Henry to ask for a further 4,000 English troops. *En route* he had encountered Leighton, who had warned him that Elizabeth was determined upon Essex's return: a report confirmed by an earlier emissary of the King's whom Mornay met at Rye. By Mornay's account,[53] his own reception at Court was hostile and em-

---

Oxford University, granted by the Queen to Buckhurst despite the electors' preference for Essex (HMC *Salis.*, vol. iv, pp. 162, 165–6).

49. d'Aubigné, p. 253.

50. BM Harleian, 4762, fo. 125 (Henry to Essex, n.d., but evidently referring to these preparations).

51. Unton, p. 246; Valdory, p. 24ᵛ.

52. Unton, pp. 260, 263–4; *LM*, vol. iii, pp. 551-2; PRO SP 78/27/37. Williams subsequently complained that this delegated authority was insufficient to enable him to govern his men (PRO SP 78/27/234).

53. Mornay's instructions and his lengthy account of the mission are printed in *MM*, vol. v, pp. 129–37, 152–88.

barrassing. Elizabeth railed against Henry's time-wasting exercises, and berated the absent Essex for 'making the king believe that it was he who managed everything, but she would soon show him the contrary'. Successive representations provoked her to recurrent displays of bad temper. On 9 January Mornay believed that his arguments had at last procured 2,000 pikemen and 1,000 musketeers, but two hours later the Queen allegedly changed her mind. Further negotiations with Burghley, Howard, and Hunsdon revived his hopes, but at his final audience Elizabeth favoured him with no more than a further review of Henry's errors, his wastage of her troops, her own general's reckless conduct, and the pointlessness of England's aiding France by any means other than prayer. While Mornay, greatly injured, set off for France, Burghley persisted in asking for at least 1,000 pikemen. He had no better success.[54] The decision, as Mornay noted, was Elizabeth's, and she would not be moved.

Understandably, Mornay attributed his failure to the Queen's pique and the emotions excited in her by Essex; and to the Earl's return he attributed her agreement some six weeks later to send 1,600 fresh soldiers after all.[55] Yet however feminine her manner of expressing it, Elizabeth's attitude did not lack reasonable grounds. In her political and strategic judgement there was still something to be said for countering likely Spanish occupation of French coastal towns with occupation of such towns on England's own account; and it was with action to that end in view that she sent her forces in March.[56] But there was far less to be said for what England stood to gain at this critical time from an open-ended commitment of scarce resources to aid so prodigal and dubious an ally as the French king. There was discouraging evidence of jaundiced attitudes towards him on the part of leading Frenchmen. Quite apart from the League, Nevers was openly dissident, Soissons resentful of the failure of his suit to marry the King's sister, Épernon unco-operative to the point of sending Elizabeth information prejudicial to his sovereign's requests.[57] Moreover, she had direct evidence of Henry's personal unreliability and impetuousness. He himself had ac-

54. PRO SP 78/27/77.

55. *MM*, vol. v, pp. 187–8; PRO SP 78/27/188; cf. Unton, p. 340.

56. For the intention of using them to seize a coastal town, probably Le Havre, PRO SP 78/27/272. Exactly one month elapsed from their ordering by the Privy Council to their arrival at Dieppe (*APC*, vol. xxii (1591–2), pp. 256–7; PRO SP 78/27/236; cf. Elizabeth's arguments, PRO SP 78/27/115).

57. *LM*, vol. iii, pp. 546, 588, 594; Unton, pp. 252–5, 223, 309; PRO SP 78/27/77, cf. 234.

knowledged in his envoy's instructions the inadequacy of his forces at
the siege, and so had implicitly conceded that the reports of his earlier
representatives had been gravely misleading and that doubts regarding
the seriousness of his intentions towards Rouen had been well
founded.[58] Now he brushed past miscalculations aside with the practical argument that Parma was in France and would reach Rouen before his own French supporters could arrive there. If what he said was
true—and if those Frenchmen meant to come at all—Elizabeth could
fairly argue the practical impossibility of raising, equipping, and dis-
patching an English force within the time available.

And indeed time had become for Henry a matter of acute concern.
He must have time to gather his forces: the voluntary supporters awaiting his summons elsewhere in France, the aid that was promised from
the Provinces, the reinforcements for which he still hoped from
England. But Parma must not be allowed time to pursue his mission
in friendly places close to the frontier, and to develop a deliberate
campaign. 'I fear nothing,' wrote Williams to Essex, 'but that the Duke
of Parma will shun fighting in all he can, persuading himself in time
the King will be forced to break with wants. If anything persuades him
to fight it must be for the safeguard of Rouen, the which is in some
want already both of victuals and munition, but no nearer to be forced
than when your lordship departed.'[59] So while Henry led his horsemen
to observe and harry the enemy and to retire before him in a venture-
some exhibition of cavalry tactics, contrary to the expectations of
interested observers he did not 'relax my grip on Rouen'.[60] At the siege
activity mounted, now about the town itself and upon the river as well
as against the fort. With Essex gone and most of the remaining English
lodged at Biron's insistence in the vicinity of St. Catherine's, the
French took their chance against the Cauchoise *quartier*. Trenches
were dug, the gate battered, a narrow breach made, and ladders raised
against the walls. The attempt was beaten off; others were essayed, by
bombardment upon the St. Hilaire gate now heavily lined with earth,
by sapping under the walls at the Martainville and Beauvoisin *quartiers*.
Such random activity, poorly co-ordinated and ill-prepared, did not
result in lasting material advances. Yet Villars's resources were severely
strained. As his losses through sortie and skirmish increased, so did

58. PRO SP 78/27/19.
59. PRO SP 78/27/180; cf. above, p. 39.
60. CSP Venetian (1592–1603), no. 8; *MM*, vol. v, p. 149; *LM*, vol. iii, pp.
564–5, 568.

complaints within the town—and with them, clamour for Mayenne's promised relief.[61]

On 5 February the Spanish and League relieving army entered Normandy near Aumale, with Henry in close attendance. On the same day the effort upon St. Catherine's was intensified. Again the besiegers won through to the ditch under the Thuringe bulwark. Supported by a furious artillery bombardment, sapping with pick and shovel was put in hand under a section of the bulwark which the defenders had lately heightened in order to counteract the improved elevation of the besiegers' guns. Villars was alarmed. While diversionary activity raged about the town he warned that no one should sortie without his express permission, and drew all available men into the fort to reinforce the threatened bulwark and to repel imminent assault. After a fortnight's labour beneath its foundations the besiegers were satisfied that the bulwark now rested upon the props and stanchions which they had inserted, and would collapse when these were burned. Soldiers were mustered; the mine was sprung. A portion of the wall subsided, but the whole remained entire. There was a further bombardment and an attempt to scale the weakened wall, in which a few besiegers gained the rampart only to be thrown back. That night work on the mine was resumed, and preparations were made to blow it with gunpowder. The garrison overheard movements below the bulwark; flares were thrown down and by chance ignited the powder trail. The mine exploded. A section of the bulwark collapsed. It took with it many of the guard. It also fell upon those who were completing the mine and upon the assault party. Shock and confusion were so great that by the time the besiegers had gathered their wits the defenders had plugged the breach with faggots, turves, and sacks filled with earth and dung, and had cleared the enemy by sortie from the immediate approaches.[62]

For Villars it had been a narrow escape. A messenger arrived the next morning from Mayenne with advice that the relieving armies would be at Rouen within a week, but that the attentions of Henry's cavalry would force them to march slowly and to camp each night with elaborate care.[63] Informed that the besiegers had other mines and other assault plans in readiness, the governor could not afford to wait, even if he so chose.[64] He resolved upon a massive sortie, planned for the

61. cf. below, p. 179. 62. Davila, pp. 268–9; Valdory, pp. 38–40.
63. ADSM PRS (Ligue), entry for 20 February 1592; cf. de Thou, vol. xi, p. 468 (vol. v, p. 118), and below, p. 178.
64. cf. Parma's view of Villars, below, p. 179; also, Davila's view (p. 283) that

small hours of 26 February. Foot-soldiers supported by cavalry made a disciplined attack upon the trenches before the Thuringe bulwark and upon the principal encampment at Darnétal. Five guns were captured outright, others spiked, battery emplacements demolished, munition dumps exploded, siege-engines destroyed, and heavy losses inflicted on the besiegers, Biron himself being wounded in the leg. The material damage constituted a grave setback to a siege conducted throughout with inadequate means. More damaging still was the effect upon the besiegers' morale. Their thrust of the preceding weeks, the best-sustained effort of the siege, had been nullified at the hands of a garrison generally supposed to have grown steadily weaker and more demoralized.[65] Efforts against the fort at last gave way to serious approaches upon the town—and in particular upon the Cauchoise *quartier*. Yet the English remained about St. Catherine's to be joined there in April by their fresh contingent, who arrived in time to witness the closing stages of the siege.

News of the sortie gave Parma and Mayenne reason not to proceed for the time being with their relieving march. Instead, a party of infantry was sent to reinforce the garrison.[66] These had little difficulty in entering the town by the Beauvoisin gate in broad daylight and without loss. But Rouen was thus burdened with more mouths to feed at a time when shortage was becoming acute and measures were at last taking effect upon the river. Women and non-combatants were ejected from the town in increasing numbers; and anxiety among the Rouennais grew with the collapse of the Cauchoise wall. For them, Mayenne's reiteration that he would come 'as soon as I hear that the king of Navarre has renewed your siege'[67] seemed as hollow as Villars's own gesture of holding a tournament outside the Martainville gate to demonstrate his *insouciance*.[68] *Te Deums* sung in the cathedral beneath the exhibited trophies of war could not obscure the renewed intensity of the siege; and with the King's Council's 'resolution to batter

---

Villars was determined to drive away the besiegers unaided if he could, without having to rely upon external assistance.

65. In verbal exchanges between sentries on both sides immediately before this 'unhappy accident' (Unton, p. 333), Villars had taken care to foster that supposition (Valdory, p. 43; La Londe, 'Mémoires', partly printed in d'Estaintot, pp. 233–5).

66. Valdory, p. 49ᵛ; ADSM PRS (Ligue), entry for 9 March 1592; cf. below, p. 180.

67. ADSM PRS (Ligue), entry for 18 March 1592.

68. de Thou, vol. xi, p. 476 (vol. v, p. 124); Davila, p. 287; Valdory, p. 52.

Rouen',[69] Villars's position became daily less tenable. Pressed by the *parlement* he agreed to send a messenger to warn Mayenne that no more than a month's further resistance could be guaranteed.[70] The next weeks were marked outside the walls by extensive approach works about St. Gervais, where a heavily fortified battery had at last been mounted and was maintained in defiance of attempts at dislodgement. Within the walls they were marked by growing unrest, perhaps fomented by fifth-columnists, and culminating in the riot of 16 April. But for the besiegers it was all too late. Three days later the relieving Dukes arrived. Henry's forces withdrew, with defiant fusillades and in good order, towards Pont de l'Arche. The next day Mayenne entered the town. To all intents and purposes, the siege of Rouen was over.

The affair had borne every appearance of ludicrous mismanagement. As a feature of the western European war, it had been extravagant of men, money, and materials at a time when Henry and his allies could ill afford wastage of any. As an exercise in siegecraft, it had been characterized by a host of elementary errors. In besieging any place capable of more than rudimentary resistance, the need for advance provision of labourers and relevant equipment to execute preliminary works was axiomatic among theoreticians and experienced soldiers alike. Yorke had outlined these requirements to the English government well before the army left for France with a siege specifically in view. Those concerned were likewise fully aware of the need for means to implement a blockade, and especially to control the river. But weeks, indeed months, elapsed before such means were provided even to a moderate degree, and still more time before they were effectively applied. In terms of tactics at the siege, the weak points of Rouen's defences were identified at the outset but were not subjected to concentrated attack until too late. Co-ordination between the various units of the besieging army was generally poor. It was well enough contrived on 11 November, as it had been before Gournay; and the ground gained in Essex's last assault and in the attack of 5 February demonstrated the value as well as the short-term feasibility of co-ordinating operations about fort and town. But over the long term attacks were random so that, with rare exceptions, Villars was able to deal with

69. Unton, p. 379; for the general strategic significance of this resolution, cf. below, p. 173.

70. ADSM PRS (Ligue), entry for 18 March 1592; Davila, p. 288; de Thou, vol. xi, p. 477 (vol. v, p. 124).

each one either before or as it materialized, by means of small-scale
counter-measures without committing his limited resources to the full.
He was able as well to maintain communications and to move troops
between fort and town as occasion arose, owing to the besiegers' failure
to occupy and hold the intervening terrain.[71]

As distinct from mismanagement, technical insufficiency was an
important factor in the besiegers' failure. Extensive reliance was placed
on artillery bombardment, the results of which were extremely disappointing. Evidently the standard of gunnery was very low. Observers
regularly wrote of day-long bombardments that did no damage, of gunners who could not hit a ravelin and had instead to fire at random into
the town. But poor gunnery alone does not explain why hastily thrown-
up earthen walls subjected to regular artillery fire over a period of
several months were insufficiently weakened to collapse when mined.
What the besiegers needed for battering fort or town was heavy guns
capable of 'tormenting, shaking, and overthrowing all'. Guns of longer
range but throwing lighter shot 'make only their hole, and so hide
themselves in the wall or rampart'.[72] In all likelihood, too few of the
former were available at the siege. The battery noted by Yorke in
November as having been planted within 100 yards of the flank of the
Thuringe bulwark consisted of four culverin.[73] He also noted the availability of eighteen 'cannons' at that time, but these may well have
been of the perier type, throwing only half the weight of shot of full
cannon. Yet the seven fully-furnished field pieces sent by Elizabeth,
from the Tower and from Guernsey well before the commencement of
the siege, included two seven-inch cannon each throwing 43½-lb. iron
round shot, as well as three demi-cannon each throwing 30½-lb. shot
and two culverin each throwing 17-lb. shot.[74] Despite the extraordinary delay in bringing them to Rouen, from mid-December the
besiegers could have deployed these and a score of other field pieces as
well within 'point-blank' range as defined by the theorists.[75] Powder
was in short supply: and, as Beauvoir remarked, guns without powder

71. cf. above, p. 152.
72. Sir Richard Hawkins, quoted in M. Lewis, op. cit., p. 190.
73. See above, p. 155.
74. I have calculated these average shot from Constable's and Bedwell's statements of artillery and munitions supplied (PRO SP 12/239/131; SP 78/26/156.
My figures for cannon and demi-cannon differ slightly from Lewis's (op. cit.,
pp. 19–21). Elizabeth invested artillery, with furnishings, powder and shot, to
the value of over £2,500 in the siege before it began.
75. See Webb, op. cit., pp. 131–8.

'are bodies without spirit'.[76] Even so, the ineffectiveness of contemporary artillery, especially against earthworks, was amply demonstrated at the siege of Rouen. By contrast, harquebuse fire was markedly more effective. Observers recorded many instances of accurate sharpshooting, by the Rouennais on the day of the besiegers' arrival and by both sides during the siege itself. Yet even the technical expert Yorke saw continued relevance in bows, for 'they be natural weapons and therefore need no training'.[77]

At the very outset of this abortive siege Burghley advised Essex to 'devise how some letters might be written into Rouen' to spread news that Parma could not come, that the Pope was dead, that Aragon had risen against Philip of Spain. 'This kind of devices,' he believed, 'might percase do as much good as a battery, if it be well used.'[78] So indeed it proved. The besiegers resorted continually to subterfuge without obtaining decisive results. In December a would-be spy, Anthony Portman, introduced himself first to Cecil and then to Unton with an offer to enter Rouen where, thanks to his father, he had useful contacts.[79] Henry already had a servant of his own inside the town, enjoying Villars's confidence and encouraging the King to think that 'this lad is not so great an enemy of mine as he would seem' and would prefer to deal with him than with the Spaniards.[80] In the same month, when Soissons and the indefatigable conspirator du Raulet presented themselves at the Old Palace, trusting to assurances that it would be delivered into their hands, the former narrowly escaped and the latter was captured.[81] Later the King allegedly took steps to bribe defending captains in order to procure Villars's death, with no better results.[82] Then, as now, undercover agents promised more than they delivered. For all these efforts the siege dragged on, far outlasting food supplies.

During the first month meat was available in reasonable quantities, and officers at least could dine quite lavishly. But by December the lack was becoming plaintfully evident of 'an English victualler after the old manner'. Through lack of food, Englishmen, it was claimed, were dying at the rate of a dozen a day; and a full day's hazardous journey was

76. PRO SP 78/26/186.

77. PRO SP 78/26/133. On contemporary controversy over the relative merits of bows and guns, see J. R. Hale's introductory chapter to Sir John Smythe, *Certain Discourses Military* (New York, 1964), pp. xli–lv.

78. HMC *Salis.*, vol. iv, p. 151.

79. PRO SP 78/26/244; Unton, p. 206.

80. *LM*, vol. iii, pp. 527–8.   81. Valdory, p. 21.

82. See above, p. 146.

necessary for carts to reach even possible sources of supply.[83] To some extent such reports were exaggerated for the benefit of the English government. As late as mid-January the Bohemian volunteer Charles de Zerotin could write from Henry's camp that 'victuals are abundant and at a reasonable price; it is amazing that so many men should not have exhausted the country long since; but it seems that the more that is consumed, the more is produced'. By March, however, 'there is very little left, and that little is outrageously costly'.[84] Meanwhile disease set in; 'plague' and a 'pestilent ague' termed 'kampe' ravaged 'this infectious place'. Endeavours, alarming to the English government, were made, to control infection by conveying sick men in unknown numbers from Rouen to Dieppe and thence to England.[85] And as conditions worsened and physical corruption spread, the spirit and manner of the engagement became brutalized. At first, chivalry and good humour were evident, in Essex's challenge to Villars, matched by the Chevalier Picard and by another 'brave fellow in crimson velvet' on the Rouennais's side; in courteous exchanges of corpses between the combatants; in pranks such as that of the English heralds in making a French counterpart so drunk that he needed no blindfold when returning from their camp. But by the end of December a captured Englishman could find himself dragged on his face into the town to have cannon balls dropped on his stomach; while by April the besiegers were cast as rapists, blinders of peasants and tearers out of their tongues. Well might Coningsby write of the 'corruption of these wars'.[86]

So those veterans of siege warfare in France and the Netherlands—Biron, Williams, Baskerville, Henry himself—manoeuvred miserably about a town divided within itself and suspect in its defences. And yet all insisted that Rouen was eminently takeable, must shortly fall, could not but fall. If their failure stemmed partly from mismanagement and material lacks, there was a further explanation. In Essex's judgement that explanation was plain: 'the expecting of the Duke of Parma makes the King afraid to do anything'.[87] This was to call into question not Henry's physical courage—no one doubted that—but his strategic thinking. Until the King's arrival, Essex and Biron, building upon their fruitful partnership before Gournay, had shown themselves capable of

83. Coningsby, pp. 36–7; PRO SP 78/26/133; Unton, p. 180.
84. Zerotin, pp. 71–3.
85. Coningsby, pp. 58, 60; PRO SP 78/26/161.
86. Coningsby, pp. 35, 61; Valdory, pp. 23, 65v.
87. Devereux, pp. 271–2.

selecting and pressing forward the most promising line of attack. After his coming, the besiegers' main effort was concentrated on the fort—mistakenly, as it seemed. To Unton, Henry protested his determination to take Rouen, and explained his unwillingness to batter the town in terms of his need to conciliate Catholic opinion within his Council. To Elizabeth he insisted, through Mornay, that Rouen was his principal aim and that he had no intention of voluntarily engaging Parma in battle. But these protestations were disingenuous. In his letters to his own French supporters Henry consistently presented a very different order of priorities. To them, his insistence was always upon his eager expectation of a decisive battle.[88] And in April he admitted to the Queen's special envoy Thomas Wilkes that such an engagement with Parma had always been his main concern, and that Rouen was ancillary to it.

Mystified by so many conflicting reports and assessments from the siege, Elizabeth had sent the experienced Wilkes specifically in order to ascertain why the affair had been so prolonged. To the points he raised Henry at last made frank replies.[89] He no longer argued that his siege of Noyon, allegedly the cause of delay at the very outset of the campaign, had been undertaken simply to disguise the attempt on Rouen. Now the King declared 'the siege of Noyon to have been of great necessity for the preservation of Picardy, which he accounted to be of far more importance than Rouen'.[90] With St. Quentin, Chauny, and other towns, it constituted an essential impediment to Parma's coming. It was the Queen who had 'constrained' him 'to hasten himself to the siege of Rouen, which he then undertook (though accompanied with many difficulties) only to satisfy her Majesty's desire'. Indeed, he 'never had any liking to attempt the siege of Rouen, but was overruled therein by his Council'. He 'never had any hope of good success of that siege till now'. His present optimism sprang from his conviction 'that if he have the victory of the battle the gates of Rouen will be opened to him'. It was in order to bring about a battle with Parma that 'he determineth not to move from the siege'. Moreover, Henry now spoke boldly of the Queen's dependence on him, 'and wished that he had such a fool as her Majesty had of him to make wars against the

88. Unton, p. 379; *MM*, vol. v, p. 167; *LM*, vol. iii, pp. 521 sqq.
89. For Wilkes's instructions and his report, PRO SP 78/27/248, 251, 285.
90. cf. Turenne's account that Picardy was far more seriously 'infected by the League' than was Normandy (PRO SP 78/26/347–9); and for the later significance of Noyon, below, p. 194.

King of Spain'.[91] The message was unmistakable. It was Parma, not Rouen, that dominated Henry's thinking and had determined his tactics at the siege. In August 1590, as Henry had waited outside Paris for the Spanish general, Grimeston had noted: 'The King doth wish his coming and as it seemeth feareth him not much.'[92] Now, with Parma on his way once more, Henry awaited him no less expectantly.

91. cf. HMC *Salis.*, vol. iv, pp. 185–6.
92. HMC *Finch*, vol. i, p. 32.

CHAPTER NINE

PARMA

'To succour those gentlemen and towns aligned with the Holy League and to bring about the raising of the siege of Paris ... is a resolution worthy of your Majesty's greatness.'[1] So much had Parma conceded to King Philip shortly before his departure for France in August 1590. When the King pronounced, his servants did wisely to respond with compliments. Parma had reserved his compliments for the more moderate features of Philip's resolution. Painstakingly, gloomily, he had explained how it placed him on the horns of an impossible dilemma. If he should leave for France, the Netherlands might well be lost. If he should not leave, the cause of the League might become irremediable. But it was quite beyond his means to take a strong enough army into France and at the same time to leave behind a strong enough army to beat off the challenge of the Provinces and their associates. There were insufficient soldiers, insufficient reserves of money, insufficient supplies.[2] Four months later, with his excursion over, his presentiments seemed to have been confirmed. The League had indeed been succoured and the siege of Paris raised, but the cost, realistically assessed, was surely unacceptable. It was not only that Maurice of Nassau had seized his chance to drive south into Brabant; that the policies of Parma's deputy Mansfeld had been both inconsistent with his principal's and inept in themselves;[3] that discontent was rife at every level of society in the tax-burdened, war-torn southern Netherlands; and that the situation in France had all too clearly shown how far the military survival of the League depended upon Spanish aid. Most unacceptable of all, in Parma's judgement, was the spread of indiscipline, mutiny, and desertion in the Spanish army. Shrunken in numbers, demoralized, unpaid, with even its core of Spanish veterans

1. AGR CS vol. 21, fo. 188. Parma's second French expedition is described at length in van der Essen, vol. v, pp. 323–55. My own interpretation differs from his both in general and in particular respects; I have used other material as indicated in the footnotes. For help with Parma's meandering Spanish prose I am much obliged to Dr. K. R. Andrews.

2. AGR CS vol. 21, fos. 187–96.

3. Lefèvre, vol. iii, pp. 550–2.

infected, that multi-racial body could hardly be relied on to discharge even a defensive role. It was above all in quest of funds to rehabilitate the army that, immediately after his return to Brussels, Parma sent to Spain a personal representative, the son of Philip's secretary Don Juan de Idiáquez, one of the few remaining men whom the King could bring himself to trust.[4]

In the past there had been good reason to respect Parma's judgement. With his expertise in military and in political craft, he had shaped a policy that had been vindicated by achievement. In addition to mastery of broad strategic principles, grasp of technical and logistical detail and tactical flair, Parma had shown sharp sensitivity to the weaknesses and divisions so prevalent among his opponents in the Netherlands, noblemen and others. By his policy, the threat and actuality of military pressure had been maintained while his adversaries' frailties were exploited through bribery and intrigue. In principle, such a policy seemed precisely what was now needed to further Spanish interests in France. But by 1591 the most significant of Parma's achievements lay in the past. His career had reached its zenith in 1585, with his recapture of Antwerp. Although there had been further gains during the next two years, upon the Meuse and at Sluys, his great reconquering drive of the early 1580s—a drive that had owed far more to his personal dynamism than to any northward redirection of Spain's augmented strength[5]—had lost its momentum. Parma's achievements were fading. His adversaries had closed their ranks. None realized better than he that his political fortunes were in decline. They could

4. van der Essen, vol. v, pp. 308–14. Successor to the traitor Antonio Pérez as secretary to Philip's council of state and one of the celebrated *Junta de Noche* at the heart of the Spanish administration, Idiáquez was broadly in sympathy with Parma's view that Spain should concentrate on the Netherlands rather than on France. But his opinion was in effect neutralised by the contrary view taken by Cristóbal de Moura, the Portuguese member of the *Junta*. For Idiáquez's career, see F. Pérez R. Minguez, *Don Juan de Idiáquez, embajador y consejero de Felipe II* (San Sebastian, 1934).

5. According to Dr. Geoffrey Parker's calculations ('Spain, her enemies and the Revolt of the Netherlands, 1559–1648', *Past and Present*, no. 49 (1970), pp. 88–90), annual receipts of money from Spain by the Military Treasury of the Spanish Netherlands had averaged nearly 7,000,000 florins (£700,000 sterling) between 1572 and 1575, but only approximately 4,000,000 florins from 1578 to 1585. In the decade from 1585 these receipts averaged approximately 11·36 million florins, mostly spent on French causes, which absorbed 3,000,000 of almost 4,000,000 florins received by the Treasury between August 1590 and May 1591—evidently without satisfying Parma's needs.

be restored only through his army's revival and the refurbishing of his military image. Such a restoration required money, supplies, time to prepare a fresh campaign. It also required immense energy: and Parma's health was in decline as well. Weakened by gout, by hydropsy, and by other ailments symptomatic of cardiac disorder, he was no longer the commanding figure whose qualities had formerly inspired his troops and merited the respect of his master.

It was unlikely that Philip would alter his plans in deference to the young Idiáquez's report of Parma's predicament. It was doubtful that he could furnish adequate means to execute those plans. In the meantime the governor-general had to find means of his own to counter Prince Maurice's spring offensive. With his forces in no condition to pursue the latter deep into Gelderland in order to arrest his progress northwards, Parma stationed them upon the Waal with a view to diverting the enemy towards the south. Maurice responded with disconcerting eagerness. His approach coincided with Idiáquez's return, bringing funds and peremptory orders from Philip that Parma must leave for France with the minimum of delay. At least this gave him an excuse for withdrawing from the Waal.[6] But however skilful that withdrawal, it was scarcely calculated to enhance his military reputation at this crucial time. It meant that he must leave for France in the aftermath of fresh setbacks, on a mission that was inherently unattractive to him. In the Netherlands he was governor-general, subject to distant direction from the Escurial but otherwise formally in control of affairs and in a position to manage his own recovery. In France it was Mayenne who headed the League and bore the formal title of lieutenant-general of the kingdom. There, too, others of Philip's accredited agents would correspond independently with the King, would receive instructions from him, and would interpret those instructions as they saw fit in relation to tactics of their own devising. As Parma had reason to know, the meddling of such as these could be damaging enough to him even in the Netherlands. On foreign soil, mingled with the machinations of Philip's other allies, it could be ruinous. Philip might believe that with Parma present in France his self-appointed role as arbiter of that kingdom would be decisively reinforced. For the Duke himself, his presence there was far more likely to damage beyond repair his own hopes of recovering his reputation.

He delayed his departure for over four months. The previous year, when Philip had ordered him to take 20,000 men into France, he had

6. van der Essen, vol. v, pp. 319–22.

insisted that 30,000 would be needed. Now his estimated figure rose to 40,000, of whom one quarter must be cavalry. Philip had sent funds, but not enough. If his commands were to be obeyed, Parma must have 400,000 gold *écus*, and an additional sum to cover outstanding debts.[7] In August he was at Spa, seeking to restore his health. In September, at Brussels, he learned that Maurice of Nassau had taken Hulst and so threatened Flanders itself. It was no consolation that six weeks later Maurice was back on the Waal, for there Nijmegen fell to him. Not until the end of November did Parma leave Brussels for Valenciennes to review the army of some 16,000 mustered there for France under *maestre del campo* Idiáquez. Recruitment and preparations were still not complete. Parma returned once more to Brussels, to exchange courtesies with the Imperial ambassadors on their futile errand of arbitration in the Netherlands.[8] A week later he was at Landrecies; and at last, on 22 December, he made his long-overdue rendezvous with Mayenne at Guise. Ill-health and lack of conviction, as well as the need to deal with dissent in the Netherlands and to organize his garrisons and army of occupation there, were responsible for his procrastination. It had provoked Philip to repeated reminders in his own hand of the urgency of the case.[9] And yet, the delay was not entirely disadvantageous.

It had been widely believed that Parma would be back in France before the close of the campaigning season of 1591. He had himself, the previous November, promised to the citizens of Paris his prompt return with a powerful army. In April Mayenne had been assuring his

7. Lefèvre, vol. iii, pp. 512, 588–9; cf. van der Essen, vol. v, pp. 279, 333. By Don Diego de Ibarra's account the Spanish paymaster-general had available at the outset of the French campaign only 258,000 *écus*, of which 100,000 were advanced to Mayenne and a further 120,000 already earmarked for one month's pay for Parma's army (*ML*, vol. v, p. 56). That gold was specified is noteworthy; on the inflationary effects of Spanish silver currency upon France at this time, and reaction to it, see F. C. Spooner, *L'Économie Mondiale et les Frappes Monétaires en France, 1493–1680* (Paris, 1956), pp. 175–6. Moreover, comparison of statements concerning funds actually at Parma's disposal with estimates of funds made available to him by Philip provokes huge misgivings regarding the efficiency of Spain's financial administration and the reliability of its officials; cf. above, note 5.

8. Their coming had long been presaged; for Burghley's efforts to forearm the Provinces against their arguments, see, for example, BM Cotton Galba D VIII, fos. 204–6. On 29 November Turenne reported to Nevers that Parma had been arrested in Brussels on Philip's orders (BN AFF 3619, fo. 103). For Alonzo de Idiáquez's office, BN AFF 3981, fo. 23.

9. Lefèvre, vol. iii, pp. 584, 590–1, 598–9.

supporters that that return was imminent.[10] King Henry, whose own winter negotiations had been governed by that same belief, had stationed himself at Noyon in July in full expectation of combating Parma on the direct route from Brussels through Landrecies to Paris. The season passed and Parma did not come. By the time of his arrival Henry had gone reluctantly to Rouen, his Germans wasted, his French supporters scattered in different provinces. Parma, it seemed, was free either to dominate Picardy as he might choose, or even to exploit at leisure the fact of his military presence within the French frontiers as a means of gaining the desired political settlement without having to strike a blow in action. As Philip's ambassador Don Diego de Ibarra had advised the Duke at Landrecies, 'he should halt at the first camp . . . for simply through seeing the entry of your Majesty's armies into this kingdom, the French will be left in no doubt of the safety of Rouen nor of all the other advantages which they can expect from them'.[11]

Parma saw matters differently. Poised at last to leave for France, he had indicated to Philip in a long letter from Landrecies some predisposition to take positive military measures. He stressed that the case of Rouen was important. It might possibly be relieved by sea, but 'if the Béarnais[12] should batter the town it seems that we should have to succour it . . . for to let such a town as Rouen be lost before our eyes would be a bad business. And on the other hand, to do battle, which is likely if the Béarnais should wish it, is no more than we can desire in order to succour that town.' By contrast, Parma was reserved on the question of the succession to the French throne. He affirmed that he would do his duty, that discussions would be put in train, and that he had taken a liking to the young Duke of Guise. But he derived no encouragement either from the League's manifest weakness or from the judgement and recent conduct of the young Duke's uncle Mayenne. Between nephew and uncle there was no love lost; yet it was upon the attitude of the latter that everything ultimately would depend. Once in France, Parma immediately pressed on from Guise to La Fère. He had sent ahead 500 infantry to garrison that town, believing that its use would be allowed him by the League leaders as a base of operations and a place of retreat.[13] But Mayenne demurred. As Ibarra was quick to

10. *CM*, vol. i, pp. 45–6; vol. ii, pp. 141–4.   11. *ML*, vol. v, p. 46.
12. i.e. Henry IV. The relevant portion of Parma's letter is printed in *MM*, vol. v, pp. 110–21; cf. Lefèvre, vol. iii, p. 613.
13. Lefèvre, vol. iii, p. 613.

perceive, this was a significant point: if the Duke was genuinely in favour of the Infanta's candidature for the throne itself, why should he object to the occupation of one town by Spanish forces?[14] And in the discussions for which, failing pressure from Henry, there was opportunity enough during Parma's first weeks in France, his long-standing doubts and Ibarra's new ones were amply confirmed.

Faithful to their royal instructions the Spanish negotiators, Ibarra and the Burgundian president of Artois, Jean de Richardot, came quickly to the central issue. The Estates-General must be convened as soon as possible. They were aware that if that assembly should prove unwilling to elect the Infanta, Philip might consider one of a number of alternative candidates: a son of the Emperor's, the Duke of Guise, though on no account any member of the house of Bourbon.[15] But for the time being prospective candidatures were not negotiable, for nothing could be decided until the Estates-General should meet. A quite contrary view was taken by the Burgundian Jeannin, representing Mayenne, and Claude de La Châtre, a former ambassador to England for Henry III and now representing Guise's interests. While their range of possible candidates for the throne was not wholly at variance with Philip's,[16] they were adamant that the Spanish must first reach agreement severally with the princes and governors of the realm, each of whom would want some tangible recompense for his support. In the French view, the meeting of the Estates-General was a secondary issue. Moreover, there were important general matters to be settled before that meeting could take place: the amount of financial and military aid to be guaranteed by Spain for the Infanta's government, the question of her marriage, the matter of reserving for Frenchmen key offices within her realm. As session succeeded session, the Spanish diplomats and Parma stressed that they could conclude no agreements upon such matters without authority from Philip. In the meantime Parma tried to put the Infanta's case to the several princes of the house of Lorraine who were present at La Fère. He met with a blank reception. The gulf between the negotiating parties seemed unbridgeable; and clear evi-

14. *ML*, vol. v, p. 55.
15. Lefèvre, vol. iv, p. 10. Philip's refusal to countenance the claim of any Bourbon prince amounted to a rejection of proposals stemming from moderates of the so-called 'Third Party' which, as he was informed in 1591, aimed either to force Catholicity upon Henry 'or, if he should refuse, to crown another, Catholic member of the house of Bourbon' (de Croze, vol. ii, pp. 210–11).
16. cf. *VM*, p. 179.

dence was emerging that Mayenne was ready to treat with King Henry
if he were disappointed by Spain. 'The French,' recorded Ibarra in
despair, 'are more concerned for their own profit than any other race I
have ever known.' And far from having his faith confirmed in the
persuasive influence of the army's presence, he now found an explanation and some excuse for French attitudes in the fact that 'after
so many months of delay, and so many promises by your Majesty and
your ministers of putting a powerful army into this kingdom ... that
which has come is so weak and so poorly equipped that even
the relief of Rouen is too risky for it, owing to the danger of a
battle'.[17]

But with his long experience of the relation between military and
political effects, Parma interpreted that fact differently. It confirmed
his existing view that the situation called for positive military action.
Continuing the talks, he sidled westwards through Picardy, away from
the frontier that daily attracted deserters from his army, and with his
conviction growing that to gain the whip hand in negotiations he must
somehow demonstrate afresh the military power of Spain. The opportunity for such a demonstration lay at Rouen. In order to take it he
must first contrive a working arrangement with the French. With the
connivance of the Spanish diplomats, he agreed to recommend to
Philip that Spain should provide the Infanta, once elected queen, with
an army of 20,000 infantry and 5,000 cavalry, and an additional subsidy
of 100,000 *écus* a month for one year. Referring these extravagant
proposals to his King, Parma was careful to hint at the possibility of
settling for considerably less.[18] But on this provisional basis he was
free to concentrate French attention and his own upon the immediate
situation. At Nesle he held a council of war, 'in which took part these
princes and many French gentlemen and all the chief ministers and
those responsible for the war who serve here in your Majesty's army'.
The proposal was made to set about the relief of Rouen forthwith. Parma
was anxious that Philip should believe this proposal to have stemmed
from Mayenne, and that the ensuing plan to approach Rouen via
Neufchâtel represented a corporate decision. Yet he did not deny that
it was entirely in harmony with his own opinion: for although 'I knew
we were having by degrees to take increasing risks, we had to decide to

17. *ML*, vol. v, pp. 50–63: quotation, p. 56; N. Garnier, *Le Président
Jeannin* (Dijon, 1913), pp. 491–5; cf. van der Essen, vol. v, pp. 337–40.
18. The letter is printed in *ML*, vol. v, pp. 63–70, and in *MM*, vol. v, pp.
137–47; cf. PRO SP 78/27/320.

come to grips with the enemy since all the other methods that could be attempted seemed to me of very little profit'.[19]

Even so, that method was extremely hazardous. Intelligence indicated that fresh forces were hastening to join the enemy, whose superiority in cavalry presented a continual and fundamental problem. By contrast, the strength of Parma's own army was rapidly diminishing. According to the muster held at Nesle on 16 January it stood at 13,546 infantry and 4,061 cavalry. But the army's weakness and disorganization were greater than those numbers implied. Only 3 of the 5 regiments of Walloon infantry, each in 12 companies totalling 1,300 men, could be accounted at full strength. The 52 companies of Spanish infantry averaged only 85 men apiece; the 15 Italian companies, only 66. Of the 3 regiments of German infantry, the first was declared to consist of 2,633 men, but 'nevertheless by the certain report that one has there are in this regiment only 1,300 soldiers'; in the second, reportedly 2,407 strong, 'I estimate that there are only 1,250 soldiers'; and as for the third, while 1,700 men passed muster many were known to be in Champagne and elsewhere, so that a mere 450 men were actually present. There were 29 companies of light horse and hargulutiers of various nationalities; and a further 9 cornets of *reiters*, paid accordingly but in fact amounting to no more than 1,500 horse. One expected source of reinforcement, the army led by the Duke of Montemarciano and funded by the Pope, had earlier been deterred by Henry's manoeuvres from entering the kingdom, had since run into difficulties with its paymaster, and was now reduced in terms of cavalry to a mere 500. Comparable difficulties faced Parma himself: pay due to his army in accordance with its reported company strength on 16 January amounted to 157,392 *écus*.[20]

In these circumstances, speed was essential; and the prospect of action might do something to restore the fading morale of soldiers who, as every commander knew, 'are never better than when they are

19. AGR CS vol. 24, fos. 92–3; cf. van der Essen, vol. v, p. 340. From his subsequent conduct it is abundantly clear that Mayenne was far from eager for Parma to relieve Rouen or otherwise to establish a military ascendancy in France.

20. BN AFF 3981, fos. 23–5; *ML*, vol. v, p. 57; cf. above, note 7 and p. 121. By 23 February Parma's army contained fewer than ten thousand effectives (van der Essen, vol. v, p. 341). Pope Innocent IX had died on 30 December 1591; his successor, Clement VII, was to show himself resistant to Spanish tutelage.

busiest'.[21] But there was much to prevent a rapid march directly upon
Rouen. Such an approach was barred by Gournay, an obstacle earlier
experienced by Essex and since turned by him to the royalists' advantage. Moreover, apart from 'the roads being so bad and broken up
that it was impossible for the waggons and especially the artillery to
travel by them ... one of the greatest difficulties to be faced was that
of food, for ensuring which it was necessary to secure the rear, and so
absolutely necessary to take the said Neufchâtel, by which means we
could get assistance from Amiens, Abbeville and all the valley of
Aumale'.[22] As Parma moved from Nesle the citizens of Amiens, who
had prepared 300,000 loaves for his army the previous month, sent him
a present of a cask of Bordeaux wine.[23] It helped fortify his belief in
that region's ability to furnish a month's supply of victuals. So he
marshalled the army westwards, in the same close and protective formation as he had employed upon his earlier retreat from Paris.[24] It was
the formation of a commander moving through hostile territory and
expecting attack from enemy forces. That expectation was well founded.
On 3 February Parma arrived at Poix. On that day Henry awaited him
at Aumale, with 7,000 cavalry.

If intelligence regarding his opponent's strength had added to
Parma's anxieties, it was partly faulty information that had brought
Henry to Aumale. In some respects, the intelligence that reached him
was very full. Captured couriers, intercepted letters, agents busy at
the camp as Parma debated interminably with the League leaders—all
these kept Henry apprised of the dispute over La Fère, of the Spanish
preference for Guise over Mayenne, even of the alternatives discussed at
the council of war. But while the nature of Parma's problems was no
secret, the details of his movements, present and prospective, remained
vague. Such vagueness was potentially disastrous to the King. It had
already destroyed his timing of his summons to his French supporters,
as well as the remaining impact of his appeals to the English government for fresh assistance. Three days before the enemy rendezvous at
Guise, Henry had issued his summons in the belief that Parma and his

21. Biron's view (HMC *Salis.*, vol. iv, p. 149).
22. AGR CS vol. 24, fo. 92ᵛ.
23. A. Dubois (ed.), *La Ligue: Documents relatifs à la Picardie d'après les registres de l'échevinage d'Amiens* (Amiens, 1859), p. 77.
24. See above, p. 9. The explanation for the slowness of Parma's progress in France lies in political and logistic factors rather than in the formation itself, with which he had made much better speed in the autumn of 1590; cf. Oman, *Art of War*, p. 516.

army had already advanced beyond Ham. Conversely, on the very day
of that rendezvous, Burghley was advising Unton that Parma was back
in Brussels. Again, on 3 January Henry had analysed the situation and
had concluded—correctly, in the event—that Parma would make for
Amiens. But within six days startling news that the enemy was in fact
approaching Beauvais drew the King towards the forces he had stationed at Gournay in readiness to apply a check. There, ten days
later, he learned that his adversary had yet to move from Nesle.[25] All
this gave him good reason to indulge his taste for cavalry activity in
personally conducted exercises of reconnaissance. Without precise information it would be pointless to pursue a strategy that embraced
co-ordinating developments at the siege with timely concentration of
his own forces and with the enemy's approach.

By 3 February he had already had two lively engagements with
advance parties of mounted Leaguers, and had ascertained the direction of Parma's own advance. It remained possible that the enemy
might proceed towards Dieppe, and necessary to observe the strength
and disposition of their main army. To prevent the former, the King
deployed most of his accompanying cavalry along a line from Auffay
through Neufchâtel to Blangy-sur-Bresle, thus balancing the defensive
screen he had already laid about Gournay. He himself meant to accomplish the latter from Aumale, with the assistance of a few hundred
light horse. But he also had in mind an ambitious tactical plan: to use
cavalry offensively as a means of harrying and disrupting Parma's careful progress, and simultaneously to step up the pressure upon Rouen
as a means of drawing him on.[26] On 5 February the attack upon St.
Catherine's was intensified. On that day Henry momentarily over-
played his hand. From an eminence east of the Bresle which Parma
must cross by the bridge of Aumale, the King observed his enemies'
combined armies, estimated at some 16,000 foot and 5,000 horse,
marching to the music of drums and trumpets, with the general himself
plainly visible, seated in a carriage at the centre of the battle, unarmed
and wearing slippers on his gouty feet. Henry laid an ambush of hargulutiers in concealed and elevated positions about the entrance to
Aumale. He himself rode forward with the object of attracting the
enemy light horse towards them. The ambushers had positioned themselves badly, and fired to poor effect. Hotly pursued, Henry shep-
herded his men across the bridge and was himself shot in the loins. He

25. Unton, pp. 203–6, 225–8, 253; *LM*, vol. iii, pp. 529–30, 542–5, 549–50.
26. cf. Zerotin, p. 74.

was carried to safety at Dieppe. Within ten days he had recovered sufficiently to sit his horse. But in the meantime Parma pressed on to Neufchâtel and took it despite its augmented garrison, while his associates crowed over the King's discomfiture.[27]

Yet Parma was in no mood to exult. What Henry intended seemed obvious: 'to await us near Rouen at a strong point of vantage so as to impede our reinforcement and, in the event of a battle, to avail himself of his artillery, his numerous cavalry and the superior position'. The Duke was no stranger to the ploy of enticing opponents towards a prepared position, which resembled his own manoeuvre upon the Waal the previous year. In principle there were several possible counters: to outflank the enemy, to confuse his preparations by delaying tactics, to respond with unexpected speed, as Prince Maurice, indeed, had done. In practice Parma had no choice. Casts from the new base at Neufchâtel disclosed that royalist cavalry were out in force, to right and left of the road to Rouen. The approach via the sea-coast was potentially a trap which Henry could easily close from inland. Owing to the effects of the long siege and of recent scorched-earth tactics by the enemy, burning possible camp locations and remaining sources of supply, there could be no question of covering the remaining distance at leisure. Owing to the effects of rain, snow, and frost, the roads were impassable to the baggage-train. Parma sent most of it back to Abbeville, and got ready for an unencumbered dash to Rouen. The exact state of affairs there was kept from him by Mayenne, who refused to communicate the contents of messages reaching him from the besieged town. Parma sent an emissary of his own to Villars, who reported that the governor's need was only for money and powder. But Villars was not to be trusted. In Parma's view he might at any moment strike a bargain with Henry, or even with the English. No more was Mayenne reliable, torn between willingness to present himself at Rouen as the bringer of much-promised aid and unwillingness to let Parma be seen

27. Propagandist reports of this famous combat at Aumale were published by both sides. de Thou's account is extremely slender (vol. xi, pp. 466–7 (vol. v, pp. 117–18)), d'Aubigné's confused (pp. 258–61), although the latter was an eye-witness according to Davila's detailed narrative (pp. 275–9). Unton had accompanied the King to Aumale but was not on the scene (pp. 285–6)—unlike Sully, whose account characteristically inflates his own role (pp. 301–6). On the use of hargulutiers to 'address an ambush', cf. *Discourse*, p. 34: their commander 'will also cause all or the most of those hargulutiers to [a]light, then place and hide themselves in such sort that 100 shot will spoil and defend ten times more than themselves'.

in that role. There was still some reinsurance against the risk of failure
to be got from letting Philip believe that it was the League leader who
pressed for the town's relief. But the real risk lay in allowing time for
the French parties to settle their several differences with their King
before the boost of some military advantage had been won for Spain.
In that event Parma, with Rouen lost 'before his eyes', would be left
in the ruins of his mission and his reputation. On 26 February, finally
dismissing all divergent counsel, he and his army set out rapidly for
the town.[28]

No sooner had he moved than the situation was transformed. A
Rouen gentleman arrived with the news of Villars's successful sortie.
The besiegers had retired and were disbanding; the town was saved
by its own exertions; there was no need of Parma. When he retorted
'that we should go on to finish what had been begun', Mayenne and
his companions loudly and unanimously protested the contrary, arguing that considerations of safety and supply were now paramount.
Political consideration notwithstanding, these were powerful arguments
to a general of Parma's temperament and experience. Reluctantly he
turned back, to Neufchâtel and thence beyond the Somme, to Pont
de Remy. While Mayenne covertly dispatched his own explanations
and fresh assurances to Rouen, Parma sent there a detachment of 650
Walloon and French soldiers with fresh supplies of powder and a
generous bill of exchange, 'so that I should not fail to do everything
that was humanly possible'.[29] As he once again expostulated to Philip,
without greater means, without reinforcements—perhaps from Brittany, from the Netherlands?—he could do no more. If any were to
reach him it could only be by sea. He set siege to Rue, to gain control
of access to the Somme and its friendly towns. The English observers
Yorke and Williams expressed alarm: was it not likely that Spanish
attentions were to be transferred to England after all?[30] But Parma
could contemplate no such ambitions; and in fact it was for Henry's

28. AGR CS vol. 24, fos. 93v–99; ADSM PRS (Ligue), entries for 19–20
February 1592; Davila, p. 283; cf. de Thou, vol. xi, pp. 469–70 (vol. v, p. 119).
cf. Henry's self-declared resolution to press the siege without battering Rouen
and 'to take the town by assault before their very eyes' (LM, vol. iii, p. 568).

29. AGR CS vol. 24, fos. 99–101; ADSM PRS (Ligue), entries for 3, 6 March
1592. It is noteworthy that Villars chose to inform the municipal Council both
that they owed this advance to his representations and that it had come not
simply from Parma but from 'messieurs les princes', collectively (RD vol. 21,
fo. 46).

30. PRO SP 78/27/194, 234; cf. above, p. 159.

benefit, not for his, that troops were arriving from the Low Countries, 'very brave in their gold lace, it will shortly discolour'.[31] With these and the long-sought English recruits the King could at last consider himself his enemy's equal in infantry.[32] And as Parma deliberated before Rue, his hopes of a military advantage grown shadowy, his prospects of a political success grew more shadowy still. The risk he had anticipated at Neufchâtel was indeed materializing. The same men who had negotiated with the Spanish diplomats in January on behalf of the League leaders were now pursuing negotiations elsewhere. Claude de La Châtre was arriving at Henry's camp to suggest terms of settlement which, untrustworthy though they might seem, included the significant proposal 'that the Leaguers offer to chase out the Spaniards and to conclude this peace without comprehending them in it'.[33] And on 2 March Jeannin was urging Villeroy to reopen his discussions with Mornay, and was indicating the possibility of 'breaking with the Spaniards . . . when we are assured of the conversion of the king of Navarre, that is to say when he gives secret assurance of it, allowing that he will need time to take instruction and to announce his conversion publicly'.[34]

For Henry, these overtures constituted an important advance on earlier demands that he summarily renounce his religion. Moderates urged him to seize his chance and respond favourably: it would make him, after all, 'not a superstitious or hypocritical idolater, a Turk, a Jew nor a Moor', but one of the majority of Christian believers. But the King replied that while he could be content in time to be converted, he could not allow himself to be constrained. Moreover, there was business in hand at Rouen that could not be finished until Parma was out of the kingdom.[35] Convinced that his earlier strategy was more relevant than ever, Henry renewed the siege.[36] Developments were swift— swifter than he had anticipated. On 12 March a section of the Cauchoise wall collapsed.[37] Six days later Villars agreed under pressure to appeal without qualification to the Dukes. For Parma, there was again

31. Unton, p. 349.   32. *LM*, vol. iii, p. 574.   33. Unton, p. 361.
34. *MM*, vol. v, p. 210; *VM*, p. 181.
35. Garnier, op. cit., pp. 497–8; *LM*, vol. iii, p. 594.
36. cf. Norris's view that Parma had retired only to obtain reinforcements, and that 'rather than Rouen shall be taken he will venture the extremity of his fortune and hasten the trial of a battle, which shall be either sooner or later as he shall be informed of the necessity of the besieged' (BM Cotton Caligula E VI, fo. 369: misdated).
37. Valdory, p. 50ᵛ; cf. Davila, p. 288.

only one possible response, however inclined Mayenne and his fellow-princes might be to linger over their double game, so rich in possibilities regarding the succession and their particular interests. Reassuring letters were sent back to the Rouennais, Parma giving the bearer separate instructions to impress upon them that he himself was motivated only by concern for their common faith.[38] He raised the siege of Rue. He settled with the Swiss infantry of Montemarciano's unpaid and discontented papal force. While Mayenne was considering a more circuitous route, Parma reformed the army, forded the Somme,[39] and, from the south bank, covered the distance to Rouen in six days. The speed of his return took Henry disastrously by surprise.

As before, spies and intercepted letters had advised the King accurately of his enemies' general intentions, inaccurately of their precise movements and strength. In the aftermath of the events of February he had licensed many of his supporters to leave his camp. Voluntary supporters and their accompanying forces must be husbanded. Without them he could not hope to match Parma in strength. But as long as they would hold themselves ready to rejoin him when the crisis came, there was no reason to exhaust their energies and purses, their stomachs and their tempers, at such a siege as that of Rouen. At the end of March he was advising them in good faith that Mayenne had appointed a rendezvous for 8 April at Montdidier, well to the east of Gournay and eighty miles from the objective. On 2 April a spy of Unton's brought intelligence direct from the enemy camp that it would take Parma five weeks to reach the besiegers. Sixteen days later Henry was visiting a sick de Chatte at Dieppe.[40] Hardly had he returned to Rouen than astonishing news arrived from Turenne, commanding mounted patrols along the road to Neufchâtel. Parma, Mayenne, Guise, and their combined armies were no more than a few miles away, brushing aside through lavish use of light cavalry the trivial obstacles put by Turenne in their path. There was barely time for Henry to raise his siege and retire south-eastwards towards Pont de l'Arche and Les Andelys. His miscalculation was complete. Not merely had Parma contrived both to relieve Rouen and to avoid the long-planned battle, but his army was far stronger than Henry had supposed. Even with his recent reinforcements, the King, with 12,000

38. ADSM PRS (Ligue), entry for 4 April 1592.
39. Unton, p. 392; Davila, p. 290.
40. *LM*, vol. iii, pp. 598–9; Unton, p. 404; cf. Zerotin, p. 75; PRO SP 78/27/305.

infantry, was still no better than his enemies' equal in that respect, and
was now the weaker in cavalry owing to the leave he had granted his
reserves.[41]

Henry's disaster seemed total. The victuals laboriously garnered for
his last effort before Rouen were now the enemy's to enjoy. His recent
recruits were already deserting, his remaining men 'suffering all manner of wants'. Parma appeared poised to destroy him, and then to
establish control over the entire coast of Normandy north of the Seine.
News was arriving from Brittany that the Infanta's claim to that duchy
had been laid before the provincial Estates meeting, significantly, at
Vannes on the south-western coast. The King was faced with the loss
of 'his own throne and the loss of [Dieppe] and all the places hereabouts'; England, with the very reality of the cross-Channel threat
from Spain that Elizabeth had schemed to prevent. Parma's suddenly-
won advantage, coupled with news brought by a Lynn privateer from
the Iberian coast 'of the great preparation of Spain for France', sig-
nalled that Philip might be closer than ever before to mastery over the
whole of western Europe. As Burghley believed, upon what should
next transpire 'dependeth the safety of our state and of the whole
Christian world'.[42]

But at Rouen it was the Duke of Guise, not Philip's general, who was
the first to inspect the fortifications upon St. Catherine's and to make
his entry into the town, through the Martainville gate. It was the
Duke of Aumale who moved warmly among the Rouennais, congratu-
lating them on their resistance. It was the Duke of Mayenne, lodged
with his army at Bois-Guillaume, whom the town's dignitaries went
first to welcome. While the French dukes attended the mass of thanks-
giving conducted by the Cardinal of Piacenza in Nôtre Dame, the
Duke of Parma was not there. His triumph was appropriated by the
princes of Lorraine who, with Villars, robbed him of more besides.
After the mass, the governor consulted with Parma, stationed with his
troops at Croisset. That evening Mayenne dined him at his camp.[43]
Conference took place. Parma and his military advisers declared that
'while [Henry] was so weak we could hardly hope for a more convenient time nor a better opportunity to bring about his destruction'.[44]
But Mayenne insisted otherwise and remained adamant in his view

41. *LM*, vol. iii, pp. 616–17; Unton, p. 413; Davila, p. 290.
42. Unton, pp. 415, 370, 432; PRO SP 78/27/315, 328.
43. Valdory, pp. 68–9; Sommménil, p. 10.
44. AGR CS vol. 24, fo. 178[v].

during the next few days, as the opportunity slipped away. Instead of immediately destroying Henry in battle, Caudebec must be recovered and the river reopened to Le Havre. This would complete the relief of Rouen and would facilitate supply and reinforcement. Tactically it did not seem an unreasonable view. The relieving army could not subsist at Rouen in present circumstances; and Henry might well decline to do battle and might retire south of the Seine, drawing the Catholic armies after him to their peril. Strategically it was absurd. To force such a retirement would in itself constitute a political victory of the first importance for the League and Spain,[45] and would simplify the task of mastering north-western France. But Parma deferred to the judgement and local knowledge of the French.[46] On his earlier approach in February he had himself entertained the possibility of taking Caudebec and noted the need to keep an attentive eye upon Villars.[47] Always heedful of logistical considerations, rarely a seeker after full-scale engagements, he allowed himself to be persuaded westwards along the river.

By doing so he surrendered his advantage instead of capitalizing on it, and delivered himself anew into Henry's hands. The King had no intention of retiring. He had reassembled his forces at Gouy and stationed them in battle formation upon high ground. Reinforcements were coming in, chiefly horsemen; while his infantry strength grew slowly to about 13,000, by the end of the month his cavalry were nearing 7,000 with still more *en route* towards him.[48] Five days after his withdrawal he was marching back past Rouen towards Fontaine-le-bourg, with the intention less of pursuing Parma than of intercepting him if he should seek to return via Neufchâtel. On the march news arrived of what had happened at Caudebec. Parma's army had come under fire from the Provinces' ships upon the river. The fire had been returned with interest, damaging several vessels of the flotilla and wrecking its commander's. Caudebec itself seemed scarcely more formidable; with its elementary fortifications of walls flanked by towers, 'the place', as Williams had written six months earlier, 'is nothing by reason of the hills'.[49] But as he placed his battery above the town,

45. cf. the advice given to Henry by his supporter Givry in August 1589: 'Who will believe you King of France when he sees that your ordinances are issued from Limoges?' (P. de Vaissière, *Henry IV*, p. 334).
46. Davila, p. 294; de Thou, vol. xi, pp. 478–9 (vol. v, p. 125).
47. AGR CS vol. 24, fos. 97, 99.
48. Davila's figures of 17,000 foot and 7,000–8,000 horse are excessive (p. 297); cf. *LM*, vol. iii, pp. 616–19; Unton, p. 419; PRO SP 78/27/353.
49. HMC *Salis.*, vol. iv, p. 148.

having scrupulously covered his rear with entrenchments, Parma was hit by a harquebuse ball which, fired from the east tower, entered his right arm below the elbow and lodged above the wrist. The wound did not seem serious. He continued to supervise the battery, saw the east wall breached, heard the garrison commander sound the *chamade*, and prodigally allowed him, together with his 300 infantry and 1,500 horse, to depart in arms.[50] Then the general surrendered himself to his surgeons. Weakened by his chronic illnesses, the exertions of the campaign, and loss of blood, he succumbed to fever. Mayenne was left in general charge of the combined armies.

It was too great a test for the Duke's uncertain authority. 'All consists in the Chief', as Williams had written;[51] without Parma the Spanish army came close to mutiny, and quarrels mounted between the disunited French.[52] In these circumstances there could be little question of prolonging the campaign in the field. From his sickbed Parma intervened to recommend retirement *en masse* to Lillebonne, where supplies could be got from Le Havre and assistance or withdrawal contrived by water. It was a view consistent with the strategic principle for which he had argued in February at Neufchâtel, of always maintaining concentration of forces.[53] But as before, Mayenne disagreed, and advocated withdrawal inland towards Yvetot. Again the tactician was disputing with the strategist, and not entirely without reason. At Lillebonne, where the estuary broadened and enemy shipping lurked, the Catholic forces might well be trapped, with all exits blocked, to be starved or beaten by Henry at his discretion. But among the woods, hills, streams, and friendly villages of the *pays de Caux*, where many noblemen had been insulted by the activities of Groulart's *chambre du domaine*,[54] it would be easier to outmanoeuvre the King, to deny him the opportunity of a battle, and eventually to withdraw overland. Mayenne won his point. In the last week of April the Spanish and League forces were en-

50. Somménil, p. 16; cf. the Gournay terms of composition, above, p. 120. With their numerically-inadequate forces, all contemporary commanders who concentrated on capturing towns, castles or other territorial strongpoints—in principle, the main strategic alternative to destroying the enemy's forces—were faced with the problem of how to retain control without alienating opinion and without having to leave in their wake for garrison-duty soldiers whom they could ill spare.

51. *Discourse*, p. 1.

52. AGR CS vol. 24, fo. 179.

53. de Thou, vol. xi, p. 469 (vol. v, p. 119).

54. See above, p. 132.

camping before Yvetot, strung out behind trenches from Louvetot
through Auzebosc to St. Clair, with Parma on the right, Mayenne in
the centre and Guise on the left.[55] The position was well enough chosen
in respect of terrain and natural cover, though scarcely tenable in the
long term by a depleted army low in morale and in supplies. As Parma
recorded in dejection, munitions were running low, horses dying
through lack of forage, men through disease spread by lack of other
drink than foul water.[56] And by now Henry was in close attendance.

From Fontaine-le-bourg he had proceeded due west, his appetite
for battle restored. Reconnaissance was poor, contact between the
various units of his heterogeneous army imperfectly maintained in the
broken country. Yet his march took him directly towards his enemies'
left. A series of disorganized skirmishes ensued until, on 28 April, a
determined royalist attack overran Guise's outposts, surprised him and
Mayenne at dinner, captured their silverware and drove them into
Yvetot. They re-formed around Auzebosc, but their position was now
gravely weakened. In effect Henry had fought his way through their
left wing, and now commanded the higher ground. He established his
camp at Valliquerville and quartered himself in the local castle, an-
cestral home of the family of Evreux. Sending to Dieppe for picks,
shovels, and wine recently taken from a Scottish prize, he meanwhile
planted artillery at Bouquelone, overlooking the enemy camp. The
danger was plain. Under Parma's desperately revived direction, the
League forces fell back to Louvetot and the relative safety of prepared
defences there. But the position was cramped. To gain room a counter-
attack was essayed upon Bosc-Himont, in co-ordination with a diversionary move upon Valliquerville. It was beaten off by the contingent
of Provinces' soldiers, who impressed observers with their 'discipline,
such as was never seen in France'.[57] A week had passed since the affair
at St. Clair. A further week was spent in fierce skirmishing. As
Mayenne had predicted, it proved possible to avoid pitched battle;
nevertheless, Parma had progressively to give ground. The camp at
Louvetot became untenable. Early on the morning of 12 May, under
cover of darkness, mist, and a screen of cavalry energetically led by his
son Ranuccio, he silently removed his entire army to Caudebec.[58]

55. Somménil, pp. 22–6.
56. AGR CS vol. 24, fo. 180.
57. C. Groulart, *Mémoires*, p. 558.
58. *LM*, vol. iii, pp. 616–28; Somménil, pp. 28–70. Unton (p. 434) and Davila
(p. 302) indicate 11 and 16 May respectively. An anonymous ms. 'Discours de

It seemed that he was caught inextricably, cut off by Montpensier to the west, by Turenne to the east and by the river to the south. Williams, however, thought otherwise. In his judgement, Parma's successful withdrawal from Louvetot destroyed all hope of forcing a decision, and indeed marked the end of the campaign. 'Touching her Majesty's forces under my charge,' he wrote from Yvetot, 'I see no reason but we should all be revoked until the King were forced to battle, which cannot be at this voyage of the Duke of Parma.' Mist had turned to heavy rain; for the royalists, movement of men and especially of guns was barely possible over the churned ground. While Parma could look for supplies to be ferried him by Villars from the south bank, Henry could only appeal yet again to the 'exhausted' town of Dieppe. But above all, the enemy were preparing 'to pass the river at Caudebec'. Although 'many is of an opinion that it is impossible for them to make it', the English at least had been aware for several days that 'They are making a bridge at Caudebec with boats, which is almost finished'.[59] As had been often enough demonstrated in the past, such a feat was well within the capacity of Parma and his engineers, breadth of waters and tempestuous weather notwithstanding. Barges and pontoons had already been brought downstream from Rouen, the merchants demanding payment for them in advance. At either end of the pontoon bridge ravelins were thrown up and equipped with guns to keep enemy shipping at bay. But if Parma saw in the possibility of naval attack his greatest remaining danger, the erstwhile besiegers were as incapable as ever of dominating the river. Whether detained by weather or deterred by earlier misadventures, no ships appeared during the days needed by Parma to carry out his operation. Owing to wind and rough water the army's crossing, made after all in the barges rather than over the bridge, could not be effected in one night and one day as he had hoped. But covered by gunfire and a sally led by Ranuccio against the approaching royalists,

---

ce qui s'est passé entre les armées du Roy et de la Ligue à Yvetot en avril 1592', dated 1 May 1592 at the camp of Valliquerville (BN Collection Moreau 745, fos. 223–4ᵛ) agrees substantially with the foregoing accounts, noting in particular the valiant service of Williams and the Flemish, and Parma's refusal to be drawn into battle even on 'the feast of St. James, whom the Spaniards hold for their patron.'

59. PRO SP 78/27/367, 350; *MM*, vol. v, p. 336; Unton, p. 430. cf. Davila (pp. 304–5), d'Aubigné (p. 268), Sully (pp. 314–15), etc.: according to the chroniclers and memorialists Parma's departure took Henry completely by surprise—a view echoed by all subsequent historians.

the manoeuvre was eventually completed without loss.[60]

Watching his enemies' escape, impotent to prevent it, Henry spoke hopefully of hurrying back to Pont de l'Arche and intercepting their retreat along the south bank. Parma was alive to such a move: in that event 'we could go to Dreux and then to Orleans, if it should be necessary'. There were some among his companions who favoured such a plan in any event, or even a march to Brittany. But for Parma these were last resorts: infinitely better if the King should delay sufficiently at Caudebec to allow time for the Catholic armies to make for Paris, recross the Seine and reach refuge at Château-Thierry on the Marne. For once, Mayenne was in full agreement.[61] In fact, the royalists were in no condition to take purposeful counter-measures. They hesitated at Caudebec; and when Henry eventually reached Pont St. Pierre, Parma was well on his way to Paris. On Easter Sunday Ranuccio and Guise dined within the capital, while Parma himself remained in the suburbs. The next day he continued his march to Château-Thierry, his army having allegedly outraged dwellers in the environs of Paris with 'innumerable murders, brigandages and extortions'.[62] But at least he had saved most of his men, and could claim to have added the relief of Rouen to his earlier relief of the French capital. Now he wrung a last concession from Mayenne, and reported to Philip in self-exculpatory but sombre terms:

in spite of the fact that absolutely everyone thinks this time inappropriate on account of the decline of the Catholic party and the weak state we find ourselves in at present, nevertheless, not to neglect to do our utmost, knowing that your Majesty as well as the Pope want the meeting of the Estates to be held as soon as possible, and how willing they are to protract matters here for their own ends, pressure has been so put upon him that the Duke of Mayenne has decided to call them to Soissons for 20 June.

Even so, Parma warned that

if the principal matter is negotiated when we are not superior to the enemy, some resolution prejudicial to the service of God, the Church and your Majesty too could result from the said meeting, for it is clear that these French are weary of these delays and our disorders, irritated at our

60. AGR CS vol. 24, fos. 180–2ᵛ. cf. Unton, p. 435; van der Essen, vol. v, pp. 353–4.
61. AGR CS vol. 24, fos. 181ᵛ–2.
62. L'Estoile, *Mémoires-journaux*, vol. v., p. 169.

weakness, wretchedness and poverty, and already lacking confidence in
our ability to liberate them.[63]

The warning was well founded. In mid-June Parma once again
crossed the Netherlands frontier, promising that he would shortly return with a powerful army and leaving behind him a detachment of
Walloons as an earnest of his intentions. As before, hostile propagan-
dists denounced and satirized his mission.[64] As before, alarming news
for the royalists was arriving from Brittany, and Henry was preparing a
fresh embassy to the English queen.[65] But the situation had taken its
decisive turn. It was not in June but in January of 1593 that the Estates-
General met. It was not the Infanta's but Henry's claim to the French
throne that was sustained. This was the outcome of the Rouen
campaign.

63. AGR CS vol. 24, fos. 187ᵛ–8.
64. *ML*, vol. v, pp. 145–51.
65. Unton, p. 469; *LM*, vol. iii, pp. 637–8; G. Groen van Prinsterer, *Archives
ou correspondance inédite de la maison d'Orange-Nassau*, Ser. ii, vol. i
(Utrecht, 1857), pp. 191–2.

CHAPTER TEN

THE SIGNIFICANCE OF THE ROUEN CAMPAIGN

THE significance of the Rouen campaign varied from individual to individual among those who had participated in it in their several ways. For the English war-profiteer Otwell Smyth it formed part of services rendered to the French king for which he was eventually rewarded with a seven-year grant of exclusive rights to import lead into Normandy and Picardy.[1] For Essex 'the French journey cost my lord above £14,000 out of his own purse besides his friends and followers', bringing his expenditure 'in her Majesty's service' by 1592 to at least £35,000.[2] His attempts during that summer to prevent 'my pawns and bonds to lie forfeited' were poorly seconded by the Cecils;[3] and his impression that they had dealt underhandedly with him during his absence in Normandy stimulated the hostility that developed between his faction and theirs in the course of the subsequent decade. For Villars his success in retaining control at Rouen culminated two years later in a final settlement with Henry which included the governor's formal recognition as *amiral* of Normandy. Incarvile was conspicuous in arranging that settlement, and had already received for his own efforts on Henry's behalf the office of *contrôleur-général des finances*.[4]

1. ADSM Série C, no. 1233 (registre), fos. 114v–16.
2. LD vol. ii, fo. 84. The figure, estimated by his steward Meyrick, does not include 'gifts to poor soldiers', 'intelligence' charges, personal maintenance and other such items.
3. W. Murdin, *A Collection of State Papers relating to affairs in the reign of Queen Elizabeth* (London, 1759), pp. 655–7.
4. BN AFF 4019, fo. 282; d'Estaintot, p. 322; G. G. Butler (ed.), *The Edmondes Papers* (London, 1913), pp. 118–19. The *contrôleur-général des finances* had emerged in the mid-sixteenth century as the chief bureaucratic member of the French financial administration, with unique responsibility for inspecting all warrants of receipt or issue though without formally participating in policy-making. The office declined in status and significance between 1573 and 1594; but following the death in October 1594 of the much criticized *surintendant* François d'O (see above, p. 109, direction of French financial affairs was entrusted to a council of nine members assisted by two *contrôleurs-généraux des finances*, of whom Incarvile was one. In 1596 Incarvile as

For Parma the wound he received at Caudebec shattered his precarious health and led to his death within the year.

Parma's wounding was one among many occasions when chance intervened directly in the Rouen campaign. Accident governed crucial incidents at the siege, such as the shortness of assailants' ladders or the igniting of their mines. Indeed, at every stage of its development the campaign can be seen as an affair of contingencies, unpredictable and uncontrollable by those involved, despite their diligence in reviewing its possibilities. For all their diplomatic and strategic planning, none of the principals had initially intended portentous engagements about the capital of Normandy. The immediate outcome of the campaign, with its abortive siege, wastage of resources, and indecisive military action, seemed to have baffled the calculations of Elizabeth, Henry, and Philip alike. Yet the reasons for their particular decisions at particular times are understandable enough. Moreover, in the context of historical analysis those decisions constitute contingency factors in themselves. Beyond tracing the interaction of such factors, judgements by historians on the merits or otherwise of decisions and those who made them are in a sense presumptions, abuses of the inscrutable logic of contingency. Nevertheless, beneath the superstructural interplay of individuals and incidents a deeper significance is discernible in the Rouen campaign, and a basis for judgement upon those principally responsible for its development.

That basis lies in the nature and limitations of the early-modern state, which illuminate the campaign and are themselves illuminated by it. The state, it is arguable, was an uneasy, a corrupt—though the term is loaded—marriage of private with public interests. Arguably, the state embraced elements representative on the one hand of a 'feudal' and on the other of a 'capitalist' ethos, and also embraced profoundly divisive attitudes where functions such as warfare, manual labour, and many more besides were in each case the business of some distinct section of society, inevitably affecting others but rarely if ever involving all members of the state directly and *en masse*. Arguably, again, the state's stability and security depended on preventing imbalance: internal imbalance between factions, internal imbalance between the

---

contrôleur-général appears to have recovered for the office its former pre-eminence within the bureaucracy (H. de Jouvencel, *Le Contrôleur Général des Finances sous l'ancien régime* (Paris, 1901) pp. 29, 420; N. Valois (ed.), *Inventaire des arrêts du conseil d'état (règne de Henri IV)*, vol. i (Paris, 1886), pp. lxx–lxxi and *passim*).

centre and the provinces, external imbalance between itself and other states in terms of alliances and the distribution of power. Arguably, once more, the state was evolving within a European system where dynastic, ideological, and material concerns continued to transcend the frontiers of individual states and might conspire to undermine their sovereignty. Each of these considerations has found its place in historical writing concerning early–modern Europe. Each may be illustrated to a greater or lesser degree from the events of the Rouen campaign. But in relation to that campaign another consideration is evident, and more important than any of these. It is that the fragile state rested ultimately upon the relation between its twin sanctions of law and force: and that their fundamental if unformulated awareness of that relation conditioned the policies of rulers.

The prominence of these sanctions in the thinking of early–modern theorists who considered the nature of the state is familiar enough. For Machiavelli, 'the principal foundations that all States have ... are good laws and good arms'; and 'there cannot be good laws where there are not good arms'.[5] For Bodin, 'the first attribute of sovereignty', that 'principal foundation of every state' is 'to give law to all in general and each in particular'; but 'in matter of state it can be taken as a certain rule that he who is in control of the armed forces is master of the state'.[6] For Hobbes, 'Covenants without the Sword, are but Words'; and 'the bonds of words are too weak to bridle men's ambition, avarice, anger, and other Passions, without the fear of some coercive Power'.[7] Without law, the state declined into corruption, tyranny, or anarchy; but if force were lacking and its lack should become apparent, law was likely to prove impotent and the state would dissolve. Theorists might vary in the precision and consistency with which they interpreted these principles, and in the constructions which they placed upon them. Their actual formulations might escape the attention of rulers as the latter concerned themselves with the practice rather than with the theory of politics. Yet in the sphere of practical politics those principles nonetheless applied. For Elizabeth, lack of coercive power meant acute preoccupation with legal forms. For Henry, neither legal arguments concerning the validity of his hereditary title to the French throne nor acts of abjuration to improve his legal standing would suf-

5. N. Machiavelli, *The Prince*, trans. E. D. (London, 1640), pp. 91–2.

6. J. Bodin, *Les Six Livres de la République* (Paris, 1583), pp. 122, 222, 521.

7. T. Hobbes, *Leviathan* (Oxford, 1909), pp. 128, 105.

fice without a demonstration of his ability to support his claims with force more effectively than his rivals could support theirs. And for Philip, the force at his disposal, apparently superior to that commanded by any of his neighbours, authorized him in his role as arbiter of law in the states of western Europe.

If the conduct of these principals during the Rouen campaign is appraised in the light of this consideration, much that must otherwise be explained in terms of personal traits—parsimony and indecisiveness, inconsequentiality and opportunism, over-ambition verging upon megalomania—becomes explicable in more coherent and more rational terms. In Elizabeth's case, legalism dominated her thinking throughout her reign, attuning her mind to Burghley's, bringing discord to her relations with zealots such as Walsingham. In the aftermath of the Armada her policy took a more aggressive and forceful turn, and she then exhibited a keener and more far-sighted strategic sense than many of her critics would credit her with having possessed. But her concern for legal appearances remained strong, as was evident in her approach during the build-up to the Rouen campaign. The campaign went far to vindicate her fundamental distrust of force as an overt instrument for her policy, to highlight its implications for her state, and to undermine any belief that the obvious impediments to sustaining its unilateral exercise by England could be overcome through contriving its exercise in co-ordination with her allies.

In Henry's case, assertion of force did not mean piecemeal subjugation of particular portions of France—least of all, of Rouen on Elizabeth's terms. This essential preliminary to the reassertion of law meant the destruction, or at least the discrediting, of rival force as commanded by those who were principally in contention with him for mastery of the state itself. In the diffuse circumstances of late sixteenth-century French politics and warfare, where concentration of forces was rarely achieved and where combat was so often inconclusive, such an object was difficult to attain. But from 1590 there was no question as to who constituted the main rival contender. Henry could master the state only by overthrowing the reputation enjoyed and the impression created by Philip's army under Parma's command. Throughout the Rouen campaign the King held the removal of this external threat consistently in view, rating it far above alternative measures recommended from various quarters, and far above any need to deal directly with internal 'revolutionary' or 'secessionary' forces. When the deputies of the Estates-General at last assembled at Paris the relevance of his policy became plain.

Philip's own concern for law was extreme, a byword among his contemporaries, manifesting itself throughout his reign. Yet he had never doubted that however staunchly he might argue the legal merits of the Infanta's case its representation to the French could not succeed without the support of force. The outcome of the Rouen campaign was the effective removal of that support, and the consequent unresponsiveness of the Estates-General which he had been so anxious to see assembled. As the astute Villeroy observed, had the deputies assembled at Soissons as Parma had desired 'this kingdom would have become irreconcilable for ever'. Paris, 'further from the frontier and surrounded by towns and places held for the king', was chosen 'to the great displeasure of the Spaniards, who wanted the assembly held in a place where they could take advantage of the army they would bring in; and I believe that if the Duke of Parma, who died at that time, had lived, they would not have allowed the change which the other ministers of [Philip] could not prevent after his death'.[8] Nevertheless, on Philip's orders an army was brought in, under Count Charles van Mansfeld. It exhausted itself in besieging Noyon, and so accelerated the awareness that was spreading in Paris of Spanish impotence. This was the determining factor. Private and public manoeuvres continued: while Mayenne negotiated on his particular account at Soissons with Philip's representative the Duke of Feria, Henry had already announced from Chartres his willingness to receive instruction in the Catholic faith.[9] In May that willingness was reaffirmed at Suresnes, where Catholic representatives of the King conferred with delegates from the Estates.[10] Undoubtedly, Henry's were timely moves. Certainly they were eagerly debated by ecclesiastical dignitaries on either side. Yet he had always indicated that in religious matters he would be guided by advice and by an ecclesiastical council, and had not yet conceded the formal abjuration upon which the League had been insistent. In terms of law, the contest between him and the Infanta was still unresolved: he being debarred from the succession by heresy, apostasy, and excommunication, she by the Salic Law which, according to the arguments of Spanish legists and their supporters, was less

8. *VM*, pp. 201–2.

9. de Croze, vol. ii, pp. 226–7, 410–11; *ML*, vol. v, p. 282.

10. The conference is recounted at length by one of the delegates, de Thou, vol. xi, pp. 719–87 (vol. v, pp. 244–76).

fundamental an issue. But without the sanction of force, Spanish arguments no longer carried conviction.

Even as the conference at Suresnes proceeded, Feria was marshalling them before other delegates of the Estates, only to be greeted with loud criticism voiced by hitherto ardent Leaguers.[11] Still the Spaniards persisted. The summer weeks passed while the deputies heard the same series of propositions in respect of candidates and the same offers in respect of military and financial aid as had been mooted two years earlier during Parma's mission.[12] Those offers were not credited. On 28 June the *parlement* of Paris made its decisive intervention, reviewing the present situation and its own past pronouncements on Henry and on the religious issue. Legal and theoretical arguments abounded, as they had abounded for so long. But the members were powerfully swayed by the exhortations of *conseiller clerc* Guillaume du Vair,[13] whose leading argument turned on a practical point: Spain's weakness, her evident inability to settle the kingdom by means of force, and the emptiness of Philip's promises in that regard. As du Vair observed, all this had been amply revealed in the course of Parma's adventures at Paris and at Rouen. The *parlement* pronounced the Salic Law inviolable.[14] One month later Henry made his famous abjuration at St. Denis. Thereafter, magnates and office-holders, provinces and towns, rallied to the King;[15] and the settlement of the state gradually went forward.

The settlement owed far more than is usually recognized to military activity in general and to the Rouen campaign in particular.[16] But that

11. A. J. Bernard, *Procès-verbaux des États-généraux de 1593* (Paris, 1842), pp. 184–5.

12. A. G. Williams, 'The Abjuration of Henry of Navarre', *Journal of Modern History*, vol. v (1933), p. 169; cf. above, pp. 174–5. For the offers as reported in Brittany in May in connection with the Infanta's continuing claim to the duchy, *MM*, vol. v, p. 413.

13. Du Vair was sworn in to this office in 1584, and ten years later became a *maître des requêtes*—an office earlier held by his father (R. Radouant, *Guillaume du Vair* (Paris, s.a.), pp. 75–6, 386).

14. Guillaume du Vair, 'Suasion de l'arrest donné au parlement pour la manutention de la Loy Salique', *Actions et traictez oratoires*, ed. R. Radouant (Paris, 1911), pp. 110–44, especially pp. 112–13, 115–17, 136; cf. E. Maugis, *Histoire du Parlement de Paris*, vol. ii, pp. 103–20.

15. cf. R. Mousnier, *La Vénalité des Offices sous Henri IV* (Rouen, 1946), pp. 543–8.

16. cf., for example, J. H. Elliott, *Europe Divided, 1559–1598* (London, 1968), pp. 350 sqq.; H. G. Koenigsberger, 'Western Europe and the Power of Spain', *The New Cambridge Modern History*, vol. iii, ed. R. B. Wernham

campaign also illuminates the limitations of the early-modern state: specifically, the limitations of its machinery, both diplomatic and domestic. This was a time when 'European diplomatic contacts were interrupted everywhere except between ideological allies';[17] and even in the latter case, agreements, when they had been painstakingly reached by heads of state operating through self-willed and self-interested agents, all too rarely embodied resolutions by which the parties expected to abide. At home it was as much the scope and quality of the administrative machinery at his or her disposal as individual temperament that conditioned the style of rule affected by each monarch.[18] That machinery was put most severely to the test when rulers attempted to draw extraordinarily upon the resources of the state in order to wage war. In the case of England the raising, equipping, and transporting of Essex's army soon revealed its limitations and disclosed the risks Elizabeth would run if she should test it too far. In the case of Spain, despite the extent and resources of his dominions and their fluctuating contributions to his means, it was basically upon Castile that Philip depended for his wars. Only there had centralization of the machinery of state evolved sufficiently to withstand the increasing strain imposed by his policies. But administrative and revenue developments notwithstanding, Castile was not enough, as the Rouen campaign made evident. At Rouen itself, on the scale and level of a municipality, Villars with his expertise in municipal management was able to recruit the instruments of the town's administration to his service sufficiently to extract extraordinary effort from the townspeople. Yet he owed his success during the siege in great measure to his scrupulousness in not riding roughshod over law through arbitrary exercise of the force at his command.

It is not always adequately emphasized how, in a century of expanding economies and expanding horizons, the states of western Europe consistently failed in their attempts to expand within Europe itself at the expense of their neighbours. Elizabeth continued to call herself Queen of France, but the title was as empty as her advisers' talk of recovering ancient possessions. Meanwhile, the state of France itself came close to dissolution; and Spain, losing control in the Netherlands, ended her golden century on a note of decline. In important respects

---

(Chambridge, 1968), pp. 305–6; J. H. Shennan, *The Parlement of Paris* (London, 1968), p. 231; Williams, op. cit., p. 170.

17. G. Mattingly, *Renaissance Diplomacy* (London, 1965 edn.), p. 195.

18. See above, chapter 1.

this age of centralization and bureaucratization was an age of contraction, as states painfully discovered their limitations. If rulers and their servants miscalculated from time to time as they contended with immense practical obstacles, those limitations did not chiefly lie in defective grasp of strategy and tactics on the part of individuals. Rather, they lay in deficiencies in the machinery of states which, owing to their very nature, were drawn irresistibly towards the exercise of force but were unable to maintain its instruments. What was problematical enough for Villars at Rouen was hardly possible as yet on the scale of international war. When it became possible, the tragedy of Europe was that the nature of the state had not changed.

GLOSSARY

amiral: officer concerned with licensing shipping and supervising the policing of the coast within his jurisdiction, and enjoying various lucrative dues including a percentage on prizes taken at sea; the powers of the *amiraux* varied from province to province.

ague: (1) an attack of acute fever; (2) any shivering or shaking fit.

approaches: entrenchments or other measures taken upon terrain to enable besiegers to draw closer to the besieged.

aune: measure of length in relation to cloth (cf. 'alnage' in England, derived from measurement by the ell). At Rouen, 'The measure is here an alne, by which all commodities of woollen and linen is measured, and is accounted $1\frac{1}{4}$ yards English, but those that have made trial thereof find it to be 46 inches, but it is here to be noted that in buying of linen cloth of this country there is allowed in the account of measure 24 alnes for 20 and is called the Merchant's Alne or measure, and by the same is oftentimes here again sold in England, and it is found that Dieppe, Caen, and some other cities of Normandy afford also this overmeasure' (Lewes Roberts).

back: back-plate: one of the two main parts of the cuirass (q.v.), and detachable from it.

bailli: crown appointee, of noble status, supervising municipal elections and retaining, despite its erosion through sixteenth-century central and local bureaucratic developments, considerable importance in civil as well as in military administration.

barricado: from Spanish *barricada*, meaning simply a barricade. Contemporary military writers were much addicted to gratuitous technicalities in the form of terminology borrowed from foreign languages.

bastile: an outwork, sometimes attached to but more often detached from, the main fortifications, with its rear open to them, and providing cover for advanced parties of defenders.

bastion: a part of a fortification jutting forward in the shape, when viewed from above, of an irregular pentagon with its base in the main line, from which stemmed two sides constituting the 'flanks' and, from them, two further and longer sides, or 'faces', meeting to form the 'salient angle'.

bourgeois: the term is used in this book in the strict sense of a citizen enjoying privileged and emancipated status within a corporate town, and yielding fixed dues and obligations.

bulwark: a part of a fortification jutting forward from the main line.

bureau: denotes both the collectivity of *échevins* (q.v.) with their functions, and their bench within the *hôtel de ville.*

burgonet: close-fitting armour for the head, with plates covering the cheeks, but leaving the front of the face exposed.

caliver: hand-gun, between the harquebuse (q.v.) and the musket (q.v.) in weight and length, fired by matchlock in the case of infantry.

cannon: a muzzle-loading field-gun with a $7\frac{1}{4}$-inch smooth bore, firing iron round-shot over a relatively medium range. There is evidence that French cannon were smaller than English.

casemate: from Spanish *casamata* meaning, literally, a slaughter-house: a work lying within the ditch and below its height, furnished with artillery to beat off any invasion of the latter by the attackers.

cavalier: from Spanish *caballero:* an earthwork raised to enable surveillance of adjacent works or terrain by those commanding it, and to support a platform (q.v.).

centenier: an office evolved from feudal origins to embrace numerous civil and military functions under the *quartenier* (q.v.).

chamade: an audible signal, such as a roll of drums, announcing an intention to capitulate.

chambre des comptes: superior court, supervising the administration of royal revenues, auditing accounts, and adjudicating in causes arising therefrom.

chambre du domaine: an impermanent division of a *parlement* (q.v.), concerned with the preservation of the *domaine* (q.v.) and with causes arising from its administration, and therefore tending, in the eyes of their interested officers, to trespass upon the jurisdictions both of other divisions of the *parlement* and of the *chambre des comptes* (q.v.).

cinquantenier: an office evolved from military origins to embrace numerous civil functions under the *quartenier* (q.v.).

collar: armour protecting the neck.

conseiller clerc: a member of a *parlement* (q.v.) ranking below the *présidents* (q.v.) in status; in principle expert in canon law and consequently prominent in civil, but largely excluded from criminal, processes; such members were increasingly outnumbered by 'lay' members in the course of the sixteenth century.

consular tribunal: a judicial body, consisting of a judge assisted by elected councillors, intended to expedite litigation in commercial matters; that of Rouen was the second to be created in France.

corselet: armour providing comprehensive protection for the upper half of the body.

counterscarp: the side of a defensive ditch that faces the defenders; surmounted by a 'covered way', shielded from the besiegers by the glacis (q.v.).

crumster: alias 'crompster': 'What a "crompster" was exactly is not known, but from its being designed to act with galleys and for river-defence it must have had oars' (Corbett).

cuirass: body-armour, consisting of breast- and back-plate buckled together and perhaps extending to cover the fronts of the thighs; but cf. 'back', above.

culverin: a muzzle-loading field-gun with a five-inch smooth bore, firing iron round-shot over a relatively long range.

curtain: the plain section of a wall connecting two towers, bastions, or other projecting parts of a fortification.

demi-cannon: a muzzle-loading field-gun with a $6\frac{1}{4}$-inch smooth bore, firing iron round-shot over a relatively medium range.

domaine: proprietary rights over lands (*domaine corporel*) and other issues and revenues (*domaine incorporel*) appertaining to the Crown of France and inalienable from it.

domaine forain: ancient export duty payable upon a wide range of merchandise at the rate of 1·75 per cent of values assessed in accordance with tables subject to revision from time to time.

échevins: senior municipal officers elected from and by the leading citizens, responsible for the direction of municipal affairs and the supervision of other municipal officers.

écu: generic term for French gold coins—*écu au soleil, écu au porc-épic, écu à la couronne,* etc.—and known in England as 'crowns' from the third of those mentioned. At the time of the Rouen campaign the *écu à la couronne* was worth approximately 60 *sous* in terms of French money of account (see *livre tournois,* below) and approximately 6*s.* 3*d.* in terms of English money.

embrasure: an opening, widening from within, made in an epaulement (q.v.) or parapet, thus enabling defenders to use missile-weapons without exposing themselves to the enemy.

en pourpoinct: in padded and quilted protective clothing, as distinct from armour.

epaulement: from French *épaule,* meaning 'shoulder': a raised mass providing cover from enemy fire, especially for defenders positioned upon the walls, etc., of a fortification.

field-corporals: chief assistants to the sergeant-major (q.v.), constituting the main link in the chain of command between him and the captains.

flux: dysentery; or, any flow of blood or abnormal flow of excrement from the bowels or other organs.

franc: silver coin worth, at the time of the Rouen campaign, approximately 20 *sous* in terms of French money of account (see *livre tournois*).

gabelle du sel: salt-tax: a major and unpopular source of royal revenue, and extremely complex in its administration.

gabion: large, open-ended wicker basket of cylindrical shape, filled with earth and positioned to afford cover from enemy shot.

glacis: the ground sloping upwards towards the top of the counterscarp (q.v) and terminating in the 'covered way' surmounting the latter.

halberd: hand-weapon, combining axe- and pike-heads on a shaft about six feet long.

hargulutier: a cavalryman equipped with a harquebuse, q.v.

harquebuse: hand-gun, lighter than the caliver (q.v.), fired from the shoulder by wheel- or flint-lock: i.e., by generating a spark through friction to ignite the powder. Generally rated inferior to the heavier hand-guns, but cf. p. 165.

imposition foraine: export duty payable upon a wide range of merchandise at the rate of 5 per cent of values assessed in accordance with tables subject to revision from time to time.

imprest: initial advance of money to one engaged upon business of state, analogous in principle to the 'consideration' required to validate a contract; thus acceptance of imprest committed the recipient to fulfil his part of the business in question, such as military service.

intendants: centralizing agents of government, authorized by royal commission to discharge inspectorial and supervisory functions usually over a specific, but increasingly over a wide, area of administration and its established officers.

lendings: the proportion of his wages issued weekly to each serving soldier through his captain, to enable him to subsist; from time to time —for example, at six-monthly intervals—the outstanding balance due would be issued and the recipient could then be accounted as having received his 'full pay'.

livre tournois: money of account (as distinct from actual currency, or 'real money'), divided into 20 *sous,* each *sou* being divided into twelve *deniers.*

maîtres des comptes: chief officers, under the *présidents,* of a *chambre des comptes,* q.v.

maîtres des requêtes: judicial officers, next in status to the *présidents* (q.v.) within a *parlement* (q.v.), but especially important as instruments of directly applied royal justice emanating from the royal household.

marshal: an army's second-in-command: 'The office of the Marshal is painful and great, for he meddleth with the whole affairs of the wars' (*Discourse*).

millier: weight of 1,000 lb.; the pound of Rouen was significantly heavier than its London equivalent, 100 lb. at Antwerp equalling 104 lb. at London but 91 lb. at Rouen (Gerard Malynes).

millones: an excise, reckoned in millions of ducats, upon articles of consumption.

mortier: headgear worn by the most prestigious senior judges of a *parlement* (q.v.), and denoting their status.

musket: hand-gun, with a barrel about $4\frac{1}{2}$ ft. long needing support on a forked rest, fired by matchlock: i.e. by touching the lighted end of a slow-burning cord to the powder in the flash-pan, which then ignited the powder in the barrel.

muster: assembly of military forces, or of civilians liable for military service, for inspection and training.

orillion: from French *oreille,* meaning 'ear': a projecting turret at the point where the flank meets the face of a bastion (q.v.), enabling the defenders to cover the latter's flank.

parlement: superior court of law, having also a *police* (q.v.), administrative and political role, but *not* a representative institution. The *parlement* of Normandy was formally constituted in 1515.

pataches: vessels of 'from twenty-five to thirty tons, "like rowing-frigates with guns close to the water"' (Corbett).

pauldron: armour protecting the shoulder, and extending over a portion of the chest and back.

pay: see above, lendings.

pays d'état: provinces whose Estates retained formal control over the assessment and collection of taxes.

cannon-perier: a muzzle-loading field-gun with an eight-inch chamber bore, firing stone shot over a relatively short range.

pike: hand-weapon, consisting of a pointed head of iron or steel on a shaft some sixteen feet long.

pioneers: auxiliary personnel equipped with implements for tasks, such as trench-digging, involving manual labour in the course of military operations.

platform: a raised construction suitable for mounting guns.

point-blank: range where trajectory of missile from projecting-weapon to target follows a straight line, so that no elevation is needed in firing.

police: the enforcement of regulations concerning sale of foodstuffs, weights and measures, labour, roads and bridges, vagabondage, public health, and related public services.

premier président: the chief judge of a *parlement* (q.v.), presiding over its sessions.

président: a senior judge of a *parlement.*

procureur-général: judicial officer responsible for safeguarding the Crown's interests in a *parlement* (q.v.), and therefore especially important in criminal cases.

provost marshal: field officer with special responsibility for military discipline.

quarteniers: civil officers, each elected to supervise the administration of a *quartier* (q.v.) especially in matters of *police* (q.v.), but with functions which varied from town to town notably in relation to the urban militia.

quartier: (1) a formal administrative division of a municipality; (2) part of a town containing a concentration of inhabitants representative of a particular occupation or nationality. The term is used in this book exclusively in the first of these senses.

quatrième des vins: purchase tax on wine, nominally at the rate of 25 per cent in Normandy, but in fact subject to wide local variations and fluctuations.

ravelin: an outwork with two faces forming a salient angle.

receveur: chief financial officer of a municipality: at Rouen, an elective office.

redoubt: a small work, made in a permanent fortification or adjacent to a trench and linked to it by a ditch, into which the occupying forces could retire.

reiters: German cavalrymen, equipped with pistols.

Salic Law: the doctrine by which women and descendants in the female line were excluded from the royal succession; its object, like that of the inalienability of the *domaine* (q.v.), was to preserve the indivisibility of the kingdom.

sergeant-major: principal executive officer of the field-command, rated by some commentators next in importance to the marshal (q.v.), with special responsibility for co-ordinating troop-movements and for training.

Sixteen: the central committee of the populist wing of the League in Paris, taking its name from the sixteen *quartiers* (q.v.) of the capital, where it exercised *de facto* control of municipal administration, attempted to coerce the *parlement* (q.v.) and contended with aristocratic and other elements for the movement's leadership.

staccado: from Spanish *estacada*, meaning simply a stockade or palisade: cf. *barricado*, above.

surintendant: in general, an officer appointed or commissioned to discharge directive and supervisory functions over other officers within a specified area of an administrative system.

tasses: overlapping plates attached to the lower part of a corselet (q.v.), to protect the thighs.

vambrace: armour protecting the arm; if the term is found used in conjunction with 'rerebrace', it refers specifically to the forearm.

INDEX